MINIMA ETHNOGRAPHICA

Minima Ethnographica

Intersubjectivity and the Anthropological Project

MICHAEL JACKSON

THE UNIVERSITY OF CHICAGO PRESS

—

CHICAGO AND LONDON

Michael Jackson is the author or editor of six previous books in anthropology, including the prize-winning *Paths Toward a Clearing* and *At Home in the World.* He is also the author of five books of poetry and two novels.

The University of Chicago Press, Chicago 60637
The University of Chicago Press, Ltd., London
© 1998 by The University of Chicago
All rights reserved. Published 1998
Printed in the United States of America
07 06 05 04 03 02 01 00 99 98   5 4 3 2 1

ISBN (cloth): 0-226-38945-6
ISBN (paper): 0-226-38946-4

Library of Congress Cataloging-in-Publication Data

Jackson, Michael, 1940–
    Minima ethnographica : intersubjectivity and the anthropological
project / Michael Jackson.
        p.   cm.
    Includes bibliographical references and index.
    ISBN 0-226-38945-6 — ISBN 0-226-38946-4 (pbk.)
    1. Ethnology—Philosophy.   2. Ethnology—Field work.
3. Intersubjectivity.   4. Ethnophilosophy.   I. Title.
GN345.J4   1998
305.8′007′23—dc21   97-49428
                                                          CIP

For Francine, Heidi, Joshua, Freya
Without whom, nothing

No man is an *Iland,* intire of it selfe;
every man is a peece of the *Continent,*
a part of the *maine;*
if a *Clod* bee washed away by the *Sea,*
Europe is the lesse,
as well as if a *Promontorie* were,
as well as if a *Mannor* of thy *friends*
or of *thine owne* were;
any mans *death* diminishes *me,*
because I am involved in *Mankinde;*
And therefore never send to know
for whom the *bell* tolls;
It tolls for *thee.*

—John Donne, Meditation XVII,
from *Devotions upon Emergent*
Occasions (1624)

CONTENTS

ACKNOWLEDGMENTS

Paul Rabinow speaks of friendship (*philia*) as "a primary site of thinking" (1996:13–14), and cites Aristotle's *Nicomachean Ethics* in affirming that friendship is essential to the good life (*eudaimonia*), socially and intellectually. "For with friends men are most able both to think and to act." Writing is always an arduous and solitary task. But during the time I have worked on this book, both in the United States and in Australia, my life has been filled with the pleasure of friendship, family, and intellectual companionship. I am especially indebted to the following friends, students, and colleagues who have made such a difference to the way in which this project has been concluded: Francine Lorimer, Robert Orsi, Richard Wilk, Anne Pyburn, Keith Ridler, Judith Loveridge, Shawn Lindsay, Kassim Kone, Steven Feld, Paul Stoller, Sonia da Silva, Franca Tamisari, Michael Nihill, Åsaa Persson, Lowell Lewis, Niko Besnier, Wojciech Dabrowski, Kathy Golski, Ghassan Hage, Alan Rumsey, Francesca Merlan, Jadran Mimica, and T. David Brent. I wish also to acknowledge the College of Arts and Sciences, Indiana University, which generously funded my fieldwork in aboriginal Australia between 1989 and 1994.

PREAMBLE

The One and the Many

I begin in the middle of a journey, pulled off the road so that I can listen to what Zack Jakamarra is saying, and take notes. We are just north of Warlarla in Central Australia. Zack points out a conical hill known as Ngardarri away to the west across the spinifex plain. The hill is the bound hair or ceremonial headdress of an ancestral hero. Then Zack juts his chin to indicate a scarf of red earth among the blue mallee below the escarpment on which we are standing. He tells me that two dogs traveling from Ngarnka—which lies beyond Ngardarri—camped here in the Dreaming. Even today you can find water at this site.

At Ngarnka the male dog had abducted another dog's wife. Camped at Warlarla, he "sang" up mist and smoke to confuse his pursuers. In the morning the fleeing pair moved west along a dried river course, stopping near Warlarla where the male dog scratched a hole in the ground and shat. From there to Yurlpawarnu the dogs walked on clumps of spinifex in order to leave no tracks.

After crossing the Tanami desert, the dogs reached Alekarenge (literally, "belonging to the dogs") where they encountered "many, many other dogs" from Kayeteje, Warrumungu, and other tribal areas. There, according to Joe Jangala, who "owns" the *malikijarra* ("two dog") myth, "they settled down and lived with all the others" (Jangala 1994, 135).

Like most myths, the Warlpiri narrative is allegorical. Its surface features belie its hidden depths. Though set in the past and recounted in the past tense, the meaning of the myth is consummated in time present. Though the story concerns two dogs, it is really about human beings.[1] And their identity is born of difference. Observes Joe Jangala at the end of his version of the narrative, "In the beginning they were all dogs, not just one but many. As this story has shown, this is how they became all one family, one people" (Jangala 1994, 135).

In reaching out beyond the borders of the Warlpiri world, the myth opens up discussion of the relationship between the one and the many. In bringing home to us that plural societies are often born of tragedy and loss, with people driven from the place inhabited by their own kind and obliged to work out a modus vivendi with strangers, we are reminded that tribal worlds are no more insular than ours. The Dreaming tracks that traverse central Australia are "open systems" that cross linguistic and ecological borders (Berndt 1969, 6; Myers 1986, 166–67; Rose 1992, 52–56). Raiding and abduction were once as common as intermarriage. Spear heads, wild tobacco, and artifacts were traded far afield. And ceremony and language have always disseminated across tribal lines (Meggitt 1966, 22–37). The two-dog Dreaming conveys something of this sense of strange smoke seen on the horizon, of one's own world always implicating the world of others. Ending in a place where three different tribal areas converge, the narrative encapsulates the notion that self has no reality except in relation to others, and that all human beings, while never exactly the same, tend to share similar differences.[2] Most pertinent to the argument of this book, however, is the way in which this narrative, like all narratives, allegorizes abstract issues as intersubjective dramas.

How THE PARTICULAR is related to the universal is one of the most ubiquitous and persistent questions in human life. The question is taken up in different ways in different social contexts and different discursive domains.

1. In central Australia dingos and dogs are assigned skin names and assimilated into the human world. In the Dreaming, say the Yallalin, "dingo and human were one" (Rose 1992, 47). "Ancestors and contemporaries, dingos are thought still to be very close to humans: they are what we would be if we were not what we are."

2. As Fred Myers puts it in his superb study of the Pintubi, a tension between relatedness (*walytja* connotes "shared identity," "kin," and "self") and differentiation (*munuka* connotes "outsider" and "other") "defines the basic lived problem of Pintupi life" (Myers 1986, 109–11, 160–61).

Thus the Upanishadic interest in explicating and mediating the relationship between the one and the many, the Judeo-Christian preoccupation with reconciling the ways of God to man, the medieval fascination with correspondences between microcosm and macrocosm, and the philosophical problem of combining the perspectives of a particular person inside the world with an objective view of the whole world that transcends any particular point of view (Nagel 1986:3) are all, in a sense, refractions of the same idea. And all bear a family resemblance to a cluster of critical anthropological questions: how do local and global worlds intersect, how can ethnographic studies of single societies enable us to say something about the *human* condition, and how is the *lived* experience of individuals connected to the *virtual* realities of tradition, history, culture, and the biology of the species that outrun the life of any one person.

My argument in this book is that such abstract ways of framing inquiry into the dialectic between local and global worlds, or between the particular and the universal, require existential-phenomenological deconstruction. This implies recovering what Milan Kundera has called the "terra incognita of the everyday" (1988, 5), where relationships are nothing if not social. As such, this work is an attempt to realize the *existential-phenomenological* implications of Lévi-Strauss's conception of anthropology as "a general theory of relationships" (1963, 95). To this end, Being is conceived, after Heidegger (1962) and Merleau-Ponty (1968), as Being-in-the-world—a domain of *inter-est* (inter-existence) and intercorporeity that lies *between* people: a field of inter-experience, inter-action, and inter-locution. Analytically, inter-existence is given precedence over individual essence. Relation is prior to relata.

Two caveats are in order here. As Heidegger notes (1962, 92, 170), a problem arises from construing *Dasein* as the being of betweenness, for by privileging relation over relata we risk overlooking the phenomenal reality of individual "entities." However, the phenomenological epoché enables us to set aside questions as to the ontological status of various human modes of comprehending and experiencing *Dasein*—idiosyncratic, cultural, or cosmic—in order to explore the behavioral *consequences* of these modes of understanding. My prioritization of the social is thus tied to nothing more than a *pragmatic* interest in redressing the biases toward subjectivism and objectivism in anthropology by demonstrating the value of intersubjectivity for ethnographic analysis. But just as we must be wary not to gloss subjectivity in the tradition of nineteenth-century romanticism—as a kind of intuitive, solipsistic, or introspective mode of experience (Dewey 1958,

11; Jackson 1996, 1, 24)—so we must not misconstrue intersubjectivity as a synonym for shared experience, empathic understanding or fellow-feeling. For my purposes, intersubjectivity embraces centripetal and contrifugal forces, and constructive and destructive extremes without prejudice. Among the Jelgobe Fulani, for example, societas is "exactly translated by the Fula noun *gondol*" which means, literally, "the fact of being together," "life in common" (Riesman 1977, 162). But, as with the Kuranko, the ideal and its negation are mutually entailed. "Neighborliness is not sweet" (*siginyorgoye ma di*), say the Kuranko. *Gondal hoyaa,* say the Jelgobe: "life together is not easy" (Riesman 1977, 175). One might also consider the way in which, throughout Melanesia, food is made "the measure of all things," *including* life-sustaining *and* agonistic modes of exchange, amity *and* antagonism (Young 1971). The same ambiguity obtains among the Warlpiri and Pintupi: giving ideally involves parity: it should be "level," or "square and square" (Jackson 1995, 149; Myers 1986, 170). But the same principle holds true for both the giving of life *and* the retributive taking of life in "payback" or revenge. Compassion and conflict are thus complementarity poles of intersubjectivity, the first affirming identity, the second confirming difference. This is why violence, though often repugnant to a European bourgeois sensibility, must be accommodated in anthropological analysis as a distinctively human modality of intersubjectivity, and not dismissed as a primitive or pathological aberration (see Elias 1994, 157).

The question of the relationship between particular and universal domains thus dissolves into a set of questions about how the give and take of *intersubjective* life in all its modes and mediations—physical and metaphysical, conscious and unconscious, passive and active, kind and unkind, serious and ludic, dyadic and collective, symmetrical and asymmetrical, inclusive and exclusive, empathic and antagonistic—prefigures and configures more discursive and categorical forms of relationship. Dilthey's hermeneutic circle (1976, 259–62)—in which the whole and its parts are conceived as interdependent—is thus construed as a *social* dialectic.

IN THIS BOOK I EXPLORE the *dialectic* of the particular and the universal as it makes its appearance in the interpersonal life of the peoples among whom I have carried out fieldwork: the Kuranko of northeast Sierra Leone (1969–70, 1972, 1979, 1985), the Warlpiri of central Australia (1989, 1990, 1991), and the Kuku-Yalanji of southeast Cape York, Australia (1993–94,

1997). My aim is to show that the ways in which the Kuranko deploy the symbolic antinomy between village and bush, and the Warlpiri mark the relationship between individuated being and the Dreaming, and Kuku-Ya-lanji deal with relations between insider and outsider are different vernaculars for negotiating the same uncertain relationship between particular and universal modalities of social identity. As such they may be placed on the same footing as the traditional anthropological discourse on difference and identity.

In exploring these social contexts I assign priority to lifeworld (*lebens-welt*) over worldview (*weltanschauung*), and give more weight to the ways in which the relationship between the one and the many arises in practical contexts of everyday life than to the ways it has been treated philosophically. Fieldwork experience has taught me that notions of shared humanity, human equality, and human rights always come up against the micropolitical exigencies of ethnic, familial, and personal identity, and the dialectic between particular and universal frames of reference often dissolves into a troubled dialogue between the privileged microcosm of anthropologists and the peoples of the Third World whose voices, struggles, and claims define with far more urgency the conditions that define our global future. The reflexive dimension of this work testifies to the ways in which one's ethnographic understanding of others is never arrived at in a neutral or disengaged manner, but is negotiated and tested in an ambiguous and stressful field of interpersonal relationships in an unfamiliar society. As I noted in 1977, any interpretive synthesis one presents is the product of dialogue: a "thinly-disguised allegory of culture contact mediated by personal relationships" (Jackson 1977, xiii; cf. Riesman 1977, 1–2). Accordingly, this book critically examines the role of anthropology in the liberal humanistic tradition and concludes with a set of reflections on the vocation of the intellectual in the late twentieth century.

The Intersubjective Turn

The history of anthropology from Lévi-Strauss to the present day has comprised a series of deconstructions of subjectivity. For Lévi-Strauss the subjective was synonymous with inwardness and affect and had to give ground to formal models of the mind if we were to grasp the structural logic that underpinned social reality. Foucault, in a famous image, dissolved the subjective into the imperious unity of discourse—a face drawn in sand erased by the sea. Bourdieu disseminated subjectivity into the habitus. And Geertz saw subjectivity as inaccessible except as it found expression in webs of shared significance and cultural symbols. However, in recent years, subjectivity has not so much been dissolved or denied but relocated. According to this "intersubjective turn" (Joas 1993, 250), selfhood is understood as a bipolar notion, arising from and shaped by ever-altering modalities of embodied social interaction and dialogue (Goffman 1967, 1971; Bakhtin 1981; Graumann 1995; Tedlock and Mannheim 1995). Accordingly, what we commonly call "subjectivity" or "selfhood" are simply arrested moments artificially isolated from the flux of "interindividual" life (cf. Sartre 1982, 99; Crapanzano 1988, 4). To echo quantum theory, the subject-object partition is an artifact of our interventional acts of *measuring* reality; in fact, selves are no more single existences than are atoms and molecules.

Genealogically linked to Buber's concept of the dialogical, Schutz's social phenomenology, the pragmatism of William James, John Dewey, and George Herbert Mead, and existential-phenomenological thought, the focus of intersubjectivity is the *interplay* of subject and object, ego and alter. Singular selves are simultaneously part of a commonalty, sole but also several, not only islands but part of the main.

In emphasizing that reality is relational I do not intend any erasure of the notion of self as intentional agent. Indeed, I share William James's view that "*the fons et origo of all reality, whether from the absolute or the practical point of view, is . . . subjective, is ourselves*" (James 1950, 2: 296–97). However, one must be careful not to conflate subjectivity or consciousness with any particular subject or self. Human consciousness is never isomorphic with the things on which it fastens, the objects it makes its own, and the selves which it constructs. Consciousness is the natural state of human existence. But notions of subject and object, ego and alter, are not given, but made. They can, accordingly, be placed in parentheses, reshaped, and unmade. This is why, subjectivity does not universally entail a notion of the subject or of selfhood as some skin-encapsulated, seamless monad possessed of conceptual unity and continuity. In fact, such a conception of the self is anthropologically atypical, and in those societies where such a conception is fostered and fetishized, a heavy price is paid. For in withholding or retracting intersubjectivity from human relations with material and natural things in the name of scientific rationality, one risks discarding those anthropomorphic correspondences that enable people, in moments of crisis, to cross between human and extrahuman worlds, and thereby feel that they can imaginatively if not actually control the universe as a particular extension of their subjectivity, much as tools allow one to manipulate matter as an extension of one's own body (Jackson 1989, chap. 9).

The notion of intersubjectivity is useful in three ways. First, it resonates with the manner in which many non-Western peoples tend to emphasize identity as "mutually arising"—as relational and variable—rather than assign ontological primacy to the *individual* persons or objects that are implicated in any intersubjective nexus. The Mande proverb puts it, *Ala ma ko kelen da*—God did not create anything single (but only sets of relations: male-female, night-day, life-death, etc.). This same principle may explain why intersubjectivity has been central to Japanese philosophy, particularly the Kyoto Buddhist school associated with the work of Nishida Kitaro (Odin 1996), as well as some schools of Indian philosophy (Chattopadhyana, Embree, and Mohanty 1992). Second, the notion of intersubjectivity helps us elucidate a critical characteristic of preliterate thought, namely, the way it tends to construe as *extra*psychic processes that we construe as *intra*psychic. The unconscious, for example, which we refer to the deepest recesses of the psyche and to time past, is in a preliterate society more likely to be called the unknown, and located on the shadowy margins of contemporary social space (Foucault 1970, 326). Thus aboriginal people construe history as ever present, and ancestral land assumes for them the same vital force that self and soul have for us. The same principle holds true of affectivity and ethics. In preliterate societies emotions are seen less as spontaneous expressions of inward sensibility than cultivated as context-bound imperitives of intersubjective life, and "conscience" is more likely to be articulated as a function of disturbed *interpersonal* relationships (shame) than as a crisis of a *personal* moral principle (guilt). It is also the case that phenomena we label as intrapsychic defenses—such as repression and displacement—are more likely to find expression in preliterate societies as coping strategies of avoidance and scapegoating. Finally, the notion of intersubjectivity helps us unpack the relationship between two different but vitally connected senses of the word *subject*—the first referring to the empirical person, endowed with consciousness and will, the second, to abstract generalities such as society, class, gender, nation, structure, history, culture, and tradition that are subjects of our thinking but not themselves possessed of life. In other words, the dialectic of subject and object implies a reciprocal and analogical relationship not only between singular persons (what Schelling called "egoities") but between persons and a world of ideas, attributes, and things that are held in common without any one person having complete control over them or the last word on their meaning. In the latter sense, *subject* does not denote any particular person but rather a field of consciousness or a set of assumptions—as in "the subject of my research," or the "subject of our conversation." However, as Adorno notes, the notion of a subject as a "logical proposition" or as "consciousness in general" always conceals a "remembrance" of the subject as a particular embodied person. Unless the vital presence of individual subjects is made manifest in our discourse, Adorno argues, the abstract notion of subject loses all meaning. The two "have reciprocal need of each other" (Adorno 1978, 498). Thus it would be impossible to grasp the meaning of a nation's struggle for independence without reference to the meaning of independence in personal and interpersonal life.

Sartre's approach to this subject is illuminating. Any individual, he writes, universalizes and objectifies his or her epoch. But the singular *I* cannot be reduced to this otherness, for each person not only internalizes and articulates it, he surpasses and subtly alters it in everything he does or thinks. Though the individual subject contains and encapsulates the general attributes of his culture, class, gender, and history, his life does not merely give these things objective form, for in subjecting them to his own will, he chooses them (Sartre 1968, 97–100; 1981; ix–x; 1982, 97–98).[3] Each person is at once a subject for himself or herself—a *who*—and an object for others—a *what*. And though individuals speak, act, and work toward belonging to a world of others, they simultaneously strive to experience themselves as world makers.

Seven Types of Intersubjective Ambiguity

Intersubjectivity is steeped in paradox and ambiguity. In the first place, intersubjectivity is a site of constructive, destructive, and reconstructive interaction. When Mauss invoked the Maori spirit (*hau*) of the gift to elucidate the threefold character of reciprocity (1954, 8–12), he glossed over the fact that the Maori term for reciprocity—appropriately a palindrome, *utu*—refers *both* to the gift giving that sustains amity and bolsters alliances *and* to the violent acts of seizure, revenge, and repossession that are pro-

---

3. Social theorists such as Wagner, Bourdieu, Giddens, and Sahlins have voiced a similar dissatisfaction with reified notions of culture, history, and tradition. Thus Wagner's notion of the "invention of culture" (1980), Bourdieu's notion of strategizing (1977), Giddens's concept of "structuration" (1979), and Sahlins's observation that cultural meanings exist *in potentia*—continually reevaluated, reauthored, and transformed in the light of changing interests and imperatives (1985).

voked when one party denies or diminishes the integrity (*mana*) of another. Intersubjectivity moves continually between positive and negative poles. In the second place, it should be noted that in any human encounter, idiosyncratic, ideational, and impersonal elements commingle and coalesce. Because Being is never limited to human being, the field of intersubjectivity includes persons, ancestors, spirits, collective representations, and material things (Luckmann 1970; Jackson 1982a, 17). Within this field, objects tend to become charged with subjective meanings and social destinies (Mauss 1954, 10; Appadurai 1986), and human beings become both subjects for themselves and objects for others.[4] Third, as Hegel observed, no matter how great the social inequality between self and other, each is *existentially* dependent on and beholden to the other; the master's subjugation and negation of the slave is countermanded by their mutual need for each other's recognition (Hegel 1971, 170–75). Fourth, although the elementary structure of intersubjectivity is dyadic, the dyad "contains the scheme, germ, and material of innumerable more complex forms" (Simmel 1950, 122).[5] Thus the dyad is usually mediated by *something outside of and alien to itself*—a third party, a shared idea, a common goal (Simmel 1950, chap. 4; Sartre 1982, 109–21). Fifth, intersubjectivity is shaped as much by unconscious, habitual, taken-for-granted dispositions as by conscious intentions and worldviews (Reynolds 1976; Freeman 1983). These elements are neither well-integrated neurophysiologically nor consonant. Thus it is possible for fear or panic (instinctual expressions of the limbic brain) to render a person speechless, but that same person can readily simulate panic or declare himself afraid when he is not (the ability to lie or gainsay reality being a more recently evolved cortical function). Sixth, intersubjectivity

4. Webb Keane's incisive analysis of representation practices in Anakalang (Sumba) makes it clear that language, signs, and symbols are never mere modes of self-expression *or* self-estranging forms of objectification but are vitally implicated in the field of intersubjective life (1997, 67,92). In a comparable vein, Elizabeth Povinelli shows how, for the aboriginal people of Belyuen (Cox Peninsula, Northern Territory, Australia), the work of hunting permeates the country with speech (*mal*) and sweat (*wenterre*) so that language and labor come to reciprocally "cause" the country to "think about" its occupants, penetrating their bodies, entering their hearing, and animating their consciousness (1993, 152).

5. For example, archetypally intimate dyads such as mother and child, husband and wife, brother and sister, brother and brother, and father and son everywhere define the ontological basis for the working of the cultural imagination, as among the Tallensi where "the ancestors are projections of parents" (Fortes 1949, 176), and among the Iatmul where "everything and every person has a sibling and the polysyllabic names are so arranged in pairs that in each pair one name is the *elder* sibling of the other" (Bateson 1958, 243).

reflects the instability of human consciousness—the way our awareness continually drifts or oscillates between a retracted, substantive, and onto-logically secure sense of self and a comparatively expanded and unstable sense of self in which one is sometimes fulfilled in being with another, at other times overwhelmed and engulfed (James 1950, chap. 10). The same oscillation occurs in somatic consciousness: at times one experiences one's body as an inert and alien thing; at other times one's body is in perfect union with one's will. Our awareness is forever shifting between ecstatic and recessive extremes—of having a sense of ourselves as fully embodied and an equal persuasive sense of being disembodied—of being pure mind (Leder 1990). Using a gestalt model, one might say that self stands out momentarily against a background of otherness, only to become ground in its turn for the figure of the other. Self is everywhere reciprocal to other selves, both behaviorally and experientially. We have as many selves as there are others who accord us recognition and carry our image in their mind (James 1950, 294). One's self is as manifold as the objects and others one calls one's own, and one's ontological security depends on these things. Without a sense of solidarity with others, one can find no meaning in one-self. As a corollary, the binary relationship of I and Thou, like the identity of self, invariably implicates ever-shifting pluralities and combinations of persons. These groupings often entail overlapping and contending frames of social reference—such as us versus them—that in practice create consid-erable ambiguity (Sartre 1982, 118–21; Jackson 1977, 71–73).

Finally, intersubjective ambiguity can also be explored as a problem of knowledge. Merleau-Ponty asks, "How can the word 'I' be put into the plural, how can a general idea of the *I* be formed, how can I speak of an *I* other than my own, how can I know that there are other *I*'s, how can consciousness which, by its nature, and as self-knowledge, is in the mode of the *I,* be grasped in the mode of Thou, and through this, in the world of the 'One'?" (1962, 348; cf. Merleau-Ponty 1964, 114).

This, in a nutshell, is one of the central dilemmas of human coexistence: I and Thou are similar yet separate, one yet not the same. This apparent contradiction of coexistence has prompted some phenomenologists to ask how one may *know* the inner experience of the Other as he or she knows it? On what grounds can empathy, transference, or analogy bridge the gap between me and you?

Scientific opinion is divided over whether self-awareness, and the recip-rocal ability to understand another as oneself, is present in nonhuman pri-mates (Byrne 1995; Povinelli and Eddy 1996). But there is no question that such cognitive mirror-imaging is developed in children by the age of two–*before* the advent of "synpraxic speech" (Luria and Yodovich 1971, 50). Observes Thomas Luckmann, learning a language "presupposes and, in a sense, 'repeats' the idealizations and the processes of intersubjective 'mirroring' which are presupposed in the constitution of language" (1972, 488). Language "arises out of social experience" (Hanks 1990, 44); it extends and augments modes of *social* interaction and interexperience which are *already in place* (Edwards 1978, 451).

Alfred Schutz regarded empathic understanding as a product of "the natural attitude of common-sense thinking in daily life" (Schutz 1973, 11). Differences between individuals are overcome, he writes, by "signitive-symbolic representation" (Schutz 1967, 100). This entails, he observes, "two basic idealizations." The first is "the interchangeability of standpoints," the second is "the congruency of relevances"—which is to say that for most practical purposes individuals take it for granted that they have much in common despite their biographical differences (Schutz 1973, 10–13; 312–16).

But the mystery of how one can know another is not invariably an epistemological or cognitive issue. Otherness, like selfhood, is initially an *outcome* or product of intersubjective engagement, not a given property of existence (Husserl 1970, 120–23). As Merleau-Ponty subsequently showed, intersubjectivity is not simply a dialectic of conceptual intentions; it is lived as intercorporeity and through the five senses as introceptivity (Merleau-Ponty 1964, 114–15, 121; 1968). Psychologists have demonstrated that intersubjectivity is present in a primary, protolinguistic form between the seventh and ninth month of an infant's life (Stern 1985, 124–37), when the mother-child bond is mediated by various modes of behavioral synchrony and affect attunement, including smell, touch, gaze, sympathetic laughter and tears, cradling, lulling embraces, interactive play, and the rhythmic interchanges of motherese.[6] Even when intersubjectivity takes

6. Papoušek 1995, 58–81; Trevarthen and Hubley 1978, 212–26. So suddenly replete is this phase with gestures and movements that engage the child with others that Henri Wallon refers to it as one of "incontinent sociality" (Wallon 1949, cited in Merleau-Ponty 1964, 141). It is only at around three that this "syncretic sociality" is modulated: "the child stops lending his body and even his thoughts to others. . . . He stops confusing himself with the situation or the role in which he may find himself engaged. He adopts a proper perspective or viewpoint of his own—or rather he understands that, whatever the diversity of situations or roles, he is *someone* above and beyond the different situations and roles." (Merleau-Ponty 1964, 151–52).

on its specific cultural trappings, these are often less a matter of conscious social learning than of unconscious mimetic and countermimetic processes, imitative games, and praktognosia (Mauss 1973; Merleau-Ponty 1962; Jackson 1983; 1995, 118; Fiske 1995).

Moreover, there are many contexts in every society where participation is emphasized over detachment. Rather than some self-conscious standing-out from the crowd or transcendence of one's egocentric standpoint, the issue is one of bringing personal proclivities and persuasions under control and so acquiring the ability to work and coexist with others in a *practically efficacious* way. Thus Kuranko people are far less exercised by the conceptual question, What is in my neighbor's mind? than by practicing social wisdom (*hankili*) and cultivating copresence—"greeting," "sitting together," "working together," and "moving as one" (Jackson 1982a, 30; 1995, 165). In Papua New Guinea, the term *wantok* ("one-talk") suggests this consensual notion of kinship (Lederman 1986, 27). Language articulates social relationship more than it expresses information and ideas. And agency is not so much self-expression as self-restraint tied to an ability to foster mutually beneficial alignments within a wide field of social and extrasocial relations. In such a world, civility, etiquette, and emotions are less matters of inward disposition than of interactive performance, and "we" replaces the discursive "I" (cf. Lutz 1988, 86–98).

Ethnography corroborates Merleau-Ponty's understanding of sociality. We understand others, he observes, not through cognition and intellectual interpretation but through "blind recognition" of reciprocal gestures, common metaphors, parallel images, and shared intentions (1962, 185–86). We are embodied social beings before we are anything else. "The social is already there when we come to know or judge it," he writes; "it exists obscurely and as a summons" (362). Beyond our words and actions, he observes in a singularly beautiful phrase, lies "the region where they are prepared" (1965, 222).

Rules of reciprocity and exchange arise out of these innate patternings of empathic bonding, synchronous interaction, and mirror-imaging in intimate interpersonal worlds.[7] Disturbances in the field of interpersonal relations

7. Lacan 1966; Schutz 1967, 1970, 1973; Winnicott 1974; Bowlby 1971; Mead 1934; Esterson 1972; Laing 1965. Furthermore, one might suppose that syntactical, logical, mathematical, and political relations between subject and object are also experientially foreshadowed by the embodied, reciprocal interactions of subject and object in intersubjective life. However, such a view—that primordial patterns of *sociality* underpin *mental* operations—would seem to be contradicted in the case of autism and idiot savants where a genius for remembering

will register as cultural contradictions, as well as show up as knots and binds in the field of bodily intersubjectivity. Such interconnections between cultural, bodily, and interpersonal domains find expression in the root metaphors of a culture, and disclose to the ethnographer the points at which the habits, idioms, and stratagems of intersubjective life become introjected as intrapsychic defenses and projected as transpersonal defenses that govern what can and cannot be said and done within the group as a whole. "Ontological metaphors" also enable us to broach the subject of the poetics of intersubjectivity (Lakoff and Johnson 1980, 25–32). By this I mean that in every culture key images of ontological presence afford the anthropologist insights into the workings of intersubjective experience, while at the same time providing data for the cross-cultural analysis of invariants. Thus, the connotations of *mana* in Polynesian, *dewa* in Sumba,[8] *miran* in Kuranko, and honor in circum-Mediterranean societies suggest that, despite cultural variations, similarly embodied sensations of amplitude—"substantiality" (cf. Laing 1965, 41–42), "weight" (cf. Riesman 1977, 185), "standing" (Straus 1966, 143), "voice" (Keane 1997, 202–3), "containedness" (Jackson 1982, 22; Riesman 1977, 226), and charismatic forcefulness—everywhere constitute our sense of existence and autonomy. Comparable metaphors suggest the loss of presence: falling, floating, drifting, shrinking, being rootless, empty, ungrounded, petrified, overwhelmed, or reduced to an inert thing (see Binswanger 1963, 223; Laing 1960, 43–49).

and computing numbers is accompanied by a conspicuous absence of social skills and a lack of empathic awareness (Luria 1968). But might it not be that in such individuals social relations have become so deeply introjected that *intra*psychic operations eclipse and supplant extrapsychic ones? And in a similar vein, might it not be argued that computers are not minds because they cannot exteriorize and body forth empathic intentions based on their own corporeal self-understanding?

8. Webb Keane's masterful account of the Anakalang notion of *dewa* nicely demonstrates that the intersubjective connotations of the word also entail a sense of subjective identity. "Dewa is not only a principle of life but also the basis of people's innate relationship to objects, of successful interactions, and, one might say, their charismatic ability to attract or otherwise move others. . . . Onvlee [1957] . . . interprets the term as "that in a man through which he is as he is, . . . his character and to an important degree, also his appointed fate," and that which differentiates one person from others. The latter remark is especially insightful, for *dewa* seems to characterize the conjunction between material circumstances, the trajectory taken by men's and women's lives over time, and the distinguishing features of their identities' (Keane 1997, 202). The Maori term *mana* carries a similar range of meaning: though a divinely derived and inherited form of authority and power that signifies *rangatiratanga* (high rank) it is also a charismatic quality that waxes and wanes according to the nature of a man's interactions with others (Marsden 1975:193–194; Mahuika 1975:89–90).

SINCE INTERSUBJECTIVITY is inescapably ambiguous, an anthropology that makes intersubjectivity its focus forfeits the search for ahistorical and determinate knowledge, describing instead a forcefield of human interaction in which contending needs, modes of consciousness, and values are forever being adjusted, one to the other, without any final resolution. Accordingly, a negative capability has to be built into our ways of thinking.[9]

As a consequence, we will reach conclusions that are more paradoxical than final, such as the fact that ties of close kinship inevitably subsume hostility *and* amity, rivalry *and* solidarity (Fortes 1969, 237; Freeman 1973). Or that the Oedipus project, in which each person assumes responsibility for himself or herself, entails the ritual repudiation of the very bonds of obligation and nurturance that define the ethos of the natal family. Every human attachment carries the seeds of its own negation.

Toward the end of his life, Merleau-Ponty spoke of a silence that was not "the contrary of language" but rather "envelops the speech anew" (1968, 179). In Bamana thought such a view is compellingly elaborated. In aphorisms enjoining silence, even speech—without which sociality is inconceivable—is sometimes seen as inimical to society: speech builds the village, silence regenerates the world; speech disperses, silence makes whole; speech burns the mouth, silence heals it (Zahan 1979, 117–18). The BaMbuti view is similar: quietness equates with social cooperation and ecological harmony while noise destroys both (see Feld's incisive commentary [1996, 2–3] on Colin Turnbull's account [1965] of silence, song, and noise in BaMbuti cosmology).

At this point, philosophical anthropology and proverbial wisdom come together.

"To study the way of the Buddha is to study the self, and to study the self is to forget the self; and to forget the self is to be enlightened by others" (Dogen, founder of the Soto sect of Zen Buddhism).

> *Tat tvam asi* ("Thou art that"); (Chandogya Upanishad VI 13.3).
> *Je est un autre* (Rimbaud).

Ã *sé do; ã tótó* (Beng, Côte d'Ivoire: "We are all one; we are all different"; Gottlieb 1992, 14).

---

9. By "negative capability" John Keats meant the capability of "being in uncertainties, Mysteries, doubts, without any irritable reaching after fact & reason" (Keats 1958, 193); see Jackson 1989, 15–16, Stoller 1989, 144–45; 1992, 212; Desjarlais 1992, 34.

Wanggany ga dharrwa; rrambangi ga ga:na; galki ga barrkuwatj (Yol-ngu, Northeast Arnhem Land, Australia: "One and many, together and alone or close and far apart"; Tamisari 1997).

No advantage without limitation.
No gains without giving.
No self-realization without self-sacrifice.

Again, one of the most striking ironies is that while there are no human universals that can be established on objective grounds, the fact remains that anyone's particular and limited experience of the world tends to have the force of universal truth. Though many religious traditions claim that the universal is revealed in the particular—"a World in a Grain of Sand," according to William Blake's *Auguries of Innocence;* "countless worlds in every dust-mote," according to Mahayana Buddhism; "by one clod of clay all that is made of clay is known," according to the Chandogya Upanis-had—it is perhaps truer to say that when one is most deeply involved in what is closest at hand, the entire world is *experienced* as being contained in that one microcosm.

And this too is a paradox of human existence—that one can be in the world only if one feels that one's own world is, in some significant sense, also *the* world. In other words, it is irrelevant whether the psychic unity of humankind is proven scientifically or accepted on ideological grounds because it is existentially imperative. Human sameness everywhere consists in similar differences. Hannah Arendt observes, "plurality is the condition of human action" because while we are all human, "nobody is ever the same as anyone else who ever lived, lives, or will live" (1958, 8).

Such a notion of the singular universal grounds the practical possibility of crossing cultural boundaries, and doing anthopological fieldwork. In his essay on the inconstancy of our actions, Montaigne noted, "We are all framed of flaps and patches and of so shapelesse and diverse a contexture, that every peece and every moment playeth his part. And *there is as much difference found betweene us and our selves, as there is between our selves and other"* (1948, 298; emphasis added). That is to say, there is always some aspect of oneself, however well hidden, that corresponds, albeit obliquely, to the beliefs and behaviors one sees in others. Methodologically, therefore, one proceeds from the latent in self to the manifest in other, and from the manifest in self to the latent in other in a demanding series of essays at recognition. Discursively, this process presumes the psychic unity of humankind. Devereux observes: "were anthropologists to draw up a complete list of all known types of cultural behavior, this list would overlap, point by point, with a similarly complete list of impulses, wishes, fantasies, etc., obtained by psychoanalysis in a clinical setting" (1978, 63–64; cf. 1976, 83). That which we designate "culture," therefore, is simply the repertoire of psychic patterns and possibilities that generally have been implemented, foregrounded, or given legitimacy in a particular place at a particular point in time. But human culture, like consciousness itself, rests on a shadowy and dissolving floe of blue ice, and this subliminal, habitual, repressed, unexpressed, and silent mass shapes and reshapes, stabilizes and destabilizes the visible surface forms. And just as cultural forms are continually being lost to this underlying and largely invisible ocean of potentiality, so it in turn continually feeds back into the visible field of intersubjectivity.

Vita Activa

The field of intersubjectivity should be understood as a forcefield charged with energy and driven by need.

In Marx's vision of the human condition, active, purposeful labor (praxis) is seen as this driving force. Work produces and reproduces both selves and societies (Marx and Engels 1947, 14–19). But work is always a matter of keeping *both* body *and* soul together. Not only does work provide the livelihood of persons, it creates modes of sociality and sustains a vital *sense* of what it means to coexist and cooperate with others. Accordingly, human labor not only generates and regenerates organic and social being; it is the means whereby human beings create and recreate the intersubjective experience that defines their primary sense of who they are. R. D. Laing calls this sense of existential integrity "ontological security" (1965, chap. 3). It implies that human beings need to belong to and engage effectively in a world of others, having some say, some voice, some sense of making a difference in the group with which they identify, yet without occluding or denying the comparable needs of others. The struggle for this balance between being-for-oneself and being-for-others is the *conditio per quam* of social existence.[10] When this balance is irrecoverably lost, and

10. I am echoing Sartre's contrast (1956) between being *en-soi* and *pour-soi,* which itself echoes Heidegger's distinction between mere objects (*vorhanden*) to whom human interest or action has given no meaning, and objects that have been picked up and charged with meaning in the light of human designs and desires (*zuhanden*).

both self and other are reduced to the status of mutually alien objects, we may then speak of pathologies of loss.

Existentially, loss is a reduction to nothingness. But as Sartre (1956) showed, Being and Non-Being are never "empty abstractions"; as possibilities they "haunt" every social relationship as emotions of attraction and repulsion, and as good and bad faith. My emphasis is on being as choosing; nothingness is, accordingly, the dispossession of choice. More precisely, nothingness is not so much an absence of meaning, a metaphysical lack, an intellectual void, a sense of being insignificant; nothingness arises out of an inability to act. It is the byproduct of being reduced to passivity, of not being able to do or say anything that has any effect on others, or makes any difference to the way things are. One of my tasks in this work is to elucidate this dialectic between givenness and choice, action and inaction, existence and inexistence, *cross-culturally*. Thus for the Kuranko, to be without kin, childless, and uncared for is tantamount to death. Among the Warlpiri being is sitting (*nyinami*), so to be without country is not to belong, to be bereft of the ontological ground of human being (Jackson 1995; cf. Myers 1986, 48). For the Maori of New Zealand being is standing-presence, and identity derives from the place where one has a right to stand (*turangawaewae*).[11] In these ways, though Being and Nothingness pervade human consciousness, the movement between these poles finds different mundane, affective, and metaphorical expression in different human societies.

Balance/Control

Normally, disease is never simply a loss or impairment of function. Oliver Sacks notes that there is "always a reaction, on the part of the affected organism or individual, to restore, to replace, to compensate for and to preserve its identity" (1986, 4). This same principle of recruitment—whereby lesions are repaired and losses made good by new growth—obtains in social life. But it is never solely individuals whose identity is at stake but *relationships* between persons as well as relationships between persons and the things that have ultimate value for them. Thus the loss of one's language, land, livelihood, and personal belongings, or the belittle-

---

11. The root *sta* occurs in numerous Indo-European words for physical, conceptual, and social Being: standing, understanding, status, estate, institution, constitution, statute, etc. (see Straus 1966, 143).

ment and shaming of those with whom one most closely identifies, are readily experienced as assaults on one's own person.

Every human encounter entails ontological risk. But from an existential point of view, what is at issue is not so much the integrity of the self but a *balance* between the world one calls one's own and a world one deems to be not-self or other. This balance is a matter of control. And it is the struggle for this control that is the driving force of intersubjective life.

No person is ever completely open or completely closed to others. There are times when one experiences oneself as a substantial, skin-encapsulated, stable unity; at other times one seems to transcend one's body and become riverine and ethereal, or merge with the body of one's family or community and have no other reality. Drew Leder, mindful that consciousness is a lived modality of *embodied* being, speaks of ecstatic and recessive extremes of bodily consciousness, a perpetual, context-specific slippage between fade-out and fade-in, absence and presence, visceral and skin depth (Leder 1990). William James pointed out in his *Principles of Psychology* that these *modes of experience* are often wrongly ontologized as competing *theories* of the self (Plato's and Aristotle's substantialist view, Kant's transcendentalist view, and Hume's associationalist view), but what really matters are the existential conditions under which these strategic modulations of self-consciousness, this perpetual movement between intransitive and transitive moments, occur (James 1950, 371).

What holds true on the subjective plane holds true *mutatis mutandis* on the intersubjective plane. Boundaries are defined only to be transgressed. But any such transgression precipitates a crisis of control. That is to say, in both the fields of interpersonal and intergroup relations, the critical issue is always whether a person is in control of this switching and oscillation between his or her own particular world and the world considered not-self or other.

This notion of *control* merges cybernetic and existential senses of the term (Wiener 1948). I use the word *control* as a synonym for "steering a course between." The word connotes governance and adjustment between self and other rather than the maintenance of a fixed line, the imposition of one person's will, or the establishment of a rigid order. As such it involves both self-reflection *and* dialogue. It is a matter of balancing, of dynamic equilibrium. But by *balance* I do not mean static equilibrium, harmony, or homeostasis. I mean to imply an ongoing dialectic in which persons vie and strategize in order to avoid nullification as well as to achieve some sense of governing their own fate. Michel Serres coins the word *homeorrhesis* for this kind of turbulent eddying in which crosscurrents and continual interchanges prevent absolute fixity and rest (Serres 1983, 74). Should self and other become so polarized and estranged that there is a complete breakdown of dialogue between them—as in structures of absolute dominance and submission—the existential loser has recourse to extreme counteractive measures to break the deadlock, to make good his or her loss, and revitalize the social system. One sees this in the work of tricksters, in ritual role reversal, in carnival, and in rebellion.

"To be in hell is to drift, . . . to be in heaven is to steer," wrote George Bernard Shaw. But the imperative need for self-determination or self-definition has always to be adjusted to the equivalent needs of others. Navaho thought nicely captures this intimate connection between subjective and intersubjective control: if there is to be balance or "social harmony" (*hozho*) in the world, "people must be able to first create *hozho* in their minds" (Witherspoon 1977, 180). This entails a complementarity of controlled statis *and* creative activity (195–96). Among the Yolmo Sherpas of the Nepalese Himalayas a similar critical balance between social and somatic life depends on each individual being able to control and coordinate his or her body-heart-mind within the context of social relationships (Desjarlais 1992, 72–77).

Existentially, then, equilibrium is a matter of striking a balance between the countervailing needs of self and other. Experientially, this is sometimes felt to be a struggle between spirit—which is vitally centered on the self—and matter, which is the inert force of the external world. But in every human society concepts such as fate, history, evolution, God, chance, and even the weather signify forces of otherness that one cannot fully fathom and over which one can expect to exercise little or no ultimate control. These forces are given; they are in the nature of things. In spite of this, human beings countermand and transform these forces by dint of their imagination and will so that, in every society, it is possible to outline a domain of action and understanding in which people expect to be able to grasp, manipulate, and master their own fate.[12] This is the microcosm in

12. Any parent anywhere will attest to the need that children have to decide things for themselves, to order their own universe, to play with the possibilities of the world in which they find themselves. This ontological imperative for "self-coherence," "self-agency," "self-affectivity," and "self-history" that constitute a sense of a "core self" is evident from early infancy (Stern 1985).

which we demand the right to have our voices heard, in which we expect our acts to have some effect, and into which we strive to extend our practical understanding.

These two domains are never discrete. They overlap. They invade each other. They may be variously described as the world of fate and of free will, the world of nature and of culture, the world of the gods and the world of human struggle, the public domain of the polis and the private domain of the individual citizen. Moving between these domains, playing them off against each other, negotiating the troubled boundary between them—between the world one claims the right to call one's own and the world one relinquishes rights in and forfeits to otherness—constitutes the central dynamic of human action.

Elsewhere I have argued that striking a balance between such ecstatic and enstatic extremes constitutes in all societies the experience of being at home in the world (Jackson 1995, 123–24). That is to say, sociality is achieved neither in masochistic abnegation, reclusiveness, or fatalism, nor in totalitarian excess, hysteria, and megalomania, but in a ceaseless cybernetic adjustment of contending needs and interests. Thus the struggle between groups of aboriginal people for native title and the counterassertions of state's rights or the "national interest" is but one example of a universal problem that is at once ethical and political (Jackson 1995). Does a woman have the right to abort a fetus, or is this right properly vested in Congress or the church? Do I have the right to take my own life, or does this right belong to the state? Where does my freedom end and the demands of the collectivity take over?

An ethics and a theory of justice are entailed in these situations. The assumption that people everywhere seek to adjust *their* world to *the* world at large implies that justice as fairness[13] is everywhere a matter of having some sense of control over one's own life, of experiencing a just apportionment of forces and of things between the particular world I consider mine and the wider world I associate with others.

Rather than view the particular and the universal as static, predefined, and opposed, I see them as terms in a dialectic that admits no final resolution. As I have already noted this dialectic embraces many refractions of

13. John Rawls uses the principle of redress as the basis of a theory of social justice, the idea being "to redress the bias of contingencies in the direction of equality" (Rawls 1971, 100–101).

the core experience that we are at one and the same time part of a singular, particular, and finite world *and* caught up a wider world whose horizons are effectively infinite. My thesis is that *control over the relationship and balance between these worlds is a central human preoccupation.*

Control, right, and *power,* in the sense in which I am using the words here, are issues of existential mastery *before they are matters of economic or political advantage.*

In his early work on power relationships, Foucault observed that we have "only two models available to us: firstly, the model offered by the law (power as law, proscription, institution), secondly, the model based on war and strategy in terms of relationships of strength" (in Lévy 1995, 372). Subsequently, however, Foucault's conception of power undergoes a sea change. The Sartrean question he had earlier shelved—how is power exercised intersubjectively?—now becomes central. Speaking of this "theoretical shift" from institutions like hospitals, asylums, and prisons to the field of the subject, Foucault noted the necessity of looking "for the forms and modalities of the relation to self by which the individual constitutes and recognizes himself qua subject" (1990, 6). Elsewhere he confesses that he had overemphasized "techniques of domination," and that his interest was now in those "techniques of the self" that "permit individuals to effect a certain number of operations on their own bodies, on their souls, on their own thoughts, on their own conduct, and this in a manner so as to transform themselves, modify themselves, or to act in a certain state of perfection, of happiness, of purity, of supernatural power, and so on" (Foucault 1980, cited in Miller 1993, 321–22).

My argument is that power must *first* be understood in precisely this existential sense of empowerment, and that we need to move away from a preoccupation with political control, and control over resources and capital, in order to understand the *modus vivendi* that is strived for in all contexts of human endeavor—imaginary or material—namely, a balance between what is given and what is chosen such that a person comes to experience the world as a subject and not solely as a contingent predicate.

In this sense one might say that an attempt to deconstruct or simply avoid such category terms as *politics, history, economics, law, religion,* and even *culture,* on the assumption that lived experience always overflows and confounds the words with which we try to capture or analyze it, is allied to the revolutionary struggle of the oppressed. But not in any crudely ideological or political sense. To declare against circumscriptive language is to declare for the phenomenal world of immediate experience, interpersonal relations, and lived events. It is to testify to the wealth of life in even the most poverty-stricken and desperate situations. It is to emphasize the *experience* of being in control rather than assuming that control must be first defined objectively as a matter of commanding wealth, possessing power, or manipulating the fate of one's fellow human beings.

To this end I abolish, or at least bracket out, any *a priori* distinctions between real and imaginary control, or scientific and magical mastery. Such a move enables us to explore, for instance, contemporary secular anxieties of losing control over one's life—which find expression in the anxiety of job loss, invasive gaze, disease contamination, terrorist attack, abuse, loss of reproductive potency and control, or abduction by aliens—much in the same way that William James explored the varieties of religious experience.

"Control is a nineties obsession," writes Kathy Bail (1997, 38), reminding us of the possibilities of vicarious mastery with which the media captivate us: fantasies of controlling cars at high speed, means of managing aging, sexuality, diets, budgets, and consciousness. But control of the balance between self and not-self is an imperative that carries us beyond postmodernity. And this control does not everywhere consist of some crassly conspicuous governance of one's world; it may entail yielding and abnegation.

Gillian Rose has recently made this point with great passion. Terminally ill, she speaks of how control may often be gained by surrendering it:

> "Control" in this context has two distinct meanings, both crucial. In the first place, "control," as you would expect, means priority and ability to manage, not to force, the compliance of others, to determine what others think or do. In the second, more elusive sense—a sense which, nevertheless, saves my life and which, once achieved, may induce the relinquishing of "control" in the first sense—"control" means that when something untoward happens, some trauma or damage, whether inflicted by the commissions or omissions of others, or some cosmic force, one makes the initially unwelcome event one's own inner occupation. You work to adopt the most loveless, forlorn, aggressive child as your own, and do not leave her to develop into an even more vengeful monster, who constantly wishes you ill. In ill-health as in unhappy love, this is the hardest work: it requires taking in before letting be (1995, 97–98).

Life Stories

That Gillian Rose had recourse to stories as a way of working through her crisis is itself telling. In the face of death, certain knowledge and medical technology may be less useful than magical or fictive resources.

Since Freud developed the psychoanalytical technique of transference, in which the analysand yields authority to the analyst in order to plumb the unconscious—recovering repressed memories and articulating them as stories—the so-called talking cure has been recognized as a powerful therapeutic technique. The technique helps us recover an awareness of words as our first objects—but objects that inform human subjectivity more deeply than any others, for, as Lacan notes, their genesis and efflorescence lies within the body-self.[14]

But storytelling is motivated by more than a compulsion to confess (Reik 1966) or a need for self-expression. Life stories emerge in the course of *inter*subjective life, and intersubjectivity is a site of conflicting wills and intentions. Accordingly, the life stories that individuals bring to a relationship are metamorphosed in the course of that relationship. They are thus, in a very real sense, authored not by autonomous subjects but by the dynamics of intersubjectivity, in which initiatives are often frustrated and desire transformed. Yet unlike material objects, which are also produced in the course of human interaction, stories always convey this twofold sense of the human subject as *both* actor *and* sufferer (Arendt 1958, 184).

Traumatic experiences challenge habitual expectations and unsettle our customary modes of understanding. In causing us to doubt the truth of what we think we know and the efficacy of what we customarily do, unprecedented experiences entail a crisis of control. We are thrown. We are confused. Our world begins to fall apart. Yet in all human societies, recounting one's experiences in the presence of others is a way of reimagining one's situation and regaining mastery over it. Stories enable people to renegotiate retrospectively their relation with others, recovering a sense of self and of voice that was momentarily taken from them. This is dramatically brought home by the effects of victim-impact statements at sentencing hearings when, by publicly voicing their pain and anger, grieving families reclaim some sense of general recognition of the humanity that the murder or rape of their loved one took away from them.

---

14. Among the Mande *kan* is the word for both language and throat. Words are said and felt to arise within the body. They are part and parcel of a person's embodied subjectivity.

Such transformations may be momentary or magical, but in relating a reconfigured yet symbolically coherent version of an event, we come to feel that the true meaning of an event that befell and overpowered us lies within our grasp—partly, if not entirely, a matter of our own insight and agency. Narrative thereby mediates a reinvention of identity. As Karen Blixen put it, "All sorrows can be borne if you can put them into a story or tell a story about them" (cited in Arendt 1958, 175). In a similar vein, Anatole Broyard has written recently of the way he used narrative and metaphor to deal with dying. Stories, he notes, are instinctual ways in which we try to confine a catastrophe, to rescue ourselves from the unknown, to bring an overwhelming and incomprehensible experience "under control" (Broyard 1992, 19–21).

The same principle holds true of ritual. In male initiation rites the world over, the passage of human life from birth to death is played backward. When neophytes are symbolically killed and reborn, a natural course of events gives way to a culturally contrived sequence, creating the impression that men have mastery over life and death. This vicarious midwifery implies that men possess the power of women to bear children and influence the destiny of their sons. Whatever the psychological and social reasons behind this sleight of hand, it has the effect of making men imagine themselves the generators of life, the measure of all things (Jackson 1977, 202–4; Thomas 1973, 407–8; Jackson 1995, 147). At funerals a similar ritual passage from passivity to activity occurs: in reenacting, remembering, and recounting the life of a loved one, the living succeed in simultaneously metamorphosing the dead into an ideal type—an ancestor, a paragon—and experiencing for themselves an ability to go on with life.

Objectively, stories and ritual scenarios seldom tell the truth about what actually happened. They tell a truth that enables people to live in the here and now with what happened *to* them in the past. In this sense, the scenarios are expedient lies; they prioritize the existential urge to remaster experience rather than the epistemological need to preserve an exact record of it.

The Itinerary of an Idea

The train stops. I gaze out at people in a city street, bent on their business, apparently oblivious to each other, creatures of habit and inheritance. At this remove they appear identical in their comportment, their attire, and their expressions. I could be watching ants industriously repairing a disturbed colony. Or a scatter of objects without intrinsic meaning, creating no meaning as they come and go, trapped entirely in the situation in which they find themselves. "Human beings, facing outward like the Seasons, moving hand in hand in intricate measure: stepping slowly, methodically, sometimes a trifle awkwardly . . . unable to control the melody, unable, perhaps, to control the steps of the dance" (Powell 1951, 2).

Yet I know that the individuals in the street below me see themselves as epicenters of conscious worlds, the authors of purposes that outrun the course of what is behaviorally evident. Schemes, fantasies, anxieties, fragments of information, memories, and preoccupations constitute for each person a unique and partially disguised microcosm that I can only guess at. Creatures of history and habit, to be sure, but in their *experience* of the world in which they make their way with such blind faith, they are each singular and significant. Each has friends and families for whom the world would be the less without them. Each has a story to tell. It is, therefore, not what they *apparently do* that wholly defines their humanity—or would suffice as a scientific description of their nature—but what they *virtually experience* in the course of their actual lives.

SEEN FROM SPACE, the earth deepens our sense of the infinite and unknown. But observed remotely, human beings are diminished, for unlike the material earth they are conscious of their own existence, and this consciousness seldom mirrors exactly the biogenetic and environmental realities that shape their lives. This is why the view from afar gives us no purchase on human reality unless it is complemented by and compared with a view from within. Recognizing this interplay between the forces that bear upon us and the projects whereby we reimagine and rework those forces makes any description of human reality *both* a matter of science *and* of art.

Though we are for the most part creatures of habit and inheritors of a cultural and biogenetic past over which we have no governance, our imaginary and our ordinary conscious life fly in the face of these brute facts of existence. Aware, for example, that we are ultimately no more significant than the billions of other human beings who have lived out their brief lives on earth, reproduced their kind, died, and been forgotten, our desire to have children, to raise them well, and to find fulfillment for ourselves is largely unaffected by this knowledge. We lead our lives according to rational planning as well as necessary illusions. In many ways our lives contradict what is the case. Indeed, most human lives gainsay the conditions that underlie their possibility. We live against the grain of the habitual. We seek to make that which is given and inevitable seem chosen and original. Human consciousness is a field of energy focused on lifting us out of the merely material and endowing it with our intentionality, just as, in Native American myth, the earth diver once dredged mud from the depths and darkness of a primordial ocean to shape an inhabitable island in the light of day.

IN 1969–70—MY FIRST PERIOD of fieldwork in Sierra Leone—I was struck by the ways in which the Kuranko periodically confounded, overturned, and played with the ideal order of their social world only to reestablish, reaffirm, and consolidate it. This vital process of negating then reconfiguring the status quo was abundantly evident on ritual occasions when a hiatus or crisis disturbed or suspended the ordinary order of things and diviners were consulted, sacrifices offered, medicines sought, initiations begun, or the dead buried. But it was equally evident in the trivial and contentious palaver of everyday life: a pedantic argument over the origin of a word, a disagreement over the refund of bride wealth, a domestic altercation, a dispute over the boundary between two farms. Kuranko people entered into such dialectic with an energy that I found mystifying and perverse until I realized I was witnessing a kind of informal theater in which people shaped their lives, not in slavish conformity to custom but through active engagement, negotiation, and struggle.

Against the prevailing structural-functional orthodoxy that analyzed how deviance was dealt with and disorder redressed, I sought to understand the antinomian in existential terms—as an imperative aspect of social being. It seemed to me that negation, resistance, and alterity were as fundamental to human existence as order, security, and routine. At the same time, I wanted to work with ideas indigenous to the Mande world itself, such as the Bamana notion that sociality is born of a rapprochement or balance between "wild" energies—symbolized by the mythical figure of Nyalé—and normative constraints, symbolized by Ndomadyiri (Zahan 1974, 3–5); or the Kuranko notion that some kind of complementarity must exist between secular and "wild" powers (Jackson 1982a, 10); or the Dogon dialectic between Yourougou, the pale fox, who is extravagance, disorder, and oracular truth, and Nommo, who is reason and order (Calame-Griaule 1965).

Where structural functionalism tended to reify the social order, finding in it the ultimate cause and consummation of human existence, I wanted to know as directly as possible something of the experiences of the individuals who in fact constituted this order. As I saw it, the driving force in any social field was the vital intelligence and energy of individuals acting alone or in concert. Antinomian moments such as ritual role reversals, narrative inversions and transformations, domestic recalcitrance, youthful delinquency, ecstatic experience, and encounters with djinn were paradigmatic ways in which people stepped outside the circle of normative village life in order to recapture and reconstitute it in ways that were charged with a sense of having *chosen* it thus, of being both conscious and in control of it.

Human social life was thus a dialectic between givenness and choice, a continual movement between an externally factitious world shaped by one's ancestors in a previous epoch and that same world recreated, reworked, and reconstrued by the living in the light of imperatives that included respect for the past *as well as* the changing exigencies of the present. Even if Kuranko society remained, from a God's-eye view, unchanged generation after generation, it was the purposeful activity of the living that determined this. Yet even here, paradoxically, the ancestral world *had to be* negated by the living in order to be affirmed.

Sartre's existential Marxism provided me with the interpretive framework I needed. According to Sartre's progressive-regressive method, one should aim to describe *both* the preexisting social and historical factors that constitute any human situation (the practico-inert) *and* the ways in which projective, imaginative, and purposeful human action (praxis) both conserves and goes beyond these prior conditions. Although the world one inherits is initially experienced as inert and objective—a world sufficient unto itself, made up of anterior choices and *faits accompli*—this world is reconstituted continually through human labor and in the human imagination, so that one's sense of being merely an "accidental individual" gives way to a sense that one makes a difference to the world in which one came to consciousness. Because one never simply conserves the world into which one is thrown, a human life is, in Sartre's terms "dialectically irreducible."

Thus we encounter the world as a fetishized product of previous activity, the work of other lives, an outcome of inscrutable designs. This given world appears to possess a life of its own, and we the living seem to dwell in its shadow. Yet without our consent and labor this sedimented world of ancestral acts and foregone conclusions could not prevail. Its perpetuation is not a matter of inertia but of the vital activity of the living who, in Marx's compelling phrase, force the frozen circumstances to dance by singing to them their own melody (cited in Fromm 1973, 83).

Dostoyevsky saw this dialectic as a matter of proving to oneself continually, even perversely, that one is a person and not a piano key (1961, 115).[15] For Sartre the critical thing about human existence was that "we are not lumps of clay, and what is important is not what others make of us but what we ourselves make of what they have made us" (1963, 49). Nikos Kazantzakis observed that "to say 'yes' to necessity and change the inevitable into something done of [one's] own free will . . . is perhaps the only human way to deliverance. It is a pitiable way, but there is no other" (1961, 274). Norman Brown, invoking Spinoza's principle of *causa sui* and Sartre's *être-en-soi-pour-soi* reconstrued the Oedipus complex as the "oedipal project"—an ongoing process of self-making in which a person moves from being a passive object of fate, an appendage of others, a plaything of the world, to active and responsible mastery of the social world (Brown 1959, 118; Becker 1975, 35–36).

But it is the way we live the *relationship* between the world into which we are born and the world we have a hand in making that defines the field of existential anthropology. In other words, existential anthropology must be careful to disengage its project from others that though akin to it, place undue emphasis on autonomous individuality and self-actualization and ignore the particular *cultural* milieux in which such existential imperatives unfold.[16] The critical issue is *intersubjectivity and interexperience*—the ways in which selfhood emerges and is negotiated in a field of interpersonal relations, as a mode of being in the world.

Playing with Reality

The existential imperative to exercise choice in and control over one's life is grounded in play. If life is conceived as a game, then it slips and slides between a slavish adherence to the rules and a desire to play fast and loose with them. Play enables us to renegotiate the given, experiment with alter-

15. This existential theme finds recent expression in Todorov's "critical humanism." He observes, not without irony, that the only generalization that seems to hold true for all human beings at all times is that they share "an ability to *reject* . . . determinations" and break free from the binding conditions that govern their lives. "My milieu unquestionably induces me to reproduce the behaviors it valorizes; but the possibility of breaking free from these behaviors exists as well, and that is essential" (1993, 390).

16. I am thinking here of notions that belong to the European romantic and heroic traditions, of a transcendent ego that stands out or struggles against the constraints of society, history, or biology—Nietzsche's "will-to-power," Erich Fromm's "man for himself" (1949), Otto Rank's "will psychology" (1936), Erik Erikson's "epigenesis of identity" (1968), Norman Brown's "oedipus project" (1959), and Dorothy Lee's "autonomous motivation" (1976).

natives, imagine how things might be otherwise, and so resolve obliquely and artificially that which cannot be resolved directly in the "real" world. What we call freedom is founded in our ability to gainsay and invent, to countermand in our actions and imagination the situations that appear to circumscribe, rule, and define us.

Phylogenetically, choice is an expression of neoteny. As Géza Róheim argued, it is this prolongation of the period of juvenile dependency and development in higher primates that allows time and space for play (1971). Culture is the outcome of this freedom to toy with new possibilities, to explore new strategies of interaction, to experiment with consciousness, and to vary points of view. Any parent will attest to how imperative it is for a child to play with a given situation as a way of deciding things for himself or herself.[17] A child's moral sensibility and sense of well-being is conditional upon having some sense of being in charge of the world—possessing a miniature space where he or she decides the order of things and defines the ground rules. This play imperative constitutes the grounds of the existential imperative: to do things in one's own time and in one's own way, to think of the world as something one creates, as well as something of which one is merely a creature.

Choosing, or *imagining* that we choose, our lives, is such an imperative aspect of our humanity that even in the face of absolute loss of freedom we will often act as though the situation were still in our hands, that our actions might make a difference, that it is possible to think our way free of the chains that bind us. Though we may disagree with Sartre's notion that relinquishing choice is itself an act of choice, the notion is not Sartre's alone, for it is realized in countless human situations where people assume responsibility for things that are not, strictly speaking, within their power to choose. Thus in the diamond districts of Sierra Leone, the Kuranko are notorious for naively owning up to thefts they did not commit. They prefer to clear the air rather than leave a crisis unresolved. And bereaved individuals sometimes imagine they did not do enough for their loved one, and

17. 29 July 1996—my eighteen-month-old daughter, Freya, loves wheeling her pram around rather than riding in it. Yesterday her mother bought her a toy pram. Freya wheels her Eeyore through the park and in the motel room, brooking no interference from us, jealous of her domain of autonomy and mastery, determined to do herself what has for so long been done to her, to assume active mastery of a situation she has so far lived in passivity. March 1997—now two, Freya's self-assertiveness is even more noticeable. "No, me do it, Daddy," is a continual refrain, except when she chooses to have her mother or father take the initiative, as at bedtime, with stories. Then it is the directive: "Daddy, read it."

failed them in some way, as though in retrospectively assuming a degree of choice in a matter over which they had no control they restore to themselves the capacity to act that "died" with the person whose life gave their life meaning. George Devereux speaks of the way humans deal preemptively with the "trauma of the unresponsiveness of matter" by entering into relationships with the nonhuman world as though it had consciousness and will (1967, 32–34). But the same anthropomorphic stratagem obtains *within* the human world when, reduced to the status of an object or panicked by encountering an unresponsive other (dead, deaf, unconscious, catatonic, comatose), a person acts *as if* agency and consciousness were somehow still present. There is something outrageous about situations that rob us of the power to act, speak, know, choose, and make a difference. So we *imagine* choosing, and lacerate ourselves with guilt that we chose badly or missed our chance. Even in the most desperate, humbling, and overwhelming situations, people seek imperatively to wrest back control, to reassert the right to govern their own lives, to be complicit in their own fate.

Play theory is essential to understanding these existential stratagems. But while most play theorists stress either the adaptive value of play in the evolution of culture or the problem-solving value of play in social learning, I prefer to emphasize the ways in which "mastery play" helps people regain a sense of control in situations that overwhelm, confuse, and diminish them.

Mastery play, observes Jerome Bruner, is a "special form of violating fixity" (1976, 31). Existentially, this largely imaginary or magical mode of play enables us to toy with, reconstrue, reauthor, and reverse a situation in which we find ourselves confounded and unfree. It is a way of acting that, while leaving unchanged the objective situation (as seen from the outside), transforms our *experience* of the situation.

One of the most paradigmatic examples of this mastery play is in Freud's *Beyond the Pleasure Principle*. Here Freud describes how a one-and-a-half-year-old child would manipulate objects that came to hand in order to exert "mastery" over his mother's going away and returning (1957, 18:14–16). Throwing a toy out of his cot and declaring it gone (*fort*), then reeling it back in with an exultant "there" (*da*), the child successfully objectified his emotional distress. In Freud's words, the game "was related to the child's great cultural achievement—. . . the renunciation of instinctual satisfaction . . . which he had made in allowing his mother to go away without protesting. He compensated himself for this, as it were, by himself staging the disappearance and return of the objects within his reach" (16). The existential point is, however, as Freud himself suggests, that the child accomplished through his improvised game a transition from a passive situation (in which he was overpowered by the experience) to an active role in "mastering it."

In *La Pensée sauvage* Lévi-Strauss offers a similar insight into the power of play. Speaking of works of art, Lévi-Strauss asks, "What is the virtue of reduction either of scale or in the number of properties?" He then notes that this tendency, evident in all art and in all magic, to miniaturize, simplify, and rearrange is driven by a desire to make the real object less formidable, and so to bring it under control: "By being quantitatively diminished, it seems to us qualitatively simplified. More exactly, this quantitative transposition extends and diversifies our power over a homologue of the thing, and by means of it the latter can be grasped, assessed and apprehended at a glance." Not only does Lévi-Strauss pinpoint the connection between play and magic; he illuminates the way in which existential control involves a reduction of the scale of the world to the scale of the self. The universal is thus rendered as a particular that lies within the ambit and grasp of the individual: "A child's doll is no longer an enemy, a rival, or even an interlocutor. In it and through it a person is made into a subject" (Lévi-Strauss 1966, 23).

In play, intersubjective relationships are remodeled as subject-object relations. We play with and relate to objects that stand for others. Winnicott called such objects "transitional objects" because they enable us to distance ourselves from interpersonal relationships that have become perplexing and anxiety provoking. As "objective correlatives" of these relationships they provide us with simulacra that we can manipulate in order to recover some measure of autonomy. Freud's anecdote of the child reeling a toy back into his cot ties in with Winnicott's clinical account of a boy preoccupied with string (1974, 18–23): in both cases the string symbolized the child's relationship and communication with the mother; playing with the string was a vicarious stratagem for regaining control over a relationship that had become fraught and confusing.

In as much as an existential-phenomenological perspective resists measuring experience against some extraneous standard or drawing a line between actual and imagined mastery, what matters most is the experiential and social consequences of such behavior. If our criterion of truth is a pragmatic one, reflecting the consummation of a shared goal, the endurance of pain, the fulfillment of an expectation, then the *outcome* of any belief or action is of more moment that the situations and states of mind that precede it. It is in this sense that artistic, ritual, and religious action may be placed on a par with scientific strategies. The models and metaphors with which a scientist makes sense of a welter of sense data—reducing them to generative principles or determinate rules—are, whatever their ultimate verifiability, means of ordering and authoring the world. Defining and redefining such worlds as Structure and History as if they were isomorphic with the world provides us with an illusory grasp of a reality that has, in fact, been replaced by language. Like models, the jargon conjures a momentary and consoling order out of the flux of experience, seeming to subordinate a refractory material world to the hegemony of reason. As such they provide a way of salvaging some sense of mastery over a world that masters us, of regaining or renegotiating a balance between what we can and cannot control.

Writing Intersubjectivity

How might one best explicate the connections between the dialectic of subject and object in intimate and familial life[18] and the syntactical, logical, and political dialectics of subject-object?

Following Merleau-Ponty, I argue that the mediation between the singular and universal *I* is accomplished through the body and through dialogue (1962, part 2:4). But though subjectivity is embodied, sensate, enacted, and voiced, neither body nor language should be seen as objects or instruments that are taken up by the subject who, as it were, conceives of an intention before acting on it.[19]

This "consummate reciprocity" that finds expression in gestural, affective, and dialogical intersubjectivity draws us inevitably into the experience of storytelling, music making, and dance (Blacking 1973; Feld 1982; Lange 1975). Stories, in de Certeau's words, are "spatial practices." They

18. Arguing for an approach to national space and national culture that recognizes the social poetics as well as the categorical forms of identity, Michael Herzfeld speaks of the intersubjective field of commonplace sociality as "cultural intimacy" (1997).

19. Merleau-Ponty 1962, 139; cf. Benveniste 1971, 224. Merleau-Ponty's notion of the body-subject is paralleled by Benveniste's notion of the speaking-subject who has a sense of self only in relation to the other he or she addresses. This complementarity between I and Thou is the condition of both dialogue and personhood (Benveniste 1971, 224–25). Merleau-Ponty's notion of the experience of dialogue as the "common ground" between self and other (1962, 354) may also be compared with Bakhtin's concept of the "dialogic imagination" (Holquist 1981) and Sartre's notion of language as a kind of circulating materiality, analogous to money, that carries my projects into the other and the other's projects into me (Sartre 1982, 98).

bear within them ghostly reminders of our quotidian journeying to and fro in our constructed environments. They convey in words a sense of the body-subject occupying, inhabiting, and moving though space, thus transforming it into places embued with particular meaning and specific presence (de Certeau 1988, 118; Tuan 1977).

Life stories are the connective tissue of social life and call into question many of the category distinctions that anthropologists construct for purely instrumental reasons—to systematize their fieldwork experience, identify themselves professionally, and promote the notion that while the world may not be subject to administrative order, it can at least be domesticated and subjugated through logic, theory, and academic argot. Accordingly, this book may be read as autobiography—as a succession of attempts to integrate particular and universal perspectives by juxtaposing essayist and narrative styles of writing. Progressively, I use life stories to counter anthropology's proclivity to flatten out difference and contingency in order to promote an illusory authority.

In the course of doing fieldwork, an ethnographer hears and records a lot of stories. Conventionally, one converts these stories or fragments of stories into anthropological essays, dissertations, and monographs. It's an academic habit that goes back to the early seventeenth century, when the rise of science entailed a "dissociation of sensibilities" in which authority shifted from direct testimony and immediate experience to abstract and imperiously panoptic forms of discursive practice. In Dr. Johnson's great dictionary, an essay was defined as "an irregular undigested piece" (cf. Bacon's definition of an essay as a "dispersed meditation"), but before long it became a vehicle for systematizing and communicating the results of scientific experimentation, "a finished treatise" (SOED).

As Walter Benjamin lamented, we live in a world where, by and large, essayist literacy carries more weight than narrative competence: "Less and less frequently do we encounter people with the ability to tell a tale properly. More and more often there is embarrassment all around when the wish to hear a story is expressed. It is as if something that seemed inalienable to us, the securest among our possessions, were taken from us: the ability to exchange experiences" (1968, 83).

To reclaim narrative is thus to retrace history to a time when direct experience constituted a form of truth, when wisdom and knowledge had not parted company, and stories were the commonest way of communicating and sharing the trials of life. And yet, as Foucault reminds us, the essay once possessed this very function—as an assay or experiment in which the author's identity was tried, tested, and put at risk. Foucault celebrates this mode of essayist writing as a form of ordeal [*épreuve*] that transfigures self in the play of truth. Instead of an appropriation, arrogation, or conquest that simplifies in order to communicate, it assumes the form of an askesis—"an exercise of oneself in the activity of thought" (Foucault 1990, 9). Adorno also celebrates the essay as an antidote to the philosophical habit of seeking only the universal and enduring, and eschewing the inconclusive, the tentative, the digressive, and the open ended. The essay, he notes, may be a bridge between science and art, at once an implicit critique of system and a testimony to the value of experience and irony in a world captivated by categorical thought (1991, 6–10). In this sense the essay merges with storytelling, which, Hannah Arendt observes, "reveals meaning without committing the error of defining it" (1973, 107). The storyteller testifies to life as it is lived rather than seeking to get beyond the particular situation of which he or she has direct experience in order to say something authoritative about the nature of the world. Stories bear witness to our search for some kind of provisional faith or wisdom that will make life bearable, rather than to our need for transcendence in a body of knowledge that ostensibly holds good for all people at all times. So it is that stories help us reconcile ourselves to the ways things are, rather than point to ways in which the world may be changed.

But the most telling difference between the life story and the scientific tract is not epistemological but social. Malinowski was perhaps the first ethnographer to explore a well-nigh universal distinction between "stories"—which function as "tools for conviviality" (Illich 1973)—and "myths and legends," which open up "historical vistas," legitimate social divisions, and are regarded as venerable, sacred, and true.[20] Malinowski's "charter myths" resemble the systematizing and authorizing discourse of science. Whereas the place of stories is intimate and immediate, evoking memories of childhood and of close family, or of crowded porches in an African village where children and adults sit spellbound by tales of djinn and tricksters, essayistic literacy implies isolation and distinction. This is because the authority of the scientific essay stems not from a *communis sententia* arrived at through shared experiences of mundane life but from

20. Malinowski 1974, 107. The Trobrianders' distinction between *kukwanebu* ("tales") on the one hand and *libwogwo* ("legends") and *liliu* ("sacred myths") on the other corresponds to the Kuranko distinction between *tilei* ("tales") and *kuma kore* ("venerable speech")—the latter being antinomian and fostering *communitas,* the second underwriting estate, age, and gender divisions (Jackson 1982a, 7).

an exclusive knowledge that defines the precinct of a professional and privileged class (Lyotard 1984, 25). Always arcane, always couched in cabbalistic language, always the preserve of an elite, essayist knowledge implicitly divides those in the know from those in the dark.

At a time when the division between the haves and the have-nots is widening, and when ethnographers are wrestling with the problem of how to articulate their understanding of other cultures in ways that do justice to the people who actually inhabit those cultures, the return to narrative is a political act (cf. Abu-Lughod 1993, 16–19). Not only does it imply a critique of metaphysics and transcendence, it attempts to undercut discursive conventions that foster hierarchy and division.

Michel de Certeau observes that the scientific essay is to narrative as topographical map is to a tour. From the fifteenth and seventeenth centuries, maps became increasingly empty of the kinds of pictorial image—sea monsters, ships, cherubs, plants, cities, and imaginary animals—that filled the spaces of medieval maps. As cartography replaced these icons and legends with abstract, scientific data, the narrative experience of the map as a territory across which one actually traveled was lost. Maps ceased to be places of sensible activity and human journeying; they became dissociated from practice, disembodied, and static. But, observes de Certeau, narratives and tours constitute a countervailing, delinquent mode of discourse and depiction that survives this geometrical distancing: "What the map cuts up, the story cuts across" (1988, 129).

ANTHROPOLOGY HAS ALWAYS tended to drift into the kind of abstractions and reifications that might define and justify its identity as a social science. Terms such as *society, habitus,* and *culture* can all too easily obscure the lifeworlds they are supposed to cover, and we must continually remind ourselves that social life is *lived* at the interface of self and other despite the fact that anonymous conceptual and material objects are sedimented there. If we are not to eclipse the interpersonal and intersubjective lifeworlds that we enter and struggle to understand as ethnographers, we must resist fetishizing the vocabularies that we have evolved to define our goals, explicate our methods, and theorize our findings. Just as any person is as manifold and several as the relationships in which he or she plays a part, so human reality is far more relational, various, and interconnected than bounded, atomistic concepts like "nation," "society," and "culture" imply (Wolf 1982, 3). To resist conflating one's experience of the world with the words one uses to name and contain it is, of course, the thrust of Adorno's critique of identity-thinking (cf. Sartre 1964, 170). Hence the title of this book, which evokes Adorno's *Minima Moralia* (itself an allusion to Aristotle's *Magna Moralia* and Nietzsche's *Beyond Good and Evil*). But my allusions to Adorno and Sartre are also intended to justify a paratactic[21] and tentative style that seeks a rapprochement between essay and story. Just as stories are, traditionally, at least, models of minimalism and parsimony, so a synthesis of essayist and narrative ethnography may help unburden anthropological texts of the weight of information they customarily have been made to carry in their attempt to convince through what Clifford Geertz calls "the sheer power of their factual substantiality" (1988, 3). Recounting in detail the lived truth of an event may convey less data with less jargon than the scientific treatise, but what it sacrifices in impressiveness and authority it may recover in immediacy, economy, and craft. The minimalization of ethnographic fact is not, therefore, evidence of a disenchantment with the empirical but rather an attempt to radicalize empiricism by emphasizing verisimilitude and contingency over system and structure.

21. *Parataxis* means placing propositions one after the other without indicating relations of coordination or subordination between them. Adorno comments: "from my theorem that there are no philosophical first principles, it follows that one cannot construct a continuous argument with the usual stages, but one must assemble a whole from a series of partial complexes whose constellations not [logical] sequence produces the idea" (cited in Rose 1978, 13).

RETURNS

Borderlines

As I write, in mid-1996, Sierra Leone is in the throes of civil war. Years of coups, corruption, and misrule have brought the country to the edge of anarchy. The economy is paralyzed. Human rights violations, ambushes, bombings, and banditry are commonplace. Indiscriminate killings claim up to a hundred lives a day. Almost half of Sierra Leone's population are now refugees.

I have not returned to the country that Graham Greene called "soup-sweet land" for ten years, nor heard from Kuranko friends in a long time. Koinadugu has become a heart of darkness.

Under such circumstances it might seem a gross abuse of the ethnographic present to write as if nothing had changed in the decade since I last visited Sierra Leone. Lacking any direct knowledge of the social world that enthralled me for twenty-five years, it might seem a travesty if I presumed to write of that world now, a suggestion that ethnography could be divorced from history.

I do so for two reasons. First, the Kuranko have long been acquainted with the vicissitudes and violence of history, and it is important to show how culture and history intersect.[1] Second, striking a balance between closure and

---

1. Settling the area of present-day northeastern Sierra Leone around the beginning of the seventeenth century, during a time of war and political turmoil in the Sankaran region of

openness to the outside world has always been an imperative dimension of Kuranko social life. Always implicit in Kuranko discourse has been the question of how can one go beyond the particular, parochial security of one's own village and chiefdom without losing one's autonomy and identity in the comparatively unbounded, perilous domain of the outside world.

In a society dominated by kinship and affinal ties, this question locates itself on an ambiguous border between the local community and the world of strangers and enemies. In the cultural imagination it is the borderline between town and bush. It is the no-man's land that the Greeks identified with Hermes, with crossroads and frontiers, mixed messages, clandestine traffic, chicanery, and theft.

In Kuranko narratives journeys back and forth across this uncertain boundary serve to bring into discussion questions about sociality and inter-subjectivity. Of particular interest to me here is a set of narratives that explain the origins of clan totems and interclan joking relationships.

IN A SENSE, CLANSHIP is kinship extended to the nth degree. Clanship begins where genealogy peters out. Clans are defined through fictive links and mythical events. And though the idiom of kinship ideally holds its value at this level, and shared clanship supposedly gives one the right to claim hospitality and help outside one's own familiar social world, a clan is quite simply "many" (*sie*), and one cannot expect such claims to be invariably met.

This ambiguity is of the essence. Played up in clan myths, it draws attention to the ways in which the borderline between kin and not-kin can be crossed. And by spelling out the origins of totemic icons, and the modes of alliance and mutuality that blur the nominal distinctions between different clans, these myths suggest how the gap between the particular and the universal may be bridged.

---

upper Guinea, the origins of Kuranko clans are as various as they are confused (some were hunters, some warriors, some praise singers, bards, and genealogists, some Muslims, some staunch pagans—refugees from Islamic jihads). It should also be noted that only a hundred years ago Kuranko suffered grievously from the incursions of the Maninka warlord Samori Turé, whose armed horsemen (*sofas*) are still invoked as a synonym for terror. During his journey through Kuranko country in 1895–96, the English explorer J. K. Trotter reported: "Hardly a town escaped destruction; except Kurubundo, every town we saw had been built within the last year or so by Kuranko who had escaped from the Sofas, hidden in the bush, and returned when the country was clear" (Trotter 1898, 84).

Here is one such myth, related by Fina Kamara, of Kabala:

> When you are in a faraway place with no towns or food to be
> found anywhere . . . you suddenly hear a sound. You go to
> where the sound is coming from, and you find something to eat
> there. But it is a bush thing and you are afraid of it. Yet it does
> not harm you. So you take it as food. You then return to town
> and explain to your clan what happened: how you lost your
> way in the bush, had no food, heard a sound, went and discov-
> ered such and such in the bush . . . how it helped you find food
> and survive to return to town. Then you declare that no mem-
> ber of your clan should ever eat that creature again, or harm it
> in any way. It becomes your totem [*tane*]. It is your kinsman
> [*nakelinyorgonu*]. You tell your clan joking partner [*sanakuie*]:
> "That creature, which saved my life, is my kinsman." That is
> how totemism began.

What is arresting about all such Kuranko narratives is that the creature
who saves the life of the clan ancestor is an absolute stranger. The bond
of kinship is thus affirmed in a free and supererogatory gesture rather than
an obligatory act. Since such freely chosen bonds are definitive of friendship rather than kinship, one is led to the conclusion that ideally kinship
is a mode of kindness, based on magnanimity rather than mandate. In other
words, instead of evoking the bond between mother and child (*nakelinyorgonu,* "kinship," literally means "mother-one-relationship"), or the intimacy of hearth and home (*dembaiye*), as Kuranko ordinarily do, clan myths
define the good in terms of the generosity, empathy, and openness that
ideally informs relations between close friends.

By associating the moral qualities of *morgoye* (personhood) with an animal with whom no prior or positive relationship exists, do the clan myths
imply that the *given* bonds of kinship depend for their very existence on
chosen bonds of amity? Are the myths suggesting that the comparatively
closed circle of kinship must open itself up to the outside world if it is to
endure?

Fina Kamara's narrative continues:

> The Kuyaté [clan] do not eat the monitor lizard. Their ancestor
> went to a faraway place. There was no water there. He became
> thirsty. He was near death. Then he found a huge tree, and in
> the bole of the tree was some water left from the rains. The
> monitor lizard was also there. The ancestor of the Kuyaté sat
> under the tree. The monitor lizard climbed into the bole of the

tree, then climbed out and shook its tail. The water splashed the man. The ancestor of the Kuyaté realized there was water there. He climbed up and drank. He declared: "Ah, the monitor lizard has saved my life!" When he returned to town he told his clan about the incident. He said, "You see me here now because of that monitor lizard." Since that time the monitor lizard has been the Kuyaté totem. Should any Kuyaté eat it, his body will become marked and disfigured like the body of the monitor lizard. His joking partners will have to find medicines to cure him.

Most clan myths proceed from an explanation of how a particular animal became the clan totem to an account of how certain other clans became allied or incorporated as joking partners or marriage partners. Just as the bond between a clan and its totem is expressed in bodily terms (eating one's totem results in a disfigurement of the skin that mimics the body markings of the totemic animal), so sharing a totem with another clan is often seen as a form of common embodiment.[2] Thus in the myth that explains the origin of the joking partnership (*sanakuiye*) between Kargbo and Sisé clans one is told that when the clan ancestors immigrated from the Mande heartland, Mansa Kama (the Kargbo ancestor) and Bakunko Sisé (the Sisé ancestor) came to a great river. There Bakunko transformed himself into a crocodile (his clan totem) and ferried Mansa Kama across. But Mansa Kama was famished after the crossing, and Bakunko cut off the calf of his leg, roasted it, and gave it to his companion to eat. To affirm their friendship in perpetuity, Mansa Kama declared that the crocodile should thenceforth become the Kargbo totem as well.

Other clan narratives deploy other stratagems to transcend difference and merge identity. The following, narrated by Keti Ferenke Koroma, of Kondembaia, explains the joking relationship between the Koroma and Kalamé clans:

> We, the Koroma, Dabu, Fofona, and Kalamé, are all *sanakuie*.
> We are all one person [*morgo keli*]. But the one that is above
> all is the Kalamé. If you observe that Kalamé men and women
> do not sit on our mat and that we do not sit on their mat and

2. By the same token, husbands and wives avoid eating each other's totems. This averts the possibility that a pregnant woman may injure her child by eating her husband's totem, but the usual Kuranko rationalization is that the avoidance is a mark of respect: one should not incorporate or arrogate to oneself (eat or marry) that which is regarded as kin and kind. Thus incest is often compared to eating one's own totem, and near neighbors, who are like kin, will not eat each other's totems.

that we do not intermarry, it is because of the wars and how
hard they were. Our ancestor, Fakoli Koroma, was away at war.
He had fought many battles. While he was away fighting, his
wife conceived a child. He rejected his wife, and she went to a
Kalamé man and gave birth to a baby girl. That man was the
ancestor of the Kalamé, and at the time had no wife of his own.
After the birth of his child, the Koroma gave the baby girl to
the Kalamé. Later, the woman bore him a baby boy. Then the
ancestor of the Koroma said: "That girl who was given to the
Kalamé is my daughter; therefore, whoever respects the Koroma must also respect the Kalamé." Then they said: "Koroma,
the Kalamé are your totem. You are all kinsmen."

Another narrative, related by Kenya Fina Kamara, of Kondembaia, explains the joking relationship between the Yaran and ruling Kamara clans:

The wife of the first Yaran and the wife of the first Kamara
gave birth to their children in the same house at the same time:
a baby boy and a baby girl. One day, while the mothers were
away, there was a fire in the house. A dog picked up the two infants and took them out of the house and placed them under a
banana tree. When the mothers returned to the house they began to cry. They thought that their children had been burned to
death. As they were crying, the dog was running around the banana tree. Then a man said, "Eh, friend, you had better go and
see what's under the banana tree." They went and found their
infants there, but the mothers could not tell the difference between them. They decided that since the two children were in-
distinguishable, each mother could take either one. That is why
we now do not intermarry, because of that mix-up. We are all
brothers and sisters. That is what our forefathers told us.

Kuranko clan myths contrive to eclipse the nominal differences between
clans by conjuring images of intermingled bodies or blood, crossed lines
of descent, confused filiation, and near identical appearance (Jackson
1982a). But this fusion of identities is never fully consummated. Even
though informants speak of *sanaku*-linked clans as "one person," as "kin,"
as "like affines," or as "close friends," the word *sanaku* connotes duplica-
tion or duplicity, and it is this ambiguous mix of identity and difference
that gives rise to the joking relationship. United on one level (as a result
of events that effectively nullify or mask their differences), they remain,
nonetheless, divided by name, status, and, often as not, a ban on intermar-

riage. Perhaps the most exact analogy to the *sanakuiye-tolon* is with successive siblings, where the status difference between elder and young is recognized yet at the same time blurred. In the words of one informant, *sanakuiye* is "when two clans originate with two brothers who are born next to one another." Alternatively, an analogy is sometimes drawn between the *sanakuiye* and the relation between half-siblings, who share one blood ("same father") but have different mothers. It is as if one cannot take the mythical fusion of identities seriously, which is why the *sanaku* link gets acted out in forms of licensed abuse and mutual denigration, which dramatically undermine status distinctions.

At a bestowal:

A man gives a handful of stones and a pariah dog to his joking clan partner, saying, "Take this kola and this cow as our contribution to the bride wealth."

At a naming ceremony for an infant:

"Ah, one more slave in the family!"

After an initiation:

A joker approaches one of the neophyte's fathers with a bundle of dirty, discarded rags, saying, "I have brought this gown of manhood for your son to put on."

At a funeral:

A joker enters the house of the deceased and binds the hands, feet, and body of the corpse with rope. "Heh, you cannot bury him; he is my slave."

Also at a funeral:

"Stop crying. We will bring him back to life."

It may be that the ideal of fused identity and common humanity can only be realized imperfectly because it depends on qualities such as goodwill, magnanimity, and altruism that cannot be enforced or ordained. It's the same reason why a social order cannot be built upon freely chosen ties of friendship, or marriage based solely on love.

And yet, in totemic icons, in the sharing of totems, and in the bonds of the *sanakuiye,* the Kuranko affirm a conception of moral personhood (*morgoye*) that goes beyond the prescriptive domain of close kinship and extends the possibility of sociality into the wider world. In so far as the outside world is regarded as bush, the mythical scenario involves ancestral journeys into the wilderness and identifies the virtues of personhood with animals. Thus totemic universalization, by extending humanity to certain animals, may be said to provide a model for transcending ethnic boundaries.

In Lévi-Strauss's words, the totemic classifications and clan correspondences in the western Sudan effectively prevent the closure of each group, and promote "an idea something like that of a humanity without frontiers" (Lévi-Strauss 1966, 166).

But this humanistic reading must be tempered by a realization that open borders and openness of heart are conditional upon relative peace and prosperity. Given their bitter memories of invasion, border disputes, and colonial rule, it is not surprising that the Kuranko people distrust strangers, seek to keep their own counsel, and are preoccupied with marking the perimeters of their bodies, houses, villages, and chiefdoms with protective charms. The bond between totemic animal and ancestor, like the bond between *sanaku*-linked clans, is steeped in ambivalence. The other to whom one owes one's life, or in whom one's identity was once lost, remains other. The very freedom of choice that united people once in friendship or kinship may be exercised to divide them. If Kuranko clan myths have any abiding value, it lies not in their power to prescribe a permanent unity between self and others but in their power to sustain an ironic sense that in the long run distinction and separation can be as inimical to one's social survival as the absolute incorporation and blurring of self in the being of another.

In a sense this ambivalent refrain—referring as it does to narrative images that closely juxtapose sameness and difference—is grounded in the problem of marriage. While the union of man and woman is a universal metaphor of convergence and incorporation, the resistance of the *I* to the *not-I* "is felt nowhere more deeply than here" (Simmel 1950, 128). To be sure, marriage is the bridge between one's own natal world and the *res publica*—the body politic—and, as Martin Buber noted, the most forceful human acknowledgment of what it means to enter into a relationship with and to be answerable to an-other: an affirmation of "the fact that the other *is* . . . that I cannot legitimately share in the Present Being without sharing in the being of the other" (Buber 1961, 83). But the very density, necessity, and intimacy of this relationship transforms it into a site where the balance between self and other, fusion and separation, is most difficult to maintain. For the Kuranko it is the husband's lineage and the wife's lineage that define these two contrasted poles of identity. If marriage transcends the difference between erstwhile strangers, confirming affinity in alliance and exchange, in-lawship remains nonetheless dependent on interpersonal relationships between brother and sister, and husband and wife. No matter how imperative and imposed are the jural ties of affinity, they are always susceptible to the vagaries of personal affection and desire. While love, forbear-ance, and respect strengthen affinal ties, infidelity, capriciousness, and de-ceit may destroy them.

"All the palavers in this world can be resolved, except the palavers caused by women," goes the Kuranko adage.

Legally incorporated utterly into her husband's household, a young bride nurtures *emotional* ties to her own family and female friends that are often seen as inimical to her role as dutiful wife and caring mother. Among the Kuranko, as in many other societies, the young wife, divided in loyalties and caught between the imperatives of structure and sentiment, is often made the focus of men's anxieties about controlling the border between their own world and the wilderness beyond (cf. Strathern 1972, 182–84). But if many Kuranko men are preoccupied by the problem of how to ensure that women do their bidding, many young Kuranko women are just as deeply preoccupied by the problem of how to escape the onerous and re-strictive demands placed on them. Keti Ferenke Koroma put it, "When women consider the fact that they bore us, yet we pay bride wealth for them and they become our wives, they get angry." Sinkari Yegbe, of Kamadugu, readily confirmed this view. Many women don't like being beholden to men simply because bride wealth has changed hands. Domestic malingering and cheating on their husbands are, she confided, "ways of getting their own back."

The hierarchical relationship between superordinate and subordinate thus finds its most troubled expression in conjugal life. Subjected to the formal constraints of marriage, and made an object in exchange, a young wife may at the same time form clandestine attachments, assert her right to make demands on her brother (whose own marriage was conditional on the bride wealth her marriage brought to his family), and rejoice in her ability to control and influence the destiny of her children. This is why men often stereotype women as seducers and traducers who poison good relations between men and, in the past, used their wiles to betray their husbands to enemies (Jackson 1977, 87–91). "*Musu kai i gbundu lon*" (Never let women know your secrets), say Kuranko men, implying that the magical medicines with which one safeguards oneself against nefarious outside in-fluences are best not shared with one's wife.

A Kuranko woman's subjective struggle to steer a course between being reduced to the status of an object and being a subject for herself is one of the recurring leitmotifs in Kuranko thought. While it is true, to paraphrase Marilyn Strathern, that women are more in between than men, this in-betweenness raises critical questions concerning existential control of the traffic of people and things across boundaries, as well as the dialectic of structure and sentiment, that find metaphorical expression in the problem of how to negotiate and manage the difficult relationship between one's own insular world and the wider world beyond.

Distance Lends Enchantment

Society *is* ourselves, and not some foreign field that we approach from elsewhere or transcend in coming into our own. We no more exist outside of it than it exists outside of us. We are social in exactly the same sense that we are bodies. Even before we recognize ourselves as socially embodied beings, writes Merleau-Ponty, the social "exists obscurely . . . as a summons." It is "already there" (Merleau-Ponty 1962, 362).

From this arises an existential paradox. I, whose sense of myself, my identity, and my needs is so well defined, only have this sense of existing by virtue of the existence of others. I is correlative to Thou. Our relationship defines us; we are because *it* is. Moreover, myself and those most immediate to me—my kin, my kind—depend for our very existence on persons and things that are nonimmediate—not-self, un-kind. The well-being of we who consider ourselves one depends on some kind of rapprochement with those who we regard as other, even as our negation. "The wife is fetched from among the daughters of strangers," say the Sukuma-Nyamwezi of western Tanzania (Brandström 1990, 179). "We marry the people we fight," declare the Mae Enga of the western highlands of Papua New Guinea (Meggitt 1964, 218).

Those who can do me the most harm are the very people who can do me the most good. At the same time, the *things* of greatest power and value always lie beyond one's ken, outside one's circle. Working out a *modus vivendi* with the other, turning a potential threat to one's life and livelihood into an actual boon, is one of the most basic social imperatives. It is the precondition of exchange, which, as Lévi-Strauss has shown with such force, lies at the very heart of human sociality.

This is why, for the Kuranko, the village must open itself up continually to the bush. Just as hunters venture into the bush at night, braving real and imagined dangers in their search for life-sustaining food, farmers must clear-cut the forest in order to plant the grain that is the staff of life, and wives must be brought into the lineage from outside. Moreover, trade with the outside world is as imperative now as it has ever been. Despite their isolation in the western Guinea highlands, the Kuranko have always been involved in trade networks and political blocs that extended over a large area of the western Sudan. When Alexander Gordon Laing, the English explorer, passed through Kuranko country in 1825, he was invited to help "open up a good road to the sea" so that the Kuranko could exchange camwood, kola, gum-copal, and rice for salt. In Kuranko villages, strangers have always come as traders. Cattle for sacrifice are acquired from itinerant Fulani herders and, apart from the obvious impact of Islam on the Kuranko worldview, it is clear from Kuranko ritual vernacular that the acquisition of protective fetishes and magical medicines from neighboring areas has long been part and parcel of defensive strategies and intertribal exchange. Indeed, this tension between unity and division, identity and difference, finds expression in the term that the Kuranko themselves use for their ethnic region: *ferensola* (literally, "town of twins").

But the necessity of ties with the outside world is not simply economic. Secular power (chieftaincy) has always struggled to strike a balance with the "wild" powers of djinn and cult leaders who can conjure and control them. In a similar fashion, the old must draw on the potentially delinquent energies of the young, and men marry women who they fear will damage the integrity of the very group to which, ideally, they should bring life.

Vitality always exists beyond. At the edge. In that place most remote from where I am. Though the wilderness is fraught with danger, it is also the source of regenerative life. Thus among the Macha Oromo, virility is exogenous. "Killing 'outsiders' and bringing home their genitals as trophies, or spearing big animals such as buffalo and taking home the tail and other spoils of the hunt as a trophy, *faacaa,* may be seen as the conquest of male fertility from the untamed 'outside' and bringing it home." Such deeds "generate the virility that is a condition for marriage" (Hultin 1990, 155). Among the Sukuma-Nyamwezi of western Tanzania the wilderness is a place of witches and sorcerers who would destroy *mhola* (the social order), "but this is also where the child-bearing wife and the rain-giving king come from; and this is also where men, hit by the disaster of *nzala,* starvation, move to find new sources of food (Brandström 1990, 178).

Curiously, too, the most distant may also best articulate the highest ideal. If the gods are to possess real power and command respect, they must be otiose—at one remove from the human world. Familiarity is incompatible with authority. The Sukuma-Nyamwezi case is again illuminating: "The figure of the rain-giving king and the figure of the child-bearing wife both symbolically derive their regenerative power from their metonymical relationship with wilderness and the world of strangers" (Brandström 1990, 181). Freed from the snares and ambiguities of the immediate lifeworld, remote and imagined worlds can promise possibilities that cannot be realized in flesh and blood in the here and now. So, among the Kuranko, totemic creatures symbolize the axioms of kinship and of morality.

But there is a catch. The greater the distance between humans and the gods, the more problematic becomes communication between them. In practice, therefore, a kind of counterpoint and tension usually exists between sacerdotal communication (in which priests keep ordinary mortals at a distance from their gods or divine kings) and mystical communication (in which direct, unregulated, spontaneous union between mortals and immortals is possible).

Just as gods and ancestors are foci of ambivalent feelings (provoking anxiety if they become too distant *or* too familiar), so too are exotic and distant places. For insular Europe, the sea and the sea voyage were for centuries the prevailing metaphors for this hunger for self-realization and riches in the Beyond (Blumenberg 1997). And like El Dorado and Shangri-la in the West, one hears rumors among the Kuranko of a fabulous town somewhere in the hazy savannah regions to the northeast, known as Musudugu—town of women—where there are no men, where women are in possession of the most powerful Kuranko medicines and means of sorcery, and where great wealth may be gained (Jackson 1982a, 199). At once attainable and beyond one's reach, this quasi-mythical Musudugu brings to mind the paradox of all power: that it must be theoretically accessible yet at the same time practically so scarce as to be almost impossible to gain. Consider the Azande, for example, whose most powerful oracle (*benge*) originated outside Zandeland and, at the time Evans-Pritchard lived among them, had to be sought in arduous two-hundred-kilometer journeys, subject to strict taboos and frontier controls, to the Bomokandi river in the Belgian Congo. When asked why they did not cultivate the poison creeper in their own country and so save themselves the trouble of gathering it under such dangerous and difficult conditions, Zande informants expressed "disapproval" of the question, alleging that a kinsman would die if this were done. "We may suppose," observed Evans-Pritchard, "that the mystical potency of the poison is derived partly from its scarcity and the pains that must be expended in procuring it" (1937, 271). But the power of the alien lies in its essential otherness, not simply its scarcity. As in medieval philosophy, *alteritas* connotes not only otherness but the possibility of transcendence. That which is furthest from my grasp and control is that which poses the greatest existential threat to my being. By making that foreign thing my own, by assimilating it to myself, by incorporating it within *my* being, by *bringing it under my control,* I disarm its menace.[3] But more significantly the existential blood, sweat, and tears that go into the taming of the alien object come to embue the object. In this way *its* power objectifies *my* power over the Other. That which was alien now stands to augment rather than diminish me.

But there is yet another aspect to this fascination with alterity. It is as if every society, like every individual, is unable to sustain its existence as an isolate, can never be sufficient unto itself. As with the classical symbolon, human beings are driven to recover the side of themselves that gets lost, eclipsed, excluded, or denied in the formation of a normative or culturally modal personality. But this occluded other is usually constructed as something inimical to the social order—a source of antisocial or wild power *at the same time as it is a means of regaining lost personal autonomy and integrity.* In short, it is construed simultaneously as a source of constructive and destructive energy.

I see no difference between the Zande preference for the poison oracle over the termite oracle (the less potent oracle they used before they acquired *benge*) and the Western connoisseur's passion for tribal art, which, in its spurious exoticism, provides its owner with a vicarious shot of the libidinous energy and unbridled power, which, it is believed, primitives possess naturally. Or, for that matter, the West's attraction to the East as a place of spice, spirituality, and inspiration. The irony is that while the wealthy European seeks the primitive vitality of Africa or the deep spirituality of the East, these cultures often seek the material wealth of Europe. The trade in primitive art objects, indigenous music, oriental sacra and exotica may, despite its mercenary, exploitative, and appropriative aspects, work to satisfy the desire of both cultures to possess what is powerful by virtue of its radical otherness.

This vital power that lies outside one's grasp and must be sought by journeying away from where one is most secure is always regarded with ambivalence. The African mask that a European collector pays so dearly for is both venerated for its exotic power and derided as evidence of a savage sensibility. The wealth a migrant villager seeks in the West is both a blessing and a curse in so far as his improved fortune makes him an

3. In this spirit the Mende in southern Sierra Leone adopted the powerful Kuranko *korté* (kuete) medicines (Harris and Sawyerr 1968, 82).

object of envy and witchcraft, or the victim of impossible demands and expectations at home. Thus the Luo speak of *gueth makech* ("bitter money")—including unearned windfalls, lottery winnings, rewards for mercenary acts, stolen money, and profit from the sale of land, gold, tobacco and cannabis—to emphasize that such income accrues to a person as a result of his denying another person's rights or claims to it. The bitterness and contagion of such ill-gotten gains stick to the person who benefits from them (Shipton 1989, 28).

The ambivalence that permeates the exotic is nothing new to the Kuranko. One sees this in initiation and narrative alike. A neophyte must go into the bush and face life-threatening forces in order to become a complete human being. A hero must risk his life in the wilderness in order to gain the powerful things on which community life depends. It is an ambiguity that also pervades all gift exchange, since the life-sustaining things one seeks in the wider world may sap one's strength to the same extent that they may increase it.

Among the Zande, princes were suspicious of gifts from distant provinces, fearing they might be means of sorcery (Evans-Pritchard 1937, 399). *Gift,* as Marcel Mauss pointed out, is in many Indo-European languages, also the word for poison (1954, 62, 127).

Penis Snatchers

In August 1996 an Associated Press story appeared in the papers concerning events in the Cameroons. According to this story "angry mobs" in Yaounde had "lynched three men accused of using evil powers to cause male genitals to disappear." The "penis-snatchers" allegedly accomplished this legerdemain simply by shaking hands with their victims.[4]

The bemused and dismissive tone of the story conjured a stereotype of "primitive superstition." Allegedly, men in the region were now hesitant to shake hands with strangers, and were sporadically grabbing their crotches. But to an anthropologist who has worked in West Africa the lineaments of witchcraft were readily discernible. It is always the enemy within who betrays a vulnerable member of one's household to a coven, who saps or steals the life of a kinsman. As the Kuranko put it, "If a stranger unearths a buried kola nut in your compound, someone who lives there must have

---

4. Similar incidents were reported in Côte d'Ivoire in 1997, implicating Hausas and resulting in mob violence in Abidjan (Paul Stoller, personal communication).

told him where to find it." An index of trust (in the Cameroons case, a handshake) is potentially a means of mischief. Gifts may be poisons.

The Cameroons story touches on another familiar African theme: male impotence. To be a man is to be able to bring children into the world and so perpetuate one's name and lineage. Impotence implies mortality: effectively, it brings one's social destiny and identity to an end.

In the news story one critical detail provides a clue as to what precipitated the penis snatching epidemic. Most of the penis snatchers were Nigerian, and "relations between Cameroons and Nigeria are bitter because of a long-running dispute over the Bakassi Peninsula, an oil-rich stretch of country claimed by both nations." In fact, this boundary dispute between the two countries was entangled with a second divisive issue concerning relations between southern (Anglophone) Cameroons and La République du Cameroun (Francophone Cameroons).

The story can thus be read allegorically: the loss of a valuable economic resource to a powerful neighbor is translated into anxieties over loss of sexual potency. Put another way, social relations between the two nations are realized and lived as a modality of immediate bodily intersubjectivity.

The analogy might seem far-fetched were it not for the fact that, in kinship-based societies, relations between states are customarily conceived as *interpersonal* relationships between kin and affines. Indeed, metaphorical correspondences linking the body politic and the human body are deeply rooted in West African worldviews.

The crucial opposition is between town and bush. Symbolically this subsumes relationships between self and other, insider and outsider, human and extrahuman, and moral and amoral worlds. Among the Kuranko the line between these domains is strictly monitored, and arrays of self-enclosing fetishes (*kandan li fannu*) and magical medicines (*bese*) are deployed defensively on the skin (the boundary of the self), above the doorway ("mouth") of a house, as well on the borders of villages, farms, and chiefdoms. There is a direct analogy between initiatory injunctions to control one's mouth (speech), ears (hearing), and emotions and these protective fetishes and medicines. They are all means of preventing uncontrolled crossing of the boundaries of the body or social body by "wild" and nefarious forces associated with witches, djinn, sorcerers, and enemies.

But passage across these very borders is vital to life and livelihood. Openness to others is the very essence of personhood (*morgoye*). Cooperation is the basis of economic life. Villagers must enter the bush to make their farms. And trade with outsiders is imperative if one is to acquire commodities such as salt, iron tools, cloth, hurricane lamps, and kerosene. Just as the acquisition of magical medicines from enemies has traditionally been the best strategy for protecting oneself from them, so face-to-face interaction with outsiders is considered a better strategy than avoidance. Better the devil you know than the devil you don't.

In the figure of the stranger (*sundan*)—who is usually also a semi-itinerant trader—these mixed feelings about the outside world find their focus, for the stranger is always ambiguously located: someone who, as Simmel noted in his famous essay, is near and far at the same time. He belongs elsewhere yet resides here, importing qualities into one's group "that do not and cannot stem from the group itself" (Simmel 1950, 402).

Among the Kuranko the ambivalent power of the other also finds expression in the figure of the djinn. And, as with the gifts of strangers, the gifts of djinn may bring mixed blessings.

Friendship with a djinn may bring a person great wealth and renown. Of a talented or charismatic individual people may say, "A djinn has come out for him." But the djinn belong to the wild, and are capricious and volatile. The powers bestowed by a djinn may cost one the life of a close kinsman. And the influence of a djinn can be calamitous. Failure to appease djinn with food offerings may incite them to injure farmers and harm their families. Djinn can cause lockjaw, one is told. Djinn can cause people to go berserk, running uncontrollably into the bush, summoned by a djinn's calling. Often they appear in dreams, in human form. Should a pregnant woman dream of making love with a male djinn, she may miscarry. Just as djinn may make woman barren, they can, when they appear to men in female guise, drain semen, cause impotence, and generally jeopardize a man's ability to have children.

The figure of the djinn encapsulates a set of axioms: (1) that the most vital powers belong to the bush, (2) that these powers are "wild" in the sense that they cannot be readily controlled or bidden, (3) that these powers are essentially linked to reproduction, (4) that relations with djinn are like sexual relations in which desire and intense emotion may undermine conjugal relations, parental responsibility, and social order.

When Europeans were first encountered, they were likened to both strangers and djinn. Indeed, many Kuranko believed that the European travelers who passed through their country were searching for djinn to capture and put to work for them. Even today, to dream of a white man portends prosperity, and I was constantly being reminded that many young Kuranko believe that minimal schooling will give them instant access to the West, transforming them magically into doctors, engineers, and men of power. The recurring image is of death and rebirth, as if the powers of Europeans, like those of the djinn, resembled the reproductive powers invoked during initiation—powers that imply the end of one incarnation and the reconstitution of the ego in another phase of life as a knowledgable and responsible adult. Thus village men who worked for the colonial administration and learned to read and write were often said to have died to their previous lives and become *tubabu morgonnu* (whiteman's persons), or *tubabu dannu* (whiteman's children).

Even after the *tubabu* were accepted as fellow human beings and not as djinn, it was still believed that they had djinn working for them, and that this was the source of their superior wealth. When I lived among the Kuranko, villagers persisted in regarding my manual typewriter as a djinn that I had in my employ. Electricity was also the work of djinn. So too automobiles and airplanes.

If relations with djinn are problematic and double edged, relations with Europeans and the social world they hail from are equally vexed. When Kuranko men left their villages to fight for the British in the Cameroons in the First World War, they were said to have given up their lives (*ka a wakale ka nie fili*) to the *tubabu*. And several times during my sojourn among the Kuranko, news of some fatal accident in Saralon (Freetown) that involved young Kuranko men would be interpreted by elders as evidence of the dangers of putting oneself outside the protective umbrella of one's own community, and of being ignorant of how to safeguard oneself against the magical medicines of strangers.

Yet young men leave the security of hearth and home in search of fortunes in the diamond districts or cities, or employment in the police force or army, regarding these migrations as initiatory rites of passage involving the same hardships and ordeals of traditional initiation. The real difference is that the power now sought in the wilderness beyond the perimeter of one's natal village is the power of wealth and of the West. Thus kids begged me to send them Michael Jackson posters when I returned to my country, without any sense of the irony in the name.

But how can one open oneself up to this dimly comprehended and elusive outside world without losing one's way, one's autonomy, and one's dignity? How can one work with the djinn of the West without sacrificing the life of one's kin to them? How can one's local world enter into a vital relationship with the global world without inviting its own destruction?

Some of the most compelling instances of this dilemma have been discussed by Michael Taussig in his analysis of certain folkloric beliefs among plantation workers and miners in South America. The existential implications of these beliefs are particularly fascinating. In western Columbia there is a widespread belief among the peasants that "plantation workers sometimes make secret contracts with the devil in order to increase productivity, and hence their wage" (1980, 94). But the price of such a contract is a premature and painful death. Moreover, the money obtained from such a contract is barren; it cannot be invested productively in land or livestock, but only spent on luxury consumer items. In other words, relations with the capitalist world are experienced ambivalently: a sordid boon. Like a comparable belief in the southern Cauca Valley of Bolivia that godparents-to-be sometimes conceal banknotes in their hands during the baptism of an infant, the consequence of getting embroiled in a market economy is that one's life—or more precisely, control over one's own destiny—is put at risk. In the Bolivian case the baptized banknote deprives the child of blessings, and its soul may be prevented from going to heaven (Taussig 1980, 126).

More recently Brad Weiss has documented some of the bizarre and poignant ways in which this dialectic between the local and the global goes awry in East Africa. Seeking a balance between closure and openness, the Haya of Tanzania have become vulnerable to the worst the outside world has to offer: AIDS. The vernacular way of expressing this sense of vulnerability is to have recourse to a traditional concern for children's teeth and speak of a new and pervasive illness that causes children to be born with or grow plastic teeth. The illness has other symptoms—diarrhea, vomiting, fever, refusal of the breast, and wasting—but the focus is on the plastic teeth and the cure of the illness that is thought to depend on having them removed, usually at great cost (Weiss 1996, 157).

As Weiss points out, toothlessness is an icon of defenselessness, dependency, and passivity. Significantly, the Haya are unanimous in declaring that the illness, like AIDS, came from a country outside Tanzania (Uganda, say some; Rwanda, others), and the disease that causes toothlessness and wasting is associated with wealthy Haya businessmen returning to Tanzania from neighboring countries. The affliction of plastic teeth thus expresses, as does the epidemic of penis snatching in the Cameroons, an *existential* loss of control over the boundary between one's own world (symbolically "inside") and the world of the other ("outside"), which in effect reduces people to the status of objects or things.

Both diseases are reminiscent of another Haya anxiety—that outsiders are stealing their blood and selling it for profit in the non-Haya world (Weiss 1996). Similar fears have recently been reported from the Luvale-speaking area of Zambia where there is allegedly a sinister traffic in body parts (Sonia da Silva, personal communication). In each instance the theme is explicitly a loss of existential power and capacity. This loss reflects a disequilibrium. The control one exercises in one's own world is vastly outweighed by the lack of control one has in the outside world that now impinges on one's own. This loss of mastery finds expression in interchangeable icons of power and potency that get symbolically lost, stolen, or rendered useless: penis, teeth, blood, and vital organs.

Given this kind of scenario one might conclude that peoples of the Third World are fighting a losing battle with the first world, that their hold on power and autonomy is being progressively undermined by the influx of Western commodities and that they can only have recourse to traditional funds of illusory knowledge in attempting to explain such loss of control and closure. But this dialectic of what Brad Weiss calls the making and unmaking of the world has always been a challenge in all human societies, whether it is articulated in measures taken to control witchcraft attack, military invasion, colonial authority, or imported diseases. In the final analysis it is a challenge born of the human condition. Though the singular person exists with and through others, he or she may be diminished rather than strengthened in this relationship, eclipsed rather than fulfilled. Though this paradox of intersubjectivity finds expression in the political problem of how to strike a balance of power between different nations, it remains here as everywhere an existential issue of how the claims of any individual can be adjusted to the claims that others make on him or that he makes on himself on their behalf, such that everyone finds validation and dignity in the many.

Auctoritas

When we question an action whose legitimacy is in doubt, we ask, On whose authority? That is to say, we seek to identify a person who has set a precedent for the action, and to identify the status of this person. If the person is someone we respect, who has authority in our eyes, we tend to accept the action. Authority and authorship are thus intimately linked.

For the Kuranko, as with numerous other tribal peoples, ancestors embody this authority and are the ultimate authors of social custom. However, for we who live in a postmodern age, authority has become so decentralized and dispersed that it is no longer possible to identify any one person or period of history to which we can confidently attribute authorship of the discourse and customs in which we now find ourselves steeped. The individual subject, as author and arbiter of her own life and times, is dead (Barthes 1977; Foucault 1977).

Such a view would seem to be anticipated in premodern societies, where ontological priority is assigned not to the individual subject but to the field of social relationships of which he or she is vitally a part and the social constraints to which he or she is subject. This intersubjective field incorporates persons, ancestors, bush spirits, God, animals, and sometimes inanimate objects. Thus for the Kuranko, being is never necessarily limited to human being. Moral personhood may be found in totemic animals, benevolent djinn, ancestors, and strangers with whom one has little expectation of altruism and good will. But the attribution of subjectivity—and by extension authorship and authority—to the group to which one belongs goes further than the recognition that human *relationships* rather than singular persons are the true loci of subjective life. The systematic masking of the role of individuals in sustaining the social order is tied to the prior value accorded the epoch of the ancestors and the emphasis placed on a person's continuous and filially pious relationship with them. To publicly place one's own creative power on the same footing as the ancestors or God (often called the "chief creator," *dale mansa*) is to invite social censure and supernatural hubris.

As a prelude to exploring the ways in which the seemingly similar premodern and postmodern conceptions of the author diverge, I want to review how one of the most creative individuals I knew among the Kuranko treated the question of *auctoritas* in a 1979 conversation with me.

I had worked intermittently with Keti Ferenke Koroma, of Kondembaia, for several years. His stories were among the most compelling I ever recorded, and his renown as a storyteller and fabulist went well beyond his own chiefdom. In our conversations he did not hesitate to admit that he originated many of the stories he told, but he always kept this to himself when he performed stories in public. Even with me he played down the pleasure he gained from his own giftedness by acknowledging that his creative genius was innate. It emerged from an interplay between his god-given gifts and his own acquired ingenuity. Storytelling was a matter of both nature and nurture.

"To begin with, my great great grandfather was a chief. Then my grandfather was a chief, and my father was a chief. When you are born into a ruling house, you will be told many things. If you are a fool (*yuwe*)[5] you will be none the wiser, but if you are intelligent (*hankili me i la*) you will scrutinize everything intently. Then, when you lie down you'll think of certain things (*i ni miri koe dunn' ma*). Though it is only Allah who gives thought to a person."

This last remark was, I thought, a gesture toward balancing his initial emphasis on his own intellectual acumen with an acknowledgment of Allah's blessings.

"What inspired you to compose stories?" I asked.

"What determines a person's destiny?" Keti Ferenke asked rhetorically. "*Sawura* [destiny] comes from Allah."

"Is it decided before you were born?"

"Yes. My destiny was to tell stories. When my father went to a diviner before I was born, the diviner told him that the child would be very clever [*hankili kolo*]."

"Can a person change his destiny?"

"No."

"Could you stop composing stories?"

Keti Ferenke laughed. "I can stop telling them, but I cannot stop thinking of them. When someone asks for a story, the idea comes to me. I cannot stop that." Keti Ferenke paused for a moment. "Do you know the calabash?"

"Yes."

"The man who cuts the stem of a calabash and the man who cuts a baby's throat, whose crime is worse?"

"The man who cuts the baby's throat."

"Not true."

"Why?"

Keti Ferenke then related the story of the calabash and the country pot (Jackson 1982a, 277–88) to show how things are seldom what they seem at first sight.

Later, I asked Keti Ferenke how he thought up his stories.

"I just think of them. They come into my mind, just like that [*an bi na la n hankili ma, kale tu*]. I am not asleep. I am not dreaming. When I think of them I put them together."

"When did you begin telling stories?" I asked.

---

5. Yuwe may mean insane or simply foolish; in the second sense it implies a failure to listen to one's elders and betters. As in many other oral societies, craziness is an expression of an aural failure, a sign that one has not heeded instructions about what is and is not socially appropriate behavior.

"I started when I was young. Whenever my father made a farm we would go there to frighten birds from the growing rice. We would sleep in the farmhouse. In the evenings we would tell stories. When one person told a story, someone else would respond. Well, many people come to a chief's place. People came from afar and told their stories, and we told ours in response. That is what happened. We were brought up telling stories."

We talked for a while about two specific stories that Keti Ferenke had composed and that I had recorded on a previous fieldtrip—"The Abuse of the Killing Word" (Jackson 1982a, 164–67) and "Gbeyekan Momori and His Deceitful Friend" (179–84). Then we fell to talking about two other stories against theft and backbiting that Keti Ferenke had related to me earlier in the day.

"I made up these stories immediately you left [in 1972]," Keti Ferenke explained. "Though you had gone, I knew you would come back and ask me to tell more stories. What you tell a person becomes that person's, so when you returned I wanted to tell you things you had not heard before."

Keti Ferenke spoke of our relationship—of the nature of intersubjectivity in fact—in terms of *sabu* (agency/cause). "Nothing happens without cause," he said. "You are my *sabu*. I am your *sabu*. There are many Kuranko and many *tubabu* [Europeans], but only we two are friends."

To be sure, stories had come to mediate our relationship. Gradually, too, they had gone from being gifts exchanged to living embodiments of our friendship: dialectic responses by the one to the other.

Perhaps this was why Keti Ferenke could so unabashedly play up his creative accomplishment in my presence, though publicly he always played it down. But there was a world of difference between performing stories for me alone and performing publicly. Whereas in my company he called all the shots, with an audience his performance was continually responsive to and conditioned by feedback. As in all storytelling sessions, meaning is constituted intersubjectively through a dynamic interplay of call and response, narrative and song, in which performer and audience are equally engaged. The subject matter of the stories and the ethical object of storytelling both constrain the subjective freedom of the storyteller. This is why, in the last analysis, Keti Ferenke sees his stories as gifts to the community of which he is a part, ways of contributing to the moral education of the young and affirming tradition.

"If you listen to my stories," he told me, "even if you are my kinsman, you will not harm me. If you listen to my stories and follow what they tell you, you will be liked by everyone and go through the world without trouble. You'll know how to behave. You won't go wrong. You'll think of my stories and remember the punishment for wrongdoing and say, 'A person should not do this!' Should you decide to steal you will remember my story against stealing and say, 'I learned from that story that stealing is not good.' Should you think of gossiping maliciously, you'll say, 'I should not spoil that man's name, lest what I do to him is done to me.' That is what my stories do for people. They teach them to be satisfied, to be friendly, to live in peace."

LET ME NOW RETURN to my earlier question concerning the deep disparity between Kuranko and postmodern notions of the subject.

First, it is important to distinguish here as elsewhere between the precepts and ideals we espouse and the rules of thumb that actually govern our everyday lives. Keti Ferenke's comments indicate an uneasy slippage between an ideological stance that plays up divine inspiration and ancestral values and a shadowy focus on his own inventiveness. This interplay between traditional and idiosyncratic emphases is also evident *in* his stories, where manifestly cultural themes—jealousy among cowives, competition between half-brothers, conflicts between the old and young—are merged with preoccupations that reflect his own biography (Jackson 1989, 31–33). Indeed, Kuranko narratives typically incorporate more than one voice, more than one persona, and this discursive openness is always increased during the telling of a story when the voices and views of the audience come into play.

A similar slippage between subject-centred and subject-decentred discourse is evident in our own society, where fashionable declarations of the death of the author are rendered self-contradictory because the declarations remain individually authored and identified with specific intellectuals rather than specific epistemes. Clearly the empirical and the epistemological are never congruent—neither in the postmodern West nor in the premodern world of village Africa.

Second, it is important to note that any superficial resemblance between the erasure of the individual subject among the Kuranko and in the postmodern West is belied by the different interests they serve and the different social consequences that are entailed by them.

Keti Ferenke made it clear that in disavowing individual authorship of his stories he gave the stories themselves greater power to affirm traditional values. The word of one man could never have the force of the ancestors' collective authority. At the same time, the author's self-effacement helps reinforce the sense that the stories are about ethical quandaries experienced in *face-to-face* encounters in the *local* community. By contrast, the postmodern erasure of the author is tied to the efflorescence of patterns of indirect communication and information processing in a global village, a virtual community.

Furthermore, the disavowal of the subject in an oral community usually reflects the ontological priority given to one's *relations* with predecessors (ancestors), successors (children), consociates (kinsmen), and contemporaries (neighbors). It reflects a social order where cooperation is essential to survival and competition inimical to *communitas*. Power must be shared—and the so-called group ethic can thus be read as a positive affirmation of interpersonal relationships and not a sign of the lack of ego strength, individualism, or sense of self.

The postmodern erasure of the subject is quite differently motivated. One way of understanding the phenomenon is to relate it to an increasing sense of individual powerlessness and insignificance in a global community dominated by electronic media of communication. This "social saturation," to use Gergen's phrase, involves a collapse of boundaries, identities, and truths (Gergen 1991). And with the shift of focus from persons to information a general malaise is born: nothing one does or says makes any difference any more—neither bringing greater justice or equality, nor altering the balance of political power. One cannot have a social relationship with a body of data, and thus the individual actor comes to feel bypassed and impotent.

Rather than see this occlusion of the subject as a by-product of the zeitgeist, I see it as a subjective strategy for dealing with the central anxiety of our times. By proclaiming that no one person can ever be the arbiter of his destiny, or invent or author a world, we recapture some sense of authoring our situation. Although we are in fact simply rationalizing our situation, we gain through the argot of postmodernism a magical sense that we are one step ahead of our times, preemptively calling the tune that we are already dancing to.

The advent of postmodernity and the demise of socialism may be traced to the same source. Socialism perished as an ideology with the dawning recognition that either there were not enough resources in the world to go around or that the entrenched interests of wealthy and powerful elites in both rich and poor nations would in any event prevent a more equitable redistribution of those resources. A belief has taken hold that the day is nigh when the poor will so outnumber the rich and be so powerless to improve their lot that their only option will be to prey on the wealthy. This neo-Gothic culture of pillage will be countered, of course, by the only survival option left open to the rich: to recruit military and paramilitary forces, build electronic fences, and engineer surveillance systems that will protect their privileged enclaves from the consumer-impoverished masses whose expectations have been raised by the popular media but whose realistic chances of meeting these expectations have been increasingly diminished. Postmodernism is the schismogenic prelude to this civil war between haves and have-nots. In its pretense to have eclipsed the subject it finds a perfect alibi for moral indifference. For if we no longer determine our world's destiny, we can have no responsibility for our own actions. To announce that the subject has been erased like a face drawn in sand at the edge of the sea is in effect to give the subject the right to act in bad faith— as though he or she were arbiter of nothing.

Another explanation for the rise of postmodernism as the secular religion of the bourgeoisie is that it reflects widespread improvements in educational standards and talent within this social milieu. So effective have these improvements been that no one stands out from the crowd any more, or if they do it is less a reflection of their native genius than of the star-making machinery of the music, film, and television industries. Excellence has now been attained by so many that the field of professional talent resembles the field of sporting talent: far fewer duds and far fewer geniuses. The mean is constant, but the standard deviation has been whittled away to almost nothing. Genius has become statistically dispersed through a larger and larger population, giving the impression that it has become scarcer. This registers as a perception that there are fewer heroes. That we are all more or less ordinary, undistinguished, and equally talented. It is a short step from this to declare the subject dead.

BUT THERE IS A POINT where the various hermeneutical conventions of premodernism, modernism, and postmodernism are unified. All these paradigms are seeded and presaged in experience, even though they are not all given ideological currency. And in all societies, and at every period of history, no matter what the extant worldview, the *experience* of authorship and authority has remained curiously constant.

The storyteller has always unsettled and called into question the structures of legitimacy. And the storyteller has always experienced his or her inspiration as stemming from a source outside the self. T. S. Eliot spoke of this ecstatic passivity as "intense apathy."

"They come into my mind, just like that," Keti Ferenke said of his stories.

"Not I but the force that flows through me," wrote D. H. Lawrence.

"*Je* est un autre [I is an other],"declared Arthur Rimbaud in a letter to his old teacher, Paul Demeny.

"I do not find it. It finds me," said Vladimir Nabokov, when asked about the source of his inspiration.

"I seem to speak, it is not I, about me, it is not about me," observes Samuel Beckett at the beginning of *The Unnameable.*

When Laurence Sterne was questioned about the design of his strange book *Tristram Shandy,* he replied, "Ask my pen; it governs me; I govern not it."

In a series of comments which follow his novel *Moravagine,* Blaise Cendrars discusses how, when he wrote the book, he had the experience of being taken over by the characters, of becoming the tool of a "mysterious other."

Malcolm Lowry confessed a similar feeling in a letter to Conrad Aiken on the writing of *Under the Volcano:* "I do not so much feel as if I am writing this book as that *I am myself being written.*"

The other to whom the creative artist attributes his or her inspiration may be identified as a god, a goddess, a muse, or simply left unnamed. But in every case, the work, like the life of the ego is inextricably linked to the existence of an alter. Each is the agent of the other, the *sabu,* as the Kuranko would say. A story or a life is thus an outcome of the play of intersubjectivity. But to downplay other or downplay self, as happens in the one-dimensional doctrinal formulations of modernism and postmodernism is to distort and mischaracterize the field of the intersubjective. Self and other are mutually entailed, as figure and ground or yin and yang. The dynamic interplay between them, which is conveyed by Keti Ferenke's remarks, makes us aware that what is projected in the worldview of any society at any epoch is only ever part of the total picture.

Chiasmus

In all Kuranko narratives it is axiomatic that the viability of the social system (the village) depends on infusing social positions with qualities such as magnanimity and intelligence whose distribution and appearance are contingent, which is to say, "wild." In cybernetic terms, the social system—

defined as a domain of nonnegotiable roles, fixed rules, given practices, ancestral values, and received wisdom—tends toward entropy. To counteract this continual drain of energy from the system, this descent into inertia, people must bring life to the village from outside it—symbolically from the bush. Obviously this involves making farms, growing crops, hunting game, marketing and exchanging produce. But it also involves ritual and conceptual strategies that tap into the "wild" and unbounded powers of the bush. In other words, the ancestral order of things cannot perpetuate itself through inertia or mandate; it must actively draw on the very energies and forces that are potentially inimical to it—the craft and intelligence of the young, the powers of djinn, the resources of strangers, and the reproductive power of women.

This exploitation of the "bush" would be uncomplicated were it not for the fact that the wild powers, dispositions, and abilities needed to regenerate the social order cannot be readily conjured, commanded, and controlled. Often the young are unruly, women are capricious, djinn are unpredictable, and strangers cannot be trusted. Even intelligence may be a mixed blessing, since the very perspicacity that is needed to make social relations viable can, if used for selfish ends, negate the ancestral order and threaten the integrity of the community.

While it may be impossible to order social reality in such a way that power holders are invariably in possession of vital capacities such as strength, courage, intelligence, and generosity, it is always possible to contrive such a fit in the imagination.

In Kuranko narratives, this adjustment or reapportionment is achieved through chiasmus.[6] A narrative characteristically begins with a polarized situation in which negative qualities are associated with a person in a powerful position (an inept or unjust ruler, a callous husband, a spiteful senior cowife, a domineering older brother), and positive qualities are associated with a person in a low-ranking position (a wise commoner, a virtuous wife, a resourceful junior cowife, an artful younger brother). The narrative proceeds to cross these elements over, so that positive psychophysical attributes come to be associated with superordinate social positions, and nega-

6. *Chiasmus:* "when the terms in the second of two parallel phrases reverse the order of those in the first to which they correspond. If the two phrases are written one below the other, and lines drawn between the corresponding terms, those lines make the Greek letter chi, a diagonal cross" (Fowler 1984, 601). A good example is the Latin phrase: *obit anus, abit onus* (the old woman dies, the burden goes away).

tive attributes extirpated through the death of an unjust ruler, the ostracism of a rogue, or the degradation of a deceiver.

If the clever and capable subordinate does not always displace the corrupt authority figure this is because the narratives are not primarily cathartic scenarios in which oppressors get their comeuppance or virtuous underlings get their just desserts; they accomplish a more formal balancing act in which justice is seen as a kind of adjustment of contingent qualities and abilities to the exigencies of the status quo (Jackson 1982a). Thus though radical changes and dramatic transitions occur in Kuranko narratives, the objective structure of rules, roles, and relationships remains intact.

Cinderella provides a paradigmatic example from the Indo-European corpus, though the story is practically universal. Pivotal to this story is a contradiction between social position and moral disposition. A virtuous and beautiful young girl (known variously as Cinderella, Rashin Coatie, Aschenputtel, Finetta, Zezolla, and Yeh-hsien) is found in degraded circumstances while her spiteful and ugly stepsisters enjoy the privileges of the well-born. The story entails a transformation, through chiasmus, in which moral beauty is transferred to the high status position (Cinderella marries the prince) and ugliness transferred to the low status position (the ugly stepsisters fall from grace). Thus the tale contrives, through legerdemain, an ideal congruence of moral virtue and elevated status.

Chiasmus may be schematized as follows:

Superior position   **Inferior position**

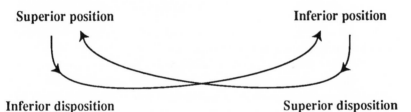

Inferior disposition   **Superior disposition**

That chiasmus is not a structure I have imposed arbitrarily or hermeneutically on Kuranko thought is borne out by evidence from another nuclear Mande people. Among the Bambara the paired terms *sako* and *dunko* connote external social necessity and inward personal desire respectively. While *sako* (literally, "death matter") implies respect for social ideals, *dunko* ("depth matter") implies idiosyncratic compulsions and emotional imperatives. Balancing the demands of one's social position (symbolized by village) with the inclinations of one's emotional disposition (symbolised by bush) constitutes for the Bambara the dynamic of moral personhood (*mogoya*) (Cissé 1973, 148–49; Kassim Kone, personal communication).

Consider now the following narrative, concerning the relationship of a ruler and his low-ranked *finaba*, Musa Kule.

> Saramba was a ruler and also a warrior of great renown. But his half-brothers became jealous of his fame and decided to kill him. They plotted to ambush him along the road. Though the conspiracy was discovered, Saramba was unable to delay his journey. A *finaba* called Musa Kule decided to disguise Saramba in his clothes. He donned Saramba's clothes so that he would die and thus save Saramba's life.
>
> On the day of the journey, they left together. A little way along the road Musa Kule took off his hat, gown, and trousers, and gave them to Saramba, his lord. Musa Kule then dressed in Saramba's clothes. They went on, riding on horses. As usual, Saramba was riding ahead. When they reached the place where the ambush had been laid, Saramba, disguised, passed by. The men in hiding said, "Oh no, not that one, it is only his poor *finaba*." Musa Kule then came, dressed in Saramba's clothes. They shot him.
>
> Therefore, since the time of Saramba and Musa Kule, they have always been together. Therefore they say, "Musa Kule and Saramba," meaning that they "go together."[7]

Bateson's notion of schismogenesis (1958, 175–97) helps us elucidate what is structurally implicit in this narrative.

One of the endemic problems of status or gender polarization is that the radical differences between such *social* categories (rationalized in terms of different essences, destinies, and inclinations) tend to set *people* apart and engender mutual antagonism. At the same time, the social order decays when there is a lack of interdependency or a loss of intimate cooperation between the old and the young, men and women. Bateson suggests that the distance between the categories must be periodically annulled or closed if

---

7. In a similar narrative (Jackson 1982b, 157–60) Muhammed is given lodgings and hospitality in a strange town by a lowly *finaba* (bard or genealogist). Muhammed subsequently declares the *finaba* to be superior to everyone else because he gave so unstintingly to strangers. "So he became known as Fisana [from *fisa*, "superior"] because he had done a good deed without ulterior motive. His moral intelligence [*hankilimaiye*] was superior to anyone else's" (Yeli Fode Gibaté, of Kabala).

this "dynamic equilibrium" is to be recovered and sustained. This may be achieved by a person from one category trading places with someone from the other in a ritually marked setting. Existentially one might say that it is only by seeing things from the point of view of the other that one can enter into a viable relationship with him or her. Others must somehow become us and be assimilated into ourselves if we are to know how to interact or get along with them. Alfred Schutz referred to these empathic and mimetic modes of chiasmus as "the reciprocity of perspectives" and "the interchangeability of standpoints" in which self momentarily becomes other and here becomes there (Schutz 1970, 183–84; 1973; 312–316).

These kinds of chiasmus occur during Kuranko initiations. As part of the public festivities that accompany the initiation of young girls, women dress as men, and the line between men's social space (*ke dugu*) and women's social space (*musu dugu*) is momentarily suspended. This, many women explain, is their way of vicariously or magically inculcating the superior strength, fortitude, and emotional self-control of men through ritual mimicry. The role reversals are thus a form of symmetrical schismogenesis that brings maleness and femaleness together in a transitory and imitative fusion, allowing the envied power of the former to be incorporated by the latter. The same principle holds true for male initiation, when men give symbolic birth to the neophytes and raise them to adulthood without the intercession of women (Jackson 1977, 212–13). Nonetheless, the Kuranko see such mimesis as ridiculous or crazy. Because the imitation of the other is inept and superficial, the project of becoming other can never be fully realized. In aspiring to be other, one only negates oneself. Similar absurdity attaches to *sanaku* performances, which, by conflating images of high and low status, create ludic confusion. Ironically, in attempting to erase difference, identity is often brought most sharply into focus—a point Victor Turner argued in his famous study of liminality. The monstrous juxtaposition of normally separated elements in Ndembu masks provokes neophytes to clarify and distinguish *in their own minds* features of their social environment that they had hitherto taken for granted (Turner 1970, 104–8).

THE QUESTION MAY BE ASKED, Does chiasmus operate between Kuranko society and the outside world in the same way that it operates within the local community to periodically and imaginatively confirm the functional complementarity of rulers and commoners, men and women?

Two narratives suggest that this is so.

In one narrative, which I have analyzed at length elsewhere (Jackson 1982a, 159–64, 184–91), a young man braves the dangers of the wilderness to bring back to his community a drum called the *yimbe*. The drum—which is associated with initiation—is initially in the hands of the hyenas. At the beginning of the story, captivated by its melodious sounds, the villagers have lapsed into a state of entranced passivity. In effect, social time has been brought to a standstill. By bringing the *yimbe* drum from the bush to the town the young hero sets time in motion again. People resume work, respect the elders, and initiate the young—a rite of passage that simultaneously confirms and regenerates the social order.

A second narrative (related by Yeli Fode Gibaté, of Kabala) involves a similar journey into the bush, and also culminates in the acquisition of a musical instrument and, by extension, the foundation of a crucial social relationship—this time between ruler (*manse*) and praise singer (*jeliba*):

> The ancestor of the Mansaré was Mande Sunyata. It was Mande Sunyata who discovered the xylophone [*balanje*] in a lake in Mande. It was in the hands of the djinn.
>
> Whenever Mande Sunyata went hunting in the Mande bush, he would hear the djinn playing the xylophone. The music was sweet to his ears. He said to himself, "I have enjoyed this music so much that I must bring it to the town." So he shot and killed the djinn and took the xylophone from them.
>
> He entered the town early in the morning, playing the xylophone and singing his own praises. He sang, "Take your gun Sunyata, take your gun and go to the bush."
>
> When people came around and listened, Mande Sunyata said, "If anyone takes from me this xylophone that I have taken from the djinn, I will kill him."
>
> When Mande Sunyata went back to the bush, Sira Kaarta declared, "I must play the xylophone today." So he picked it up and began to play it. He praised Sunyata better than Sunyata could praise himself.
>
> Far away in the bush, Sunyata heard the xylophone. He returned to the town and demanded to know, "Who played my xylophone?"
>
> No one dared answer him because of the threat he had made. But Sira Kaarta said, "Sunyata, I played your xylophone. But before you kill me, ask me why I played it. The reason is that no one should praise himself. One should praise others. In the first place, I praised Muhammed, so there is no reason why I

should not praise others. In the second place, your mother carried you in her womb for four thousand, four hundred, and forty years, four months, and four days. During that time you left your mother's womb at night and hunted game and brought it to the town so we would have food. Now that you are a man there is nothing you cannot do to help us live. So if this is true, your praise word is now *keita,* because you have the power to seize people's property without asking, and your name is Sunyata."[8]

Thus was his name made up of his deeds. They named him for what he did. Sunyata because he could trouble your heart. Keita because he could seize your property. Mande Sumaworo because when he became annoyed, anyone who saw him would be so afraid that they would contract elephantiasis of the testicles.[9] These were the words Sira Kaarta used to praise Sunyata.

After explaining all this, Sira Kaarta said, "Now that I have explained why I played the xylophone, I shall not return it to you, but continue to play it, praising you, because one should not praise oneself."

Then Mande Sunyata became pleased, and agreed. He took one hundred of all that he had and, together with the xylophone, gave it to Sira Kaarta. Wherever Sira Kaarta went with the xylophone, people came and gave him things. Therefore his descendants are called *jeleba.*

These narratives frame Kuranko thinking about the mixed hazards and rewards of venturing into the world beyond their local boundaries. But this ambiguous relationship between microcosm and macrocosm remains abstract and unreal until it is understood in terms of the interpersonal relationship between self and other.

The viability of the social order is grounded in an ability of one person to see things from another's point of view. The importance of this "abstract attitude" is driven home during initiation when a child learns to overcome narcissistic inclinations (symbolized by a child's attachment to the mother) and think symbolically and disinterestedly about his or her place in the wider community. Thus the force of the adage: *keran sa afoli n'kelale dinke*

8. A folk etymology is invoked here. The ruling clan name, Keita, is derived from *ke,* "inheritable property," and Sunyata, "heart burner," from *sun,* "heart," and *ya,* "dry and searing."

9. According to the folk etymology, the name derives from *sume,* "elephantiasis of the testicles," and *woro,* "calf of the leg."

la, koni a ta fo a kelale foama—"a squirrel could say it is alone in its hole, but never that it is alone in the field," that is, a person could claim to be unique in his family, but never that he or she is unique in the entire world.[10] This occlusion of self is accomplished by putting oneself in the place of another—symbolically donning new clothes or changing one's habitus. In narratives, crossing between different domains implies crossing between different social essences, and heroic journeys to and fro between town and bush articulate a series of empathic transpositions that imply that the social order can only be sustained if the self acknowledges the other *directly and experientially,* and not merely nominally and objectively as a partner in a system of economic exchange. For the Kuranko this entails interactive rather then merely empathic modes of being with another: cooperating, "moving together," or "sitting together." To share the world knowingly with others entails *praktognosis*—a practical engagement with others in everyday productive tasks. This interactive openness to the other informs all gift exchange, which the Kuranko see as a way of affirming that the life of others has the same value as one's own life and the life of one's kin. Such openness between self and other is likened to a clear path or an open field in which the grass bends one way as a person or gift passes through it, then bends back the other way when the movement is reciprocated: *nyendan bin to kile a wa ta an segi.*

This is, of course, the same field through which the ethnographer moves, and so the question arises, What does he or she give in return for what he or she gains, that like the *yimbe* drum or the xylophone is music to the other's ears?

Sacrifice

In the dry season of 1972 Lansana Kargbo came home to his natal village of Kamadugu Sukurela. After several years living and working in the Kono diamond districts, Lansana had had little luck. "My hands are empty," he told me, and that same day he sought the advice of a diviner. In the course

---

10. Cf. the Bamana proverbs: When you hear people say that such and such a blind man is intelligent, it is only in his hometown that he is so; if he travels to another town you will hear of him falling in a well (*n'i y'a men fiyento hakili ka di. a wolola dugu min na ko don: n'o te n'a tora duguwere la. u n'a binkan men kolon kono*); When you hear people say *ladle,* it is because of its handle; remove the handle and the water ladle becomes a drinking cup (*n'i y'a men ka fo ko galama. a ku de ko don; n'i ye galama ku kari k'a b'a la, a be ke jiminfilenni ye*) (Kone 1994).

of the consultation, Lansana was told that he had failed to keep in touch with his village and ancestors. He should offer a sacrifice (*ka sarake bo,* literally, "take out a sacrifice") to clear and open the pathways.

On the day of the sacrifice, representatives from every social group in Sukurela gathered in Lansana's father's brother's compound (*luiye*). Apart from elders representing the main clans in the village, invited guests included: the Kamadugu section chief; the Sukurela town chief; the leader of the young men; myself as representative of the *tubabu;* my field assistant as a representative of his chiefdom, Barawa; a visiting town chief from Fasewoia whose mother hailed from Sukurela; and a Muslim officiant. We sat on porches, in the shade of thatched eaves, waiting for the sacrifice to begin.

The cough of a pestle rising and falling in a wooden mortar in the yard behind Lansana's father's brother's house signaled that women of the household were pounding rice flour. While I scribbled down observations or took photos, and the men around me talked desultorily, Lansana and his "father" busily ensured that every last detail of the diviner's instructions was recalled and respected.

At last two enamel dishes of rice flour were brought out from the house, each with four white kola nuts atop it. This was the cue for a xylophonist to begin playing praise songs for Lansana's family, the ruling lineage in Kamadugu, as well as for his mother whose labor had made her sons prosper and brought upon them their father's blessings. "A child's destiny is in its mother's hands."

Lansana's father's brother, as the senior man of the compound, then distributed the kola among the guests, naming the social categories that each represented. Thus kola given to the leader of the young men was symbolically given to all the young men of the village, and kola given to me was symbolically given to all Europeans. The whiteness of the kola signified the spirit of amity and openness among us.

Once the kola had been given out, we squatted around the dishes of rice flour, our right hands extended, while Lansana's "father" called the names of the agnatic ancestors. The most recently dead were first named, then others as they came to mind. Finally, Lansana's mother's name was called, and to ensure the sacrifice reached all the ancestors Lansana's "father" asked one of them to "pass on the sacrifice to everyone, named and unnamed." As each ancestor was called we murmured *amina* in collective acknowledgment and assent.

An elder from the joking-related Sisé clan now distributed rice flour (*dege*) to all present: those who had received kola, as well as the women, the children, the xylophonists, and the Muslim officiant. It seemed to me that every effort was being made to transcend the particular person and particular lineage that was offering the sacrifice, to embrace not only every category and group in the community but those beyond it as well.

The second sacrifice was now prepared. This was to be a red goat, offered to God.

After consecrating it in the same way as the rice flour—though with Lansana's "father" now invoking the ancestors to act as intercessories with God—the Muslim officiant stepped forward. Several young men then tipped the goat on to its side and bound the feet closest to the ground with rope (since cuts of meat from the lower half of the animal would remain in the household). Then, as the men pinned the goat to the ground and Lansana held its head, the *karamorgo* slit its throat.

The goat was butchered on some banana leaves under the close supervision of Lansana and his "father." If the sacrifice was to be efficacious, it was imperative that the diviner's instructions be followed to the letter. So when the town chief from Fasewoia, who was Lansana's classificatory sister's son, pushed forward and seized the neck, as was his due, there was great commotion. On this occasion the diviner had instructed that the neck remain in the household. Otherwise, the division of the meat conformed to custom: lower body to the household and immediate family; upper body to other households and families in the village; lower foreleg to the head of the family; upper foreleg to the town chief; neck to sister's sons; rump to sisters; stomach to slaves; heart and liver to some respected individual; hide to the leather workers; hooves to the genealogists and xylophonists.

Godfrey Lienhardt observes that sacrifice "includes a re-creation of the basis of local corporate life, in the full sense of those words." Thus for the Dinka, "the whole victim corresponds to the unitary solidarity of human beings in their common relationship to the divine, while the division of the flesh corresponds to the social differentiation of the persons and groups taking part" (1961, 234). In the words of one Dinka informant, "The people are put together, as a bull is put together." (23). In exactly the same way, the Kuranko make the body of the sacrificial animal a surrogate for the social body. Partaking of *its* flesh is an expression of social solidarity and untroubled intersubjectivity. At the same time, the strict division of the body affirms lines of distinction between estates, between clans, between patrikin and affines, and between villagers and strangers. Thus the distinction between lower and upper halves of the animal, expressed as a difference between earth and sky, affirms the distinction between those of that place (*dugu* means both ground, earth, and locality) and those from elsewhere (*sundan*).

But while these social distinctions are affirmed in the customary division of the meat, they are momentarily transfigured in the consecration of the sacrifice to the ancestors and to God. Accordingly, Lansana's particular world implicated the world of others. His life was symbolically linked to the life not only of his immediate kin but of his affines and of other clans in the community. While the rice for the *dege* is homegrown, and therefore a symbol of the patrilineage, the goat, like other livestock, has to be purchased from outside the village. It thus symbolizes identifications and values that go beyond the circle of kinship and compound (*luiye*). Conceptually, the distinction is one between the ancestors, symbolizing the unity of the lineage through time, and God, symbolizing bonds of humanity that embrace a wider spatiotemporal domain. To invoke the name of God is to transcend or override the particularistic identifications of estate and descent, even to eclipse generalized ties of affinity and cognatic kinship within the village, and recognize, albeit momentarily, one's involvement in a world that is far more extensive than that of family or village.

But behind these shifting frames of symbolic reference in Kuranko sacrifice is a search for ontological security, for a degree of control over the forces of destiny.

Lansana's sacrifice was typical. For many generations, young Kuranko men have journeyed away from their natal villages in search of their fortunes. Many worked for the British as surveying assistants, court messengers, or policemen. Others saw service in the Sierra Leone army, police force, or security police. Others have spent many years in Kono prospecting for diamonds. Others have traveled further afield to the gold mines of Guinea, or to serve apprenticeships with medicine masters and Koranic teachers. Yet all have experienced unsettling and arduous periods alone in a place of strangers, cut off from close kin, intimidated by people with better local knowledge, prey to changing fortunes.

Consider the diamond districts of Kono. Perhaps more dramatically than elsewhere, the diamond workings bring home to the fortune seeker the fickleness of fate. It is an unpredictable world in the extreme, where danger and luck in the fields mingle with corruption, violence, chaos, and political anarchy in the country as a whole—a place ruled by powerful others, powerful intrigue, inscrutable designs. To lose one's footing in this world is the fate of most young men. When they return home they seek a different

balance between the field of their own agency and the field of the world—
a relationship with a wider world they *can* control.

Better to be in the hands of a djinn than the hands of Kome, runs a
Kuranko adage (*Morgo benta nyina bolo komo ko*), implying that it is always preferable to be under the influence of something you can control
and comprehend than to be at the mercy of forces that are unpredictable
and unfathomable. In the contexts of divination and sacrifice the world of
the ancestors and God signifies this wider yet more manageable world.
Though it extends beyond the self and the local community, it can be
reached and controlled through ritualized and magical communication.
With God and the ancestors there is room to maneuver, to exercise agency,
to act and bargain, to manage and grasp. The no-man's land between one's
local world and the world beyond is no longer impersonal and impenetra-
ble; it is intersubjective and social, and as such, can be cultivated and
crossed.

Sacrifice has always been a way of redressing a loss of balance between
one's immediate world and the wider world. It accomplishes this through
the gift that, in the Kuranko view, transforms the *relationship* between
persons or categories of persons and bestows a state of blessedness (*baraka*)
upon them. This is because the gift creates life. It opens up a path between
people. It transforms darkness and distrust into transparency and openness.
Giving to the ancestors is like giving to the living when they are far away.
It brings them close. By eating the meat or rice flour consecrated to them,
one makes them like guests sitting in one's presence. Kuranko say that the
ancestors have accepted a sacrifice when vultures flap out of the sky and
alight on the thatched eaves of houses around the *luiye* where the meat is
laid out. The act of commensality is thus also an act of social incorporation
in which beings who, while distant, always remain potentially inimical to
one's welfare are brought close and recreated as kin. Sacrifice is the ritual-
ization of the incorporative meaning of commensality.

But there is an intersubjective dynamic in sacrifice that deepens our understanding of this ritual use of commensality. As Evans-Pritchard observed, sacrifice implies more than giving something away in order to bargain for an improvement in one's lot or pay homage to one's ancestors
(Evans-Pritchard 1956, 277–82). The gift, as Mauss pointed out, always
incorporates something of oneself. "All gifts are symbols of inner states,"
writes Evans-Pritchard, "and in this sense one can only give oneself; there
is no other kind of giving" (279). In Kuranko sacrifice the gift is said to be
"taken out" of oneself; it embodies one's deepest intentionality—a fervent,

focused, and sometimes desperate concern to consummate in one's relationship with God or one's neighbors a totally unguarded openness of spirit. But this eclipse of self, this relinquishment and abnegation of one's idiosyncratic identity, must be understood existentially. In sacrifice, what is yielded and immolated is one's selfhood. Sacrifice is a form of self-effacement; suicide is its logical extreme. The giving of the life of an animal one owns (which is metonymically one's self) simply mediates and objectifies *vita pro vita* this occlusion and absenting of self. But that which goes from one's self augments one's sense of the ancestral or divine field of which one is a part. It restores to the ancestors both presence and force. If misfortune is a result of forgetting one's place in the field of ancestral being, then expiation necessitates a self-forgetting and, as a corollary, a recollection of the others in whose hands one's identity and destiny ultimately lie. The ancestral and divine domain is the temporal equivalent of the social space in which one stands—the space of one's kin and community.

In a very real sense, sacrifice is a way of ritually countermanding situations in which a person has come to stand outside his or her society. Such ecstatic situations may arise from death, illness, and ill fortune, or from any new departure in life—brush cutting to create a new farm, building a house, going on a journey, initiating a child, or contesting political office. If such events are experienced as singular or aberrant, isolating or singling one out from others, sacrifice mediates an experience of reincorporation and reabsorption into enstatic normalcy. Like all rituals, sacrifice simply exaggerates the ecstatic and enstatic extremes in order to promote a transformation *in experience* from being alone and estranged to recovering one's place within.

BUT ONE QUESTION REMAINS. Though one can readily understand the impulse to maintain this existential balance between oneself and one's ancestors (who, if neglected, may withhold protection and so make one vulnerable to ruin), it is less obvious why Kuranko should adopt the Muslim God, particularly since many Kuranko clans historically sought refuge from Islam and Islamic jihads in the West Guinea Highlands. How might we understand this transition from a "traditional" to a "world" religion—a transition that has been gathering momentum for twenty years now, not only among the Kuranko but throughout West Africa?

One explanation is that people have been faced with an existential crisis of control in their dealings with the outside world. Increasingly confused and oppressed by rumors of coups and countercoups, crisis, and corruption in the nation of which they are a part, people seek ways of clarifying, coming to terms with, and controlling their relations with it. How to deal with the unsettling sense that one is implicated in this world, subject to its changing political storm and stress, potentially at its mercy? In two seminal papers on African conversion published in 1971 and 1975, Robin Horton wrote of the perennial problem of striking a balance between individuation and *communitas,* of controling relations between human and extrahuman worlds (1971, 100). His persuasive argument was that modernity expands the range of one's social contacts and communications, making the balance between the social microcosm of the village and the wider world increasingly difficult to achieve. Under these conditions a belief in the power of the "lesser spirits" associated with one's natal environment begins to give ground to a belief in the power of supreme beings associated with the world as a whole. This is accompanied by a concern for practical and ritual means of tapping that power (ibid., 102; cf. Simmons 1976; Werbner 1989, 223–44). Hence the increasing interest in the global religions of Islam and Christianity.

But, cautions Horton, this interest is not based on "intellectual allure" (because the new gods are compatible with the old, or their proselytizers are persuasive). It is based on a changing social situation in which people are drawn into a struggle to balance traditional modes of autonomy in their local moral worlds[11] with new modalities of economic and cultural life that follow the "weakening of microcosmic boundaries" (106; cf. Horton 1993, 315–16).

In working out a *modus vivendi* with the world of new commodities, new media, new ideas, and new customs, the Kuranko struggle not to be engulfed by otherness but to negotiate some kind of control over it. Faced with a choice between Western materialism and Middle Eastern religion—which is, roughly speaking, the alternative that is presented—people tend to embrace Islam. It is not just that the supreme being, Allah, provides a focal symbol of universal humanity, nor that Islam has been associated historically with trade with the outside world; rather, the practical demands of Islam—often a simple matter of daily prayer—are amenable and flexible enough to allow one to feel in control of what one is doing rather than overwhelmed by new routines and doctrines. Thus my old friend Saran Salia could retain his personal loyalty to his fetishes and djinn if he paid

11. The phrase is Arthur Kleinman's (Kleinman 1992, 172).

lip service to Islam by attending the local mosque every evening (Jackson 1986). Some balance could be struck between the divinities of his microcosm and the divine powers of the world beyond his village.

But the need for some unifying symbol in a world of multiplex social identities based on kinship, occupation, and belief has always been felt among the Kuranko, which is why Allah and Islamic medicines have figured in their ritual life for so long. To invoke Allah at a sacrifice is thus to express a *social* need for a transcendent icon betokening unity and commonality; it implies neither depth of faith, nor shared belief, nor identification with Islamic culture. In this opportunistic embrace of a concept that belongs to a world outside one's borders, one can affirm the unity of one's own particular community as well as feel that one exercises some control over the unpredictable boundaries that lie between it and the world beyond.

Fetish

A corollary of the interpersonal dynamic that reduces subjects to objects and persons to the status of things is the metamorphosis of things into persons. But in broaching the subject of animism and the "social life of things" I am less interested in the conceptual and analogical implications of the phenomenon than in the conditions under which the experiences of things-as-persons arise.

One way of exploring this question is to take up the subject of the fetish, which, as a fabricated object allegedly possessed of consciousness and will, has often been cited as the exemplary case of inanimate animism and anthropomorphic thinking. But what I aim to do here is to suspend all consideration of the fetish as an artifact of thought, logical or illogical, and explore it as an particular modality of human intersubjectivity.

THAT WE EXIST SOLELY IN relation to others is dramatically borne out by studies of human responses to loss. The universal and primordial patterns of separation trauma, documented by John Bowlby and his colleagues (Bowlby 1971; 1975), undoubtedly form the basis of most restorative and retributive ritual. Thus the psychological movement from protest through withdrawal to acceptance finds cultural expression in rites of passage that proceed from separation through marginality to reincorporation (Turner 1970, 93–111). But we should remember that the reason why *social* marginalization, rejection, or ostracism has the same force as the forms of loss that we associate with *personal* events such as bereavement, dispossession, and exile is that they are mutually entailed; they are simply alternative ways of describing what is, in reality, a rupture in *intersubjective* life.

When robbed of the family, community, or circle of friends that sustains a sense of self, an individual feels diminished. For the Kuranko, such diminution through isolation is social death, and feared more than physical demise. Though such loss is variously experienced in different societies and in different individuals as a loss of presence, a fall in self-esteem, a weakening of body boundaries, a loss of face, a void, an eclipse, or a susceptibility to some invasively alien presence, the *existential* constant in all such cases is that a person is reduced to passivity, inertia, and nullity.

When people are invalidated or made "to feel small" in this way—effectively rendered nonentities—they may react either by willful abnegation (sinking masochistically into the slough that has been visited on them), or with angry protest (retaliating with projective gestures that reassert the lost identity). Violence against powerful or anonymous others restores a sense of being able to act, of possessing presence and substance, of being able to have an effect on the world that seems to have rubbed one out or cast one down. One thus reoccupies the space from which one has been banished or dismissed, "shooting daggers," shouting, brandishing, cursing, and using words of sexual abuse that express the kind of phallic rapacity one believes will magically restore one's lost impotence and frustrated intentionality.

The use of fetishes belongs to this field of intersubjective reclamation. Fetishes objectify a violent inner protest against being put down, against being cut out, against the occlusion of presence.

"FETISH" COMES FROM THE Latin *facticius* ("to do"), though the earliest English use of the word, in the late fifteenth century, derives from the Portugese word *feitiço*, which was applied to the "charms" used by Africans on the Guinea coast (Ellen 1988, 214). The archetypical fetish was possibly the BaKongo *nkisi* (plural: *minkisi*) from the region that today encompasses Cabinda and western Zaire (MacGaffey 1977, 172).

The word enters European discourse with perjorative connotations, a synonym for idolatry, primitivism, and savagery. Early anthropologists such as Tylor and Frazer considered fetishism to be a form of irrationalism, magic, and superstition precisely because it denied or blurred the distinction between persons and things.[12] How could an inanimate object be imbued with intentionality and moral consciousness, addressed, fed, and cared for as though it were human?

They protested too much. Those who were most repelled and outraged by the African's apparent indifference to the ontological divide between persons and things were, as often as not, engaged in the kind of colonial ventures—such as slave trading—that conspicuously reduced Africans to the status of beasts, chattels, and mere things. Moreover, the European Enlightenment's excoriation of anthropomorphism was from the outset a rhetorical device for concealing its pervasive presence in European discourse. In fact, in no human society is it possible to draw anything but a transient and ambiguous line between subject and object. In our practical lives, the line is infringed continually. The field of intersubjectivity inescapably involves an ongoing reciprocal movement in consciousness between a sense of being a subject for oneself and being an object for others.

A rejoinder to this point of view would be to admit that we often *liken* persons to things and things to persons, but that this should not be taken to imply that we *confuse* them. It is a matter of metaphor, so to speak, not a reflection of how we think things really are.

But the pathetic fallacy that erases the distinction between subject and object issues from direct experience and is not conjured out of nowhere—a mere figure of speech. Similes that merge persons and things are grounded in our continually shifting sense of ourselves as having and not having autonomy, of being embodied and disembodied, of acting and of being acted upon. And the similes arise in specific contexts, and have to be understood as such.

Consider Kuranko thought on this subject. If sacrifice is a form of gift giving that opens and clears paths between people, creating transparency and reciprocity, fetishes work to seal off, enclose, safeguard, and protect. Accordingly, Kuranko social life vacillates between openness and closure. For every adage that encourages generosity of spirit (*morgoye*), there is one that extols guardedness.

Yani wolen na don sise na don (literally, "let the chicken rather than the bushfowl eat it)—rather than give to a stranger, give to someone you know so that the gift will come back to you.

---

12. The word *nkisi* belongs not to the class of things but to the class of nouns that the linguist Laman calls "the semi-person class or the class of trees" (Jacobson-Widding 1979, 135).

Ni ya bolo kolon kononto ko i lile mala a tan nyorgo la (literally, "if you give to nine poor people you'll be the tenth to be poor)—don't be so generous as to leave yourself in need.

Thus while gifts and sacrifices serve to clear channels of communication, fetishes serve to monitor and reinforce boundaries where uncontrolled traffic jeopardizes a person's sense of autonomy and threatens his or her security. The difference between fetish and gift is that the fetish withholds or prevents communication, sealing self off from other, while the gift opens and mediates communication. The fetish closes gates; the gift opens paths.[13]

However, in no human society are people so open to others that they are able to forfeit their self-identity completely. Even the most charitable and self-sacrificing individual feels personally gratified or somehow saved by giving unstintingly. Without possessing some sense of ontological security and substantiality, others are experienced as destabilizing influences or threats. For the Kuranko, fetishes may be understood as a specific instance of the imperative to "have *miran*," that is, to be self-contained and self-possessed. The analogy is with a container like a calabash or country pot.[14] Thus *miran* can denote qualities such as self-confidence, self-possession, a commanding presence, and charisma, as well as material posessions, particularly those things that bolster one's sense of self-containedness and autonomy—personal property, clothing, a dwelling or granary, protective charms, and magical ointments.

Just as these things can be stolen or spoiled, so too can a person's self-confidence and sense of autonomy be taken away. *Miran,* like *mana* for the Polynesians, is continually waxing and waning.

To strengthen *miran* the Kuranko have recourse to fetishes and magical

---

13. A similar logic governs the distinction between (for)giving and cursing. One of the most powerful instruments of cursing is the blacksmith's bellows. The bellows are said to generate life because they fan the flames in which the smith shapes the machetes, knives, hoes, and axes with which people make their farms. Using the bellows backwards brings death; the victim's belly swells, not with food, but with the curse. The same principle of dialectical negation obtains in witchcraft, where upended cooking vessels and inverted mortars signify life-taking compulsions.

14. Jacobson-Widding notes that the "object in which a *nkisi* spirit (or the reflexion of a *nkisi* spirit) is contained is generally a bag," but sometimes a horn, shell, or basket, which is often attached to a sculpted human image (1979, 139). A Kongo author, writing in 1915, observed that the fetish is "like a man, but invisible. Also he is like a large pot in a well-made basket." As MacGaffey notes, the *nkisi* is clearly a personality (from the land of the dead) inhabiting a material object (1994, 125), but the container is not *nkisi* until *bilongo* (medicines) or *sacra* have been included in it (1990, 51).

medicines that boost their sense of substantiality or, as we might say, ego strength. When used to protect farms, villages, or chiefdoms, they act as symbolic containers, rendering that unit of social space impermeable to unlicensed extraneous influence. Commonly known throughout West Africa as jujus (from the French *jou-jou*), among the Kuranko these magical artifacts include guardian angels (*kanda malika*), djinn (*nyenne*), and magical medicines (*bese*). In short, though some are man-made objects and others are quasi-human, all are considered to have the ability to bolster the power of one's own will.

What are the grounds on which this belief rests?

First, let us remember that fetishes are deployed when a person feels vulnerable or overwhelmed by the will (usually the ill will) of others. Second, it is important to recall that human intentionality is embodied. Vulnerability implies an inability to physically combat the will of the other, sensed as a palpable force invading or engulfing one's own body-self. This is most dramatically expressed in the symptoms of a person at the mercy of witchcraft: a sense of claustrophobia and immobility, of a weight pressing down on the chest, constricting the breath.

Thwarted in one's bodily intentionality, unable to physically withstand the other, one has recourse to the fetish as a tool or instrument that extends the range and power of one's own intentionality. But it is more than this, for the fetish is also a surrogate body. It literally embodies, objectifies, and unblocks the will of the besieged individual. It facilitates vicarious action. In this sense the fetish is a negative or inverted gift. The gift immolated in sacrifice is also a surrogate body-self, but one that effectively assists the sacrificer to give ground to the ancestors and to God. Self is nullified in order that the other regain presence. In the case of the fetish, it is the other who is nullified and negated in order for the self to regain presence and control.

This is why Kuranko fetishes are defined not in terms of static intrinsic attributes but in terms of their modes of intersubjective action. For instance, the action of the djinn that assists hunters (it is called *Sogori*) is described as a kind of leeching or sucking that robs a game animal of its strength and allows a hunter to safely approach and shoot it. Magical medicines known as *besekoli* (literally, "shooting medicines") have the power to penetrate or lance the body of the other, again with the effect of immobilizing and weakening him. And magical powders (*nyenkofuri*) are cast into the wind, to be blown toward the victim and afflict him with skin disease. Frequently, the use of such artifacts requires incantations (*haya*), which are themselves ways of bodying forth the will and strengthening the hand of the user.

But intersubjective realism is never abandoned in fetishism. If the other is well protected with antijujus, then one's intentions, words, shots, or barbs will rebound against oneself. It is for this reason that the Kuranko often prefer to use protective or defensive devices rather than risk aggressive acts that may ricochet or rebound, harming the user instead of the person for whom the action was intended.

Rather than being a domain of mistaken causation and blind superstition, fetishism reveals itself to be a domain of troubled intersubjectivity where ego and alter vie for dominance and mastery. As such it embodies and objectifies many of the defense mechanisms that we tend to locate intrapsychically.

Consider the array of fetishes a Firawa friend kept in a locked box under his bed. All *kanda li fannu* ("protective/enclosing things"), these included *gbogure* ("padlock")—a real padlock with a page of Koranic verses folded lengthwise, wrapped around it, and bound with thread. Here as elsewhere, it was the *action* of the fetish that enabled one to grasp its meaning. As the bar of the padlock is closed, one wraps first white, then red, then black thread around it, reciting words from the Koran and the name of the person whom one wants to "lock up." *Gbogure* is used to gain an advantage over an adversary in a legal battle. The action described has the effect of immobilizing the victim or rendering him speechless.

Another device had a similar use. Called *yuluba* ("rope"), it consisted of a knotted cord with a noose at one end. The cord is smeared with cow's-milk butter. One holds the knotted end away from the hand, utters words from the Koran together with the victim's name, then pulls the noose tight within a clenched fist. The victim is thus tongue-tied and bound.

A third device was called *fele*. Made of twisted black and white threads, it is placed on the threshold of one's room to prevent enemies entering.

Then there was *nisi,* which is a generic term for concoctions that contain Koranic suras washed from a slate. The concoction is smeared on the body to give it protection. It works in the same way as *sebe*—small paper charms or suras sown into leather sachets and worn around the neck.

Often, on the lintels of houses, one sees miniature gates, bundles of bound cane, and knotted cords. These too may be seen as products of surrogate enactments in which subjective intentions, thwarted or uncertain in reality, find embodiment. To create a gate or tie a knot or twist threads is thus to body forth that which is initially experienced in intersubjectivity as an obstruction or double bind. Existentially, it is an attempt to come to terms with inner frustrations by objectifying them in a form that is responsive to one's will, tractable, and manageable. The balance of control is thus shifted from the unknown other, whose intentions are inscrutable and threatening, to the self.

But this adjustment of balance between ego and alter rests entirely on a transition from passivity to activity. Through the fetish one magically regains control over a situation in which one's mastery was undermined or lost. The fetish makes a person feel more ontologically secure and restores self-confidence (*miran*) because it mediates a passage from powerlessness to empowerment, from passivity to activity. This is why the fetish becomes like a person. The will, work, and energy put into the object (often a container), animates it. It is this experience that Marx alluded to when he observed that any material object on which one expends valuable time and energy becomes a "prolongation" of one's body (1964, 89). In the case of the fetish, the body of the thing becomes the surrogate body of the maker and user; as such it becomes an extension of his or her intentionality and consciousness. *It* becomes *I*. The value of the thing cannot therefore be understood as a function of scarcity; rather, it is a function of desire. The fetish is a specific instance of a universal human tendency to ontologize experience: as the effort and desire dedicated to a thing become more intense, so the experience of its ontological substantiality and value deepens.

These processes of fetishization effectively make the fetish an instrument of existential control—a means of magical resistance and reprisal in intersubjective space. Mauss understood this phenomenological process perfectly when he evoked the spirit of the gift as an explanatory principle (1954, 9). For the Maori, the *hau* that imbues any valued gift (*taonga*) is an expression of the vital identification or bond one feels with something that one has worked on with focus and devotion, in which one has invested time and energy, or that one has possessed for a long time. It is similar to the vital power that the Bambara call *nyama*. Seen as "the energy of action" (Bird 1976, 98), *nyama* is said to inhere in every action, and in every one and every thing that is in effect part of the forcefield of human interaction and human labor, including persons, iron ore, language, excrement, and food scraps (McNaughton 1988, 15–21). Just as a material gift enables one to control one's relations to the person to whom the gift goes, so, for the Bambara, it is vital to get a "handle" on *nyama* and harness it for the good of the social order.

The fetish becomes a body-subject, therefore, to the extent that a person makes it the medium of his or her consciousness and will, and invests his or her intentions in it. To speak psychoanalytically of the fetish as a pathological instance of object-cathexis, or to speak in a Marxist vein of the fetish as a chimerical conclusion of a thought process that habitually anthropomorphizes the natural world (Godelier 1977, 208), is no doubt reflective of the Eurocentric view that it is irrational to treat objects as persons. For a phenomenologist, this misses the point. For it is only when we bracket out *our* essentialistic notions of what is and is not a thing that we can fully explore modes of experience that *practically* transform objects into subjects, *and vice versa.* The crucial point is not to define the fetish essentialistically but to describe the consequences of its use.

This turns Marx's notion of fetishism on its head. For the Kuranko a fetish has meaning in use; it is an integral part of the field of interpersonal relations. Outside of such contexts of use, the fetish has no life of its own. As such, it makes little sense to speak of it as the finished product of activity, estranged from the labor that brought it into the world, or as the fantastic form of social relations rendered as relations between things (Marx 1970, 72). Its sole reality for the Kuranko consists in its being a vital and integral part of the process of intersubjective life, at once the bodily expression of one's need for autonomy and the means of restoring control when the boundary between ego and alter becomes so confused that one risks annihilation in otherness. George Devereux has argued that anthropomorphic thinking is a way of alleviating "the trauma of the unresponsiveness of matter." By imputing will and responsiveness to things, the alien and obdurate character of the material and natural world may be experienced as less threatening (1967, 32–34). But the same cosmic panic and anxiety that arises in our relationship to inert things arises in our relations with human others who confront us as alien, inscrutable, unsympathetic, and antagonistic. This is why fetishism, as a stratagem of existential control, inevitably makes its appearance in the field of subject-object relations, whether this is between persons and things or solely between persons.

Color Triad

One of the oldest anthropological mysteries is the universality of the color triad—white, black, and red. Why is it that so many languages identify only three color terms, even though all colors of the spectrum are perceptually distinguished? More specifically, when a lexicon includes only two colors, why are these invariably white and black; and when it includes three, why is it that the third term is always red (Berlin and Kay 1969, 17)?

In a notable paper on Ndembu color symbolism Victor Turner "threw caution to the wind" and suggested that we understand the basic color triad preconceptually in terms of universal human bodily and visceral experience (1970, 88–90). The three colors—white, black, red—"stand for basic human experiences of the body (associated with the gratification of libido, hunger, aggressive and excretory drives, and with fear, anxiety, and submissiveness)" (89–90).

Turner's incautious gesture effectively reverses the Durkheimian view that relations between social groups determine the logic according to which sensible and natural objects are classified. In seeking to explicate Ndembu color terms in a way that did not depart too radically from Ndembu experience and exegesis, Turner emphasized the links between color terms and "the main kinds of universal human organic experience" [88]. Accordingly, he suggested, red is universally a symbol of blood, white a symbol of breast milk and semen, black the color of urine and feces.

Though I share Turner's view that "the human organism and its crucial experiences are the *fons et origo* of all classifications," the Freudian bias in his interpretation prevented Turner from exploring in depth the intersubjective character of these crucial experiences.

Let us consider Kuranko color terms. Like the Ndembu and many other African peoples, the Kuranko have only three color words: white, black, red. Their meanings, however, can only be clarified by considering their contextual uses. To compare them momentarily with persons, one might say that their essence is defined solely in their existence.

White (*gbe*):

"When a diviner tells you to put a white sacrifice outside your house, the sacrifice will have the effect of clearing/cleaning out the ill will of anyone who approaches your house with the intention of doing you harm. The white will change his mind, so that he will no longer wish to harm you."

"A corpse is wrapped in white cloth so that the white will clean and purify the body and enable the spirit to go to *lakira* ['heaven']."

"Whiteness is like water. Just as some streams are murky, then run clear, so whiteness washes away darkness. Widows are dressed in white, but after their quarantine the white clothes are discarded and they are washed clean. The water purifies them in the same way that the white clothes did."

"The hearts of those who live together should be white."

"I trust you" (*n'de ya n gbe i le ye;* literally, "I make myself white for you").

"This is an honest person" (*morgo gbe le kela;* literally, "this is a white person").

Black (*fin*):

"Witches have black hearts."

"His ways are the ways of enemies" (*morgo fiennu;* literally, "black people").

Red (*wulan*):

"Before we the blacksmiths begin making an axe or hoe or machete, we kill, cook, and eat a red cock as a sacrifice to the ancestral smith. We sacrifice a red cock because the work is dangerous. We play with fire and hot iron. The red cock shows that our work is dangerous."

"*Saseh* [an antiwitchcraft medicine bag] is made from the skin of the red patas monkey [*kulawulan*] or the red squirrel [*tumban*]. The red wards off evil."

These phrases, culled at random from my fieldnotes, indicate the fan of referents for each color. White connotes happiness, clear conscience, untroubled state of mind, openness or transparency between people, purity, and ritual order. Black negates these attributes. It signifies animosity, nefarious intentions, death, inscrutability, and misfortune. Attributed to social and extrasocial worlds beyond one's own, it has similar connotations to the nineteenth-century European notion of Africa as the heart of darkness. Finally, red is associated with danger, trouble, anxiety, and emotionally disturbed ("hot") relationships.

It is clear that the Kuranko color triad is not primarily descriptive. The Kuranko do not stereotype themselves as "black," and many hues are typically assimilated to the primary triad: blue (*bulu,* from the English *blue*) is equivalent to black in many ritual contexts, and light colors are often substituted for white. Phenomenologically, black and white articulate two extremes of intersubjective life. While whiteness signifies trust, openness, transparency, and sincerity, blackness signifies suspicion, closure, inscrutability, and duplicity.

Witkowski and Brown argue that such color partitioning is "wired" or "programmed" in the human brain (1977; 1982). Berlin and Kay explain it phylogenetically, using an analogy with the labial stage in phonological development when an infant says only *pa* (minimal energy *p* plus maximal energy *a*) (1969, 104–5). Thus the basic ("stage 1") two-color lexicon is based on a contrast between white (maximum brightness, maximum energy) and black (minimum brightness, minimum energy). But the problem with this formulation is that it is contradicted by the facts of experience. For the Kuranko, as for many other African peoples, white is a synonym of coolness, and therefore connotes minimum energy, while red conjures up images of heat and turbulence, and therefore maximum energy.

In reviewing Berlin and Kay's seminal work, Sahlins argued that colors are "selective orderings of experience" that follow "a natural-logic" (1976, 8–10). I share this view that cultural and semiotic variations in color schemata are grounded in protocultural experience and primitive relationships, but I prefer a phenomenological conception of what is "natural." As I see it, the color spectrum is not Newtonian but intersubjective. What phenomenologists call the "natural attitude" implies that one's knowledge of others, though based most immediately on one's knowledge of self, reflects shared social *and* biological horizons—a common stock of knowledge. The polarization of white and black arises naturally within this field of reciprocal perspectives, part of the dynamic of intersubjectivity itself. As tonal extremes, black and white have the same potential for marking modalities of social relations as bitter and sweet tastes (Kuipers 1991), good and bad odors (Devisch 1985, 596–97; Classen, Howes, and Synnott 1994; Howes 1991), or touching and not touching. Eugène Minkowski's account of intersubjective space is helpful here. The contrast Minkowski draws between "clear space" and "dark space" signifies a distinction between intimacy and distance. When people are close there is a sense of clarity; when people are closed off to each other "vital space is narrowed, space is desocialized," and delusions of persecution fill the darkness (Ellenberger 1958, 111). White and black are not simply metaphors for these modalities of intersubjective apperception, they are native to the experience itself. At one extreme the intentions and views of the other are experienced as clear, and one's own intentions and views are reciprocally acknowledged without distortion and without unpredictable consequences: the other is seen for who he or she really is, and I am seen as I really am; we have nothing to hide from each other; there are no mixed messages, no hidden agendas, no ulterior motives. This condition of openness and mutual trust is experienced as a state of transparency or whiteness. (It is interesting in this regard that the Ndembu often associate whiteness with the relationship of feeder and fed; it signifies the generosity of the dominant partner and the gratitude of the junior (Turner 1970, 75)). At the other extreme, the inner worlds of self and other are mutually exclusive and mutually antagonistic. They are hedged about with defenses, deceptive stratagems, and patterns of with-drawal and withholding. Communication is garbled, and there is no clear way of reading the other's true intentions. This condition of mutual misrec-ognition is experienced as a state of invisibility or darkness. Of the Yaka, René Devisch notes that black conjures up the image of abusive sorcery—the negation of sociality, the clandestine taking of life (1993, 68). This is equally true of the Kuranko.

Phenomenologically speaking, the color contrast between white and black objectifies this extreme case in which self and other are antagonisti-cally polarized. Red would, according to this logic, signify the temporary dissolution of the boundary between self and other, a loss of identity in difference, an overlapping of domains, a merging of selves.[15] Whether this is conceptually elaborated as an image of fire and flame (as in Hinduism) or as shed and mingled blood (as in Africa), the connotation is always of a dangerous yet potentially empowering fusion of separate identities.

But these color terms do not simply give interobjective form to intersub-jective states. As objective correlatives of those states, they can be manipu-lated ritually to vicariously manage, transform, or manipulate intersubjec-tive relations—as in the case of blacksmiths in Africa who both forge tools for productive work and make weapons for war and hunting, who are mar-ginalized yet mediate disputes, promote fertility, and counteract the forces of sorcery (Devisch 1993, 69; McNaughton 1988, 11–14).

The manipulation of states of consciousness through the manipulation of color also underpins Kuranko fetishism. Protective fetishes are made of twisted white, black, and red threads, and deployed when self and other are at odds. The white thread is said to stand for self, black for the other, and red for the state of danger between them. Twisting the three colors together and winding it around the fetish, then placing the fetish on the threshold of a room or the lintel of a house, is said to clear away the dark intentions from the other's mind. The white thread, standing for self, annuls the will of the other.

Here red is the active agent. Associated with heat, it is the color of a troubled or contested relationship. Moreover, as an icon of ambiguity and

15. In the Lower Congo white and black stand for the inner and outward aspects of a person, while red is the shadow (Jacobson-Widding 1979, 305–29). Phenomenologically, the triad may be said to objectify the relationship between two *relationships,* the first relatively ethereal, the second decidedly embodied: self in relation to self (white), and self in relation to other (black). The shadow (red) is where intrapsychic and intersubjective domains overlap ambiguously and unpredictably.

transition, it signifies the dangerous possibility that instead of things moving toward separation and order (purity) they may descend into deeper confusion and darkness. Self may be engulfed by other, and the balance between the visible world of one's own kith and kin and the invisible world of strangers and enemies may be lost. As the Ndembu say, "Redness acts both for good and ill."

DIGRESSIONS

Roads and Bridges

In the dry season of 1970 I was the first person to drive a vehicle into Kamadugu Sukurela. For several months the men of the village had worked collectively—as they did when clear cutting farm sites—to build a laterite road from Namfayi over three miles of hilly and swampy ground. Streams were bridged with heavy logs, cuttings excavated, and marshy hollows filled. When the work was completed I was summoned from Kabala, nine miles away. Since I had spent so much time in the village, it was only appropriate, people said, that I should be the first person to drive along the new road.

When I arrived in the village and parked my Land Rover in the chief's *luiye,* everyone was rejoicing. Men, women, and children clamored around the vehicle, clapping, dancing, and singing. Even the town and section chiefs joined in, as xylophonists extolled the virtues of their forebears and sang praise songs for the Kargbo rulers.

Several of the young men prevailed upon me to give some of the old women a ride around the village. The women had never before seen a vehicle. Their faces betrayed both elation and fear. They half expected the djinn under the bonnet of the Land Rover to take control and speed them away into oblivion. The young men found their anxiety amusing.

After the commotion died down I sat with the chiefs and elders and received gifts of rice, chickens, and kola. It was, the elders declared, a historic day in the life of the village. Everything would change for the better now. Trade stores would open. People would come to Sukurela from more remote villages to buy food. There would be a dispensary and a school. People would be able to truck their rice to market. The village was at long last connected to the outside world.

But over the celebrations hung a pall. The chief's younger brother had died the previous day. The old men confessed to feeling confused. It wasn't only this death, but a spate of other deaths as well. They hinted darkly at witchcraft. They apologized for not being able to celebrate my arrival with unalloyed happiness.

Late in the afternoon I went to a house where a young man lay desperately ill. I'd been told that he had been cursed, though rumors also circulated that his affliction was caused by witchcraft.

Outside the house, the man's female relatives were gathered. Their faces were grim and tense with anxiety. Inside the house, older men of the young man's lineage were keeping vigil. As my eyes grew accustomed to the gloom I made out the figure of a man lying on a mat, feverishly throwing himself from side to side, his arms and legs flailing. His eyes were wide with terror.

Given the seriousness of his condition I told the elders that he should be taken to Kabala at once and hospitalized. I would drive him there in my Land Rover.

No, I was told. We should wait.

That night, a witch finder from a village four miles away was summoned to Sukurela. It wasn't the first time he had come. On a visit two weeks ago a woman had confessed to being a witch. She said that she and her coven had worked to bring about her brother's death because he had refused her some rice. After owning up to this crime the woman was bound hand and foot and buried alive in a shallow grave (Jackson 1989, 88).

I could not sleep, listening to the witch finders move about the village. Once during the night I went out to see what was going on. I refused to succomb to the terror that Gbangbane attempts to instill in those who huddle behind closed doors, hearing the guttural voice, the shuffling feet, the staccato *gban gban gban* of wooden clappers, imagining the worst.

Next morning I learned that Gbangbane had given the house of the cursed man a wide berth. Accordingly, it was concluded, witchcraft was not the cause of his condition. Everyone now, except the young man's close kin (who were implicated whether they liked it or not), decided to avoid him lest they be contaminated by the curse. The elders were adamant that I not be allowed to take the young man from the village.

With my hands tied, I sought to understand the background to the unfolding tragedy.

The young man was the Kometigi ("Master of Kome") in Sukurela. Some time ago he had run away with another man's wife and brought her back to Sukurela to live with him. When the husband came to fetch his wife back, the young man rebuffed him. Soon afterward the woman's father-in-law begged the young man to let his daughter-in-law return to her husband. His words also fell on deaf ears. The young man's sole response was to send friends to the woman's father, begging him to allow his daughter to divorce her husband.

Repudiating this option, the woman's husband and father-in-law now took the matter to the chiefdom court in Kabala, but the court referred the case back to Sukurela. When the Sukurela chief failed to influence the young man, rumors circulated that he considered his powers as Kometigi proof against any secular authority. This was why he had thumbed his nose at the court rulings.

At this point the woman's father decided to take matters into his own hands. He traveled to Kunya in the chiefdom of Sambaia Bendugu and hired the services of Mansa Kona, one of the most powerful sorcerers in Kuranko. A few days later, while working on his farm, the young man suffered pains in his neck, chest, and stomach. It was the first time he had ever been seriously ill. He returned to Sukurela, but his condition worsened by the hour.

Having already got wind of the curse that had been placed on him, the young man now lost no time in dispatching his elder brother to Kunya to beg Manse Kona to annul it. Manse Kona said he could do nothing until the cursed man's kin lodged an appeal with the Paramount Chief of Sambaia Bendugu. By the time the party returned to Sukurela with this news, the young man was dead.

He was buried without ceremony, with only his close kin in attendance. Contrary to custom, no one outside the family offered sympathy gifts or shed tears. Such condolences would have brought the curse down on them.

A day after the funeral the dead man's wives and children took the rice from their farm granary, together with all their moveable property, and walked to Kunya, where, for a fee of fifteen leone, the medicine master lifted the curse from them.

THE YOUNG MAN PROBABLY died from insect-borne encephalitis; other deaths in Sukurela at this time may have had the same cause. But what struck me, apart from the tragic hubris that I had witnessed, were two coincidences. First, it was uncanny that the young man should contract this disease within days of being ensorcelled. Second, it seemed to me both poignant and telling that this epidemic illness should afflict the village at the very moment it was celebrating the opening of a road that would connect it to the outside world. Would the road indeed bring a dispensary to the village and so help prevent this kind of death in the future? Would the road spell the end to witchcraft and sorcery? Or would it prove to be as much a curse as a blessing?

A little over a year after leaving Sukurela I returned. Little had changed. There were a couple of Fula traders residing there, selling matches, salt, sodas, kerosene, medicines, sugar, and teabags, but no dispensary, no school, and no sign of the improvements that the village had labored for. None of the things that people had hoped would come down the new road had eventuated. Indeed, the rains had washed away many sections of the road and termites had destroyed many of the log bridges, rendering it impassable.

IF SUKURELA PUT ITS FAITH in a road, Firawa—a more remote village where I did most of my fieldwork—placed its hope in a bridge.

When I came back to Firawa in 1979 after a seven year absence, walking the ten miles from the Seli River with my wife, my daughter, and old Kuranko friends, the talk was all of how the bridge would soon be completed and Firawa would gain access to the outside world.

While I was secretly and guiltily pleased that Firawa still remained beyond the reach of roads, almost every Kuranko man and woman I spoke to yearned to be more fully incorporated into the nation state. Bridging the Seli River had become imperative. "If it were possible to ask an unborn child what it most desired most in this world it would say 'the bridge,' so that trucks could come to Firawa," said one woman, complaining of an aching neck and sore limbs from having had to tote headloads of supplies for her husband's shop from the riverside.

Now the dream was about to be realized. As part of an international aid and development project for Koinadugu, funded by the European Economic Community (EEC), the Seli would be bridged at Yirafilaia. The Sierra Leone government would put up 20 percent of the required capital, and a

Peace Corps engineer would supervise construction. But even before these negotiations were completed, Chief Tala Sewa of Barawa mobilized his people. Invoking the traditional right of a chief to exact tithes and take such initiatives, Chief Sewa collected together money, cows, rice, and cement, then organized the labor to build concrete bridge piers. The work was done in the space of only two months.

Chief Sewa explained to me that some people had stored rice in their granaries for two years, waiting for a chance to truck it to market. He pointed out that fruit went rotten on the trees or was eaten by monkeys because people had no means of transporting it down-country for sale. Stressing how liberating it would be if people did not have to tote headloads of roofing iron, bags of cement, and commodities into the village, he told me that the bridge would enable a school and dispensary to be build. The bridge would improve everyone's lot, he said, and he had worked for many years toward that end.

This same desire that Tala Sewa expressed for controlled contact and trade with the outside world was in evidence when the very first white man passed through Kuranko country, in 1822. When Maj. Alexander Gordon Laing arrived in Kamato, then the largest town in northwest Kuranko, he found that rumors of the white man's presence on the coast had preceded him. So too had merchandise from Europe: several of the praise singers and soldiers of the Barawa chief, Balansama, were dressed in brand-new uniforms of the 4th West India Regiment and the Royal Africa Corps. When Kuranko praise singers welcomed Laing, they sang of the white man's warehouses full of money, and of beads and fine raiments that every Kuranko man worth his salt would desire to see his wives dressed in. Balansama[1] gave Laing a gold earring to present to Governor McCarthy on his return to the coast "as a token expressive of his desire to be on terms of friendly intercourse with him and his people" (Laing 1825, 433). Balansama then sent word to his subjects that he desired the road to be open so that Kuranko and Sankaran men with gold, ivory, and other trade goods might accompany Laing back to Saralon (Freetown). He also made it known "that he felt so desirous of encouraging commerce that he would not only send his brother, but also his son, and Dinka, one of the chiefs from Kamato, with them" (433).

---

1. The present Barawa chief, Tala Sewa, is the twenty-first in line of succession. Balansama was the twelfth Barawa chief.

WHEN I WAS VERY YOUNG I longed to live and work in a "traditional" society sealed off from the outside world and inaccessible to all but the occasional privileged stranger. Such longing is, of course, based on a fictitious image of the other as outside history, and the nostalgia and romanticism that informs this attitude is spurious. Indeed, as Johannes Fabian has so brilliantly shown, the stereotypical contrasts in Western discourse between closed and open, cold and hot, or traditional and modern societies, only serve to discount the humanity of others and rationalize our continued exclusion of them from "our" world.

Though Barawa lay beyond the reach of roads, it had never been outside the pale of history and never been isolated from its neighbors. If its respect for the ancestors, its disdain for Islam, and its preoccupation with military and magical means of sealing off its borders suggest a reserved or negative attitude toward the outside world, there is abundant evidence that Barawa also used trade, alliance, and detente as strategies of national security.

I was not alone in my "structural nostalgia" (Herzfeld 1997, 22). There was a parallel between my youthful, mistaken view of the past as an unbroken continuity, of traditional society as insular and isolated, and the Kuranko emphasis on respect for the ancestral order—a habit of extolling the virtues of the past even as they departed from it. In his passionate commitment to helping me document a social order that was passing, my field assistant, Noah Marah, regarded the old regime as superior. But he tended to conflate it with the world of his childhood. Blurring biographical and historical time, he sang the praises of a past that was as personal as it was ancestral, so collapsing into a single nostalgic image his earliest memories of his relationship with his beloved father and a cultural ideology which made the ancestors exemplary figures. Helping me place on record the world into which his father was born was an act of filial piety, a way of redeeming the "untraditional" turn his own life had taken. As for my friend Sewa—Noah's older brother—whose collusion in my project was equally significant, his motives were more political. Active in the Sierra Leone Peoples Party (SLPP) since independence, and a minister in two governments, Sewa was quick to see that a book about his people and his illustrious past would enhance his own political future.

I always claimed that I wanted to do justice to the Kuranko people in whatever I wrote about them. Noah and Sewa always claimed that it was necessary to document traditional Kuranko life before it was changed so utterly that their children and grandchildren would have no access to it.

All our avowals were in good faith, but we left unconfided many of the ethical quandaries in which our ambitions placed us. By 1979 I thought I had exhausted my anthropological ambitions. I had proved that I could do the sort of thing my teachers had done, but in the process I had become estranged from the Kuranko lifeworld. I believed that I had allowed anthropological abstractions to displace in-depth descriptions of the intersubjective field of which I become so much a part, and that I needed to reaffirm the importance of what phenomenologists call "the natural standpoint"—the position in which one finds oneself simply by being in a particular social space, in relation to others, at a given moment of time (Husserl 1962, 91–95).

That dry season in Firawa, lodged in the house that my friend Saran Salia Sano had given me and my family for as long as we remained in the village, I felt that a phase of my intellectual life was being brought to a close. At first, sitting down day after day with the old medicine master, talking about fetishes, medicines, and cult mysteries, I was convinced that what was ending was an era. Pressured by his classificatory sons (who had converted to Islam) to give up jujus and magical medicine, Saran Salia's knowledge would probably die with him. And as I taped accounts of Barawa history with *jelibas* who had, on previous visits, been loathe to confide such information to me, I told myself that I was documenting material that might not survive another generation.

But I gradually realized that what was coming to an end was not something in the world about me but something within—an engrained habit, a cast of mind, a driving ambition.

The crisis came with the onset of a bout of malaria. For five days I lay in bed, feverish and hallucinating, fearing I would die. On the sixth day, depressed and debilitated, I found the energy to scribble a few notes.

> Vague light infiltrates the gap between broken matting and a
> rough wall. The muffled thud of the mosque drum. Mist
> streams into the room through the slats of the shutter. I am
> haunted by snatches of poems that I knew by heart in my twen-
> ties. Dylan Thomas. Hopkins. Yeats. A time that predates my
> academic life, my journeys into places where, as Conrad said,
> "you don't belong." My head is swirling, ears ringing, and I
> can hardly steer this pencil across the page. Yet I feel strangely
> free. My hands, which grasped and clutched at this world like
> grim death for so many years, have been forced to relinquish
> their hold. The malaria has made me let go. I have nothing

more to do now except sit. Except listen and let be. I do not
want to abandon poetry ever again.

In the following months the idea of *Barawa* was born.

It grew out of my conversations with Saran Salia, out of the oral histories
I had taped with the *jelis* and *finas,* and library research on early European
explorations of the Sierra Leone hinterland that I did in Freetown, and then
in England. These elements provided a bridge between my life and the
lives of the whites who had gone to Barawa before me. And it enabled me
to compare and contrast European journeys into Africa and African journeys into the European world.

I began with a series of analogies. Most central was an analogy between
person and place, in which the body of a country, the body of a people,
and the body of a ruler (in whose hands the people place their destiny)
were fused. This lived metaphor found its most dramatic expression in the
suicide of Marin (Bolo) Tamba in the late nineteenth century, following
the invasion of the country he had sworn to protect. Yeli Maliki Kuyate
had recounted for me in detail the story of this sixteenth ruler of Barawa.

BEFORE THE EPOCH OF European rule, Marin Tamba's word was law (*ara
duge ke kuma ko*). Wherever people gathered, Marin Tamba was lord (*kun-
tigi,* literally "head owner"). He controlled the thunder and lightning (*saan
gbalme*), and even in the dry season he could use thunderbolts to kill any
ruler he disliked. When he used them, *balabalo,* he would bind his enemies
and take them away.

Ferensola gathered for a meeting. From all over our country, the chiefs
assembled: Fan Kolai of Neya, Fina Bala of Mongo, Maran Lai Bokari of
Morfindugu, Bamba Fara of Nieni, Ba Fara of Kalian. All came together.
During their meeting, Marama Sandi of Diang said: "This is what we can
do in the name of Allah and Anabi (Muhammed). Let us take this country
and give it to Marin Tamba, so that we can live without fear [*ma lan fere*]."

At the chiefly sacrifice (*korfe*) that followed the death of Marama Sandi
at Kamaron, all the chiefs took the country and handed it over to Marin
Tamba. They said, "Let you be the guardian of the entire country" (*i ni i
yili to ferensola ko*). Then they said, "Let Maran Lai Bokari of Morfindugu
be on the bird-scaring platform [*bende*] to watch over his borders."

When Almami Samori came to invade our country, he said, "Who is in
ferensola?" People said, "It is Marin Tamba who is there." Samori asked

that Marin Tamba come to him. "Let us meet. If he has his country there, let him come and take an oath[2] so that neither of us threatens the other."

Marin Tamba left for the meeting. He left Barawa to meet Samori. But at Kawaia he learned that the Kono had invaded from the south, from Sando. They came through SaNieni. Neighborliness is not sweet. It was a conspiracy by neighbors (*siginyorgo yanfe*). Because Marin Tamba had left the country, Sa Nieni said, "Marin Tamba is not there right now." So they got up and enlisted the support of the Kono to plunder ferensola ['The nation']. Thirty-four towns were destroyed.

As soon as word reached Marin Tamba that war had entered his country, he said, "Accept my dead body now." Immediately he entered a house and killed himself.[3]

When Almami Samori heard of this he said, "Ha, what he has done is a brave thing. But before taking his own life he should have come and told me." Then Samori sent some of his war boys and drove away the Kono.

Then all of Barawa came together and said, "Now that Marin Tamba is dead, let us leave this place."[4]

A SECOND ANALOGY I DREW alluded to nostalgia and loss. I wanted to write about Noah's cultural nostalgia, as well as the sense of alienation that he and many Kuranko admitted to feeling when they spoke of their relationship to the nation-state. I wanted to link this motif to intersubjective questions of controlling one's own destiny, and to deal with my own disquiet at having emphasized systematic understanding and abstract relations to such an extent that my anthropology had come to eclipse the very Kuranko lifeworld that mattered to me most. A third analogy connected the destinies of certain Kuranko individuals who had risked their lives going to work or fight for the British, and certain white explorers, administrators, and anthropologists who had staked their reputations on what they might discover in Africa. In a way, I wanted to come to terms with my own ambition by writing of the hubris that ended the ambitious lives of the nineteenth-

2. Dege mintine: an oath that guarantees honest dealing by drinking white-rice-flour gruel together.

3. A parallel episode is cited in Sayers (1927, 70). When the sofas besieged and sacked the Yalunka capital of Falaba in 1892, Manga Denka, the Yalunka chief, blew himself and his family up with the powder magazine rather than surrender.

4. In the power vacuum that followed the death of Bolo Tamba, Barawa people sought the protection of the British, who by then had established a military headquarters in Kabala.

Lannan

In Pursuit of **Cultural Freedom**

NOAM CHOMSKY WITH **DAVID BARSAMIAN**

WEDNESDAY 18 MARCH 2015

In Pursuit of Cultural Freedom is a lecture series on political, economic, environmental, and human rights issues featuring social justice activists, writers, journalists, and scholars discussing critical topics of our day.

NOAM CHOMSKY is internationally recognized for his writing, lecturing, and teaching on linguistics, philosophy, contemporary issues, intellectual history, international affairs, and U.S. foreign policy. Born in 1928 in Philadelphia, Pennsylvania, he studied linguistics, mathematics, and philosophy at the University of Pennsylvania, where he received his PhD in linguistics. He is Institute Professor (Emeritus) in the Department of Linguistics and Philosophy at Massachusetts Institute of Technology where he taught for more than 50 years.

One of America's foremost social critics, Professor Chomsky is the author of numerous best-selling political works that have been translated into scores of languages worldwide. Most notably among these works are *Hopes and Prospects; The Essential Chomsky; Hegemony or Survival; For Reasons of State; Occupy;* and *Fateful Triangle: The United States, Israel, and the Palestinians* (new edition now available by Haymarket Books as part of a series of his classic works).

Professor Chomsky is a recipient of a Lannan Literary Award for Nonfiction.

DAVID BARSAMIAN is the founder and director of *Alternative Radio*, an independent award-winning weekly series based in Boulder, Colorado, now in its 29th year. He also lectures nationally on world affairs, imperialism, the state of journalism, censorship, the economic crisis and global rebellions. Author of numerous books, Barsamian's recent publications are *Occupy the Economy* co-authored with Richard Wolff and *Power Systems: Conversations on Global Democratic Uprisings and the New Challenges to U.S. Empire* co-authored with Noam Chomsky. *Propaganda and the Public Mind*, also co-authored with Noam Chomsky, is forthcoming this spring.

UPCOMING CULTURAL FREEDOM EVENTS

TA-NEHISI COATES with **MICHELE NORRIS**
WEDNESDAY 8 APRIL 2015
(tickets on sale now)

NAOMI KLEIN with **KATHARINE VINER**
WEDNESDAY 29 APRIL 2015
(tickets on sale now)

All events will be at the **Lensic Performing Arts Center** at 7pm

Lannan Foundation is a family foundation dedicated to cultural freedom, diversity, and creativity through projects that support exceptional contemporary artists and writers, as well as inspired Native activists in rural indigenous communities. The Foundation recognizes the profound and often unquantifiable value of the creative process and is willing to take risks and make substantial investments in ambitious and experimental thinking. Understanding that globalization threatens all cultures and ecosystems, the Foundation is particularly interested in projects that encourage freedom of inquiry, imagination, and expression. The Foundation supports this mission through funding in the program areas of Contemporary Visual Arts, Literature, Indigenous Communities, Cultural Freedom, and a Writers' Residency Program.

ALL PHOTOGRAPHY: **DON USNER**

Video and audio recordings of all events are available at

www.lannan.org

century explorers Laing and Reade. But rather than judge myself or excoriate these adventurers for exploiting Africa and being complicit in the tragedy of colonialism, I wanted to explore the issue of cross-cultural relations as it is lived and worked out in interpersonal relationships. In this enterprise I wanted to realize a goal that I had announced years before: to write history allegorically as a kind of multiple biography, and to explore culture contact at the specific level of intersubjectivity (Jackson 1997, xiii).

If the metaphor of the road or path is central to Kuranko thought, it is equally important to ours. To keep the path of human intercourse open and clear, to work against absolute closure and darkness, is as urgent for Kuranko as it is for any European committed to the project of intercultural understanding.

But how can one enter the world of another?

Clearly, it cannot be achieved mimetically. Attempting to go native by decking oneself out in the costume of the other can only end in parody. A white man in native dress cuts as foolish a figure as Balansama's praise singers did in their English military uniforms.

It can, I believe, be accomplished through analogy. Unlike imitation, analogy does not eclipse self in an attempt to become other. Its strategy is, by contrast, to have recourse to common images—such as the metaphors of paths or bridges—that are already part of the discursive repertoire of human relationships.

Analogy does not, therefore, presume a merging of self and other but a comparison that begins with something already held in common. It is inspired by empathy rather than mimicry. However, it is not an empathy based on abstract gestures derived from the humanist or romantic traditions of European thought. Such gestures are invariably condescending and self-serving. They mask projections of one's own notions of humanity, and suspend none of one's own social assumptions, or ever put one's own security at risk. Ethnographic empathy, on the other hand, is grounded in engagement. It begins with the social skills without which an ethnographer simply cannot endure life in the field, and is augmented by a praktognosis born of cooperating in quotidian work with others—farming, fencing, threshing, parleying. It is a mode of embodied, intersubjectively negotiated understanding that comes of coexistence and coordination in common tasks; it is not a form of knowledge consolidated in precepts and enshrined in dogma. What Schutz called "the reciprocity of perspectives" is too ideal. The "interchangeability of standpoints" can never be accomplished intellectually through "common-sense thinking" or shared assumptions (Schutz

1973, 10–13, 312–16); it must entail a psychophysical going beyond one-self in shared practical activity.

ONE DAY, NOT LONG BEFORE we left Firawa, my daughter came in from playing with some other children in the compound in front of our house. In her cupped hands she held a small bird. She had found it in the dust, near death. The bird had been the plaything of a group of small boys. They regularly caught birds in the bush by placing on a branch a dollop of chewed gum (tapped from a bush vine and mixed with lime juice) with seeds embedded in it. The bird's feet get stuck in the gum when they come to eat the seeds. The boys then make cages from raffia pith and bring their catches back to the village. My daughter had found such a bird, exhausted and bruised from being too long in the boys' hands.

There was, I told her, little we could do for it. It was almost dead.

She protested; she wanted to save its life.

I suggested she give it water, and showed her how she could drip-feed it with a piece of straw. Then she went outside with the bird, while I returned to whatever it was I was doing at the time.

Perhaps half an hour passed before she came back into the house. Her chest was heaving, her face was ecstatic, she could hardly speak. And her eyes were filled with tears. The bird had flown away, she said. She had given it water, just as I told her to. Then all of a sudden it had revived and flown away. She cupped her hands and lifted them slightly as if imploring a gift, to show me how it had felt as the bird's weight was lifted from her hands.

The Other Island

Were it not for my good fortune in enlisting the help of a research assistant as able and adroit as Noah Marah, my Kuranko fieldwork would have foundered at the outset. So deep is my debt to him, and so positive the memories of the years we spent together in the field, that it might seem churlish of me to rake over, these many years later, the troubled and unresolved aspects of our relationship. But cross-cultural relations are never abstract, even though we commonly construct them as if they were. They are lived immediately and interpersonally, and I agree with Michel Tournier that a genuine anthropological novel would have as its true subject "the confrontation and fusion of two civilizations personified by two representative narrators"

(1988, 190). To be sure, what eventuates in intersubjectively is to a large extent a result of culturally conditioned mindsets, but the character and course of any human relationship cannot be reduced to the social, historical, and cultural elements that constitute it. Nor should it be subject to sweeping generalizations before painstaking attention has been paid to its specific dynamics.

From the very beginning, Noah and I were destined to be at loggerheads, though neither of us perceived this at the time. We were almost the same age, committed to the same task, and felt a deep affinity for each other. But our relationship was fraught with ambiguity and asymmetry.

When Noah quit his teaching position in the district council school in Kabala to work as my field assistant, things boded well for us both. From Noah's point of view I could pay him more than he could earn as a teacher, my wife and I would help him study for his General Certificate of Education, and we were embarked on an ethnographic project that he embraced wholeheartedly. For my part, Noah would teach me Kuranko and help me make contacts in remote villages.

The problem, however, was our unrealistic expectations of each other. Though made in good faith, our pact resembled an arranged marriage; it failed to take into account our idiosyncratic backgrounds or the pressures our relationship would have to withstand. When, after several months of work, tutoring him for his GCE, Noah decided not to proceed, I felt cheated and angry.[5] Noah, in turn, experienced intense exasperation at my tardiness in learning Kuranko and my seeming insensitivity to the fact that his social life could not be completely sacrificed to my fieldwork.

Our difficulties lay in the incompatible ways we each constructed the terms of our relationship. In the highly politicized atmosphere of the late 1960s (I had experienced the legacy of Belgian colonial rule in the Congo in 1964 and been active in left-wing politics throughout the decade), I was determined not to be some latter-day Crusoe with his man Friday. But despite our commitment to base our relationship on reciprocity and mutual benefit, Noah and I each regarded the other as occupying the superior and pivotal position. Paradoxically, we were *both* cast into a "dependence com-

---

5. Though I never regarded Noah as an 'ingrate,' it is worth reminding ourselves that in every relationship of existential inequality (where one person has more say, greater power, and more privileges than the other), the more advantaged individual expects his or her passive partner to accept her or his relatively inactive role *while receiving the other's bounty with effusive gratitude.* Mannoni has documented this "lack of gratitude" leitmotif in the colonial context with great insight (1956, 42–48).

plex" (Mannoni 1956, 61–109). Initially unable to speak more than a few phrases of Kuranko, I was wholly dependent on Noah both for my fieldwork and for finding my way around the villages and chiefdoms. Without his willing assistance I could go nowhere and speak to no one. If my relationship with him broke down, or he was unable to work with me, my project would come to a standstill. But though I was utterly reliant on him, Noah saw me as a mentor (*yugi*)—someone in whom he "placed his hope," who could teach him to drive a vehicle, pay his way, rescue him from hardship, and ultimately help him travel abroad.

The roots of Noah's attitude became clearer as he told me more about his upbringing and background. He was born in Firawa in 1942, his mother's last child. His father worked as a court messenger and was transferred often to various parts of Sierra Leone. "I was my father's favorite," Noah told me. "I started school late because my father wanted me to be with him. I was all the time with my father, slept with my father, moved with my father, until his death in 1954. Only then did I really get to know the woman who bore me."

In 1953, a year before his father died, under circumstances about which Noah remains unclear to this day, his elder brother took him out of school and pledged him to a trader who was traveling south. It was a way of postponing payment of a debt, and Noah's elder brother was not to know that the trader would pledge the bewildered boy to a woman who owned a small store on a tidal island, surrounded by mangroves, in Mendeland. Noah remained in the house of Mammy Kasan for a year or more, living under a new name, a virtual slave. Then one day, Noah's elder sister, who was married to a man from Bonthe and living in the south, overheard some Mandingo traders talking about a boy who seemed to answer the description of her little brother. Following this lead, she located Noah. But Mammy Kasan did not want to give the boy up. Nevertheless, after careful planning, Noah's sister helped Noah escape from the island and return home to Firawa where his father, overjoyed to see his youngest son again, offered a sacrifice to the ancestors in gratitude.

But the deep bond between Noah and his father may have been his undoing. It fostered a habit of dependency that Noah found hard to break. And it may have made him the unwitting object of his older brother's envy.

In conversations with me Noah consistently projected a self-image as hard-done and long-suffering. Sold into slavery. Always deprived of any chance to improve his lot.

"Since my father's death I have been paddling my own canoe," he said, then went on to describe what it was like living with his married sisters while attending school in Kabala.

"It was not an easy time I had then. I remember one time my sister Mantene remarked that my father had petted me; now that my father was dead I would have to fend for myself. So I was there struggling—going to find food, laundering, doing everything in the morning before going to school. I had to take care of myself."

But Noah was always looking for someone who would take care of him.

"I remember one Lebanese, Mr. Hassan Mansour, who took pity on me at one time and told me I could always go to him when I needed help. As a small boy I often went to Hassan Mansour."

In 1959 Noah passed his selective entrance exam and went to high school in Magburaka. But in 1962, in the run-up to the first general elections after independence, Noah found himself traveling throughout Kuranko country, campaigning and canvassing votes for his elder brother. When he returned to school, the principal warned him that further absenteeism would not be tolerated. This was why, when his elder brother summoned him in 1964 to help in another political campaign, Noah's school career came to an end.

"I couldn't go on because of hardship. I had to leave school and return to Kabala."

Here is how Noah described the next ten years:

"I was there in Kabala for some time, struggling. One day I went to Lansana Kamara's shop to buy kerosene, and met Wing Commander Macdonald, the then district officer. We talked for a while and he asked me whether I would like to work. I told him I would, but there were no jobs. He asked me to find him in his office the next morning. I went to the office and found him. He offered me work as a native administration court clerk. But I had nothing of my own. He had to give me twenty leone to buy some soap and clothes.

"After I had been there for some time, he posted me to Musaia, in the Fula Saba Dembelia chiefdom. I was there doing the work. Then I decided to leave the native administration work because I felt that I was deteriorating educationally. I then decided to pick up teaching. I was given an appointment in the district council school, the same school I had earlier attended as a pupil. So I was there fighting hard. At this time, while my contemporaries were still at school, I was struggling hard to earn my living.

"Then I came into contact with Dr. Michael Jackson, who had come from Cambridge to do his research."

Just before I left Sierra Leone, at the end of 1970, Noah passed his entrance examination for the Freetown Teacher's College and, after completing teacher's training, took up an appointment in the municipal school at Berry Street, Freetown.

EVERY HUMAN life encompasses vicious circles and self-fulfilling prophecies. While I struggled for many years to overcome a childhood sense of exclusion and rejection, proving myself the equal of my peers, Noah struggled against a similar sense of having been done wrong, constantly craving his elder brother's approval.

It was a relationship that bore all the hallmarks of displacement. In this sense it was not untypical, for the vexed relationship between father and first-born son (the father's imminent successor) among the Kuranko is carried over into the relationship between successive siblings (Jackson 1977, 161–71). In the first instance, the father customarily berates and disparages his first-born son, rationalizing this show of antagonism as a way of preventing the younger sons envying his successor. Unfortunately, the first-born son commonly experiences this as a denial of affection, and though separation and avoidance between father and first-born may be publicly necessary as a stratagem for masking the succession and preventing challenges to the father's position, it often creates a mood of rejection and resentment in the belittled son. Meyer Fortes refers to this as "the syndrome of the first-born" (1987, 229).

After their father's death, the relationship between Sewa and Noah became firmly constituted in these oedipal terms. In the company of his elder brother, Noah became circumspect and withdrawn, while Sewa hardly deigned to acknowledge his little brother's presence. Yet out of earshot of his elder brother, Noah made no bones about his ambivalent feelings.

"Really, I feel very very bitter when he tells people I am not serious. People who really know him blame him for what I am. In fact, some people feel I would have been in a better position and been a better person had he not tampered with my destiny. But you know, I hold no grudge against him, except when he makes those remarks about my not being serious. I used to agree with him. I used to say, 'You could say I am not serious; if I *were* serious I wouldn't have gone all out to make *you* what you are today.'"

Noah sometimes imagined he might have traveled the same road as his famous brother: "You know, some people blame Sewa that he doesn't help me. I could easily have been someone else. But I have always been struggling, all by myself."

Noah spoke of how he wanted to become a candidate in the political party that was contesting the 1967 general election in opposition to his elder brother's party, but his mother, speaking on behalf of Sewa, begged him to stand down. Noah commented, "She cried that she would be blamed and that people would laugh at us if I went in against my brother. She said people would say, 'Oh, the two brothers are fighting against themselves.' You see. So, thinking about all this, I had to give up the candidacy."

DESPITE OUR AVOWALS OF FRIENDSHIP, Noah understandably depended on me to take all the initiative, give all the direction, and provide all the support. He saw me as a cross between his previous patrons—Wing Commander Macdonald and Hassan Mansour—and his elder brother. But I depended on him almost to the same extent. In times of anxiety or loneliness, it was to Noah that I turned to voice my misgivings and seek reassurance. He was, however, often perplexed by these emotional demands and unable to respond. Was I not a white man, an authority figure, always in command, with inexhaustible material and intellectual resources?

Yet it was not always so. One time in Firawa I found myself besieged by feelings of loss and vulnerability. My anxiety found expression in Kuranko metaphors, so that one night, when I saw a falling star, and the next morning when Senegalese fire finches flitted around the porch of the house where I was staying, I took these auguries of death to heart and imagined that my wife, a long day's journey away in Kabala, had lost the child she was carrying. When I confided to Noah that I was concerned about Pauline and wanted to return to Kabala forthwith, he fell in with my plans without hesitation, confessing that he too was missing his wives and children.

But in this instance our empathy was centered on someone else. Some third party, on whom we could project our common tribulations. And women, in Kuranko thought, were conveniently considered weaker than men.

THESE WERE OUR FAILINGS. They reflected our idiosyncratic personalities as well as our different cultural backgrounds. And they reflected the structure of colonialism, the long shadows of which still fell across West Africa in the late 1960s.

When I now ask myself to what extent we were free to renegotiate these givens and restructure our relationship in egalitarian terms, I come up against the force of need.

For a long time our needs transcended our differences. We could set aside or bracket out the contradictory and incompatible elements in our relationship because we both had immediate and urgent need of each other. Noah needed me to help him get the education that would improve his lot. I needed him if I was to complete my fieldwork and get a Ph.D. For as long as these objectives were before us, the latent contradictions in our relationship could be overlooked.

But there were deeper needs as well. My association with Noah brought him considerable prestige among his people. Here was a white man who was wholly dependent on the goodwill of his Kuranko hosts for his security and well-being. And here was Noah, leading this white man around. "Heh, Noah," neighbors would call. "How is your little white man today?" So Noah was seen to have, and seen to enjoy having, the upper hand—Prospero to my Caliban. At the same time, his liaison with me undoubtedly gave him a sense of having an edge over his elder brother, whom I did not know well in those early days of my fieldwork.

As for me, I needed Noah to bolster my sense of humanity in a situation that constantly threatened to undermine it. For as long as I remained socially inept and linguistically incompetent, Noah was indispensable to me. I drew strength from him and felt inadequate without him. This explains, no doubt, why I thought of him as a close friend. It was consistent with the way anthropologists have always extolled the virtues of "their" people, played up the emotional significance of their adoption into local families, and referred to individual informants as personal friends. But there is often a world of difference between these bonds of kinship and friendship in the field, and nominally identical bonds back home. The intimate and incorporative bonds of fictive kinship and friendship that belong to the fieldwork situation are frequently opportunistic and transitory; what they often connote is a deep sense of gratitude that the ethnographer feels toward his host community for having saved his or her sense of dignity in a culturally disorientating and debilitating environment. It is an overcompensatory gesture to the other for having recognized one's humanity, rescued one's ego, saved one's face (La Barre 1972, 52).

As our circumstances and needs changed, Noah and I began to confront the paradoxical core of our relationship. But the confrontation was already presaged during my first period of fieldwork.

My personality was an odd mixture of reticence and ambition. Though undemonstrative, I possessed my father's passive-aggressive proclivity for "innocently" embarrassing people as a way of subverting their self-confidence and bending them to his will. In West Africa I must often have resembled the impatient figure whom the Kabyle call *el ah-ammaq*—one who throws himself into things without thinking, does his work too fast, and lacks all sense of proportion—one whose "haste is seen as a lack of decorum combined with diabolical ambition" (Bourdieu 1963, 57). Often pressed and hassled, I pursued my ethnographic project with such single-mindedness and passion that villagers would have quickly tired of me had they not preferred to see the comic possibilities I was throwing their way. Poor Noah was drawn into this vortex, but not without resistance. Invoking the needs of his family, the bidding of his friends, and general malaise, he always had a ready excuse for avoiding my excessive demands. With my first year in the field passing all too quickly, I often became irritated by his lassitude and distractedness—my way of construing the fact that he was not constantly at my beck and call.

One afternoon, in exasperation, I withdrew. I drove back to my house on the outskirts of Kabala, determined to take a break from fieldwork.

In retrospect my motives probably had more to do with the birth of my daughter two months before, and with the demands neighbors were making on my time to truck their garden produce to market, than with my annoyance with Noah. Why, I asked myself, was I always helping strangers and allowing my own family life to go into eclipse?

That night my wife and I closed the shutters and doors of our house and fell to talking about Cambridge and the life we would return to when my work in Africa was done. Our daughter lay asleep under a mosquito net.

Suddenly we heard voices approaching the house. We stopped talking, waiting for a knock on the door.

It was Noah and his wives. They had come to greet us.

I shouted that we were in bed, and bade my wife be quite until they went away.

They remained on the porch for half an hour, talking from time to time, occasionally knocking softly at the door as if to remind us that they were waiting. Then they went away.

Though I apologized to Noah next day, my remorse is still with me.

The difficulty of living intensely and unrelentingly at the heart of another culture is identical to the difficulty of living too close to another human being. It's not only a case of being too close for comfort, of having no breathing space, or of losing one's own identity in the identity of the other. When a dyadic situation admits no respite through the intervention of a third party or a shift of focus to some outside subject, individuals are reduced to stasis and passivity. This disempowering deadlock explains why ethnographers, like unemployed workers or homebound spouses, are prone to periods of profound ennui, alienation, and sheer inertia.

Here is a passage from my journal, dated 21 July 1970:

> I am suffering from having been out of my own element for far too long. Everything lies outside my control. It is not that the Kuranko world is alien and exotic to me any longer; rather that I am passive and powerless before it. There are times when I feel paranoid, as though the will of others is menacing me. I listen, I attend, I observe, I register, I record . . . but I never act! In the villages I make nothing happen. I change nothing. I make no difference to anyone. I show no feelings. I do not indicate pleasure or pain. I keep myself to myself. I have been laid low, passified, stilled. I have become a thing to which things happen, against which other's actions rebound and echo. But I am nothing because I have lost the power to act.

Regrettably, I visited my existential crisis on Noah as though he personally were to blame for the difficulties I was experiencing in his social world. One afternoon, when he came to my house to see if I had any work planned for the following few days, I found myself unable to engage with him, and turned on the radio. A BBC interview with Iris Murdoch had just begun. The good person, Iris Murdoch observed, is not necessarily someone who *does* good to others but rather someone who *abstains* from visiting his or her desires onto others, so allows *them* to come into their own. In the company of such a person, she noted, one often experiences such a sense of peace and self-fulfillment that it seems as if a divine gift had been bestowed. Allowing this gift to be given is the essence of the good.

As the radio program continued, I relished Noah's discomfort. It was as though I were avenging myself on him for my own inability to receive the gift of acceptance.

Many years later, when Noah and I began to drift apart, I thought of these episodes with chagrin.

IN 1979 I BEGAN TO DISTANCE MYSELF from the academic goals that had driven me during the previous ten years. It would be too blunt to say that

I no longer needed Noah, or that he no longer needed me, but as the ethnographic project that had bound us together ceased to be central to our relationship, we certainly came to see that we had less in common than we had once presumed. We had shared an illusory belief in a traditional way of life: Noah because he identified the historic past with his happy childhood, I because I sought an Africa that had successfully resisted the West. As we both yielded to the pressures of the present day, we relinquished our sentimental focus on the past.

Things came to a head when Noah asked if I would pay him an advance of fifteen hundred leone on his salary so that he could buy rice in Freetown to store until its market value increased. He would then sell the rice up-country and use the profit to start a small business. I gave the money but disliked the idea of exploiting the anticipated national rice shortage for personal gain.[6]

As we began to spend less and less time together, I began to exaggerate what I saw as the negative traits in his personality. It was like a divorce, when erstwhile lovers resort to acrimony as a way of distancing themselves from their shared past, reclaiming their own autonomy. I grew indifferent to Noah's hard-luck stories. I found his lassitude infuriating. And his pedantic and laborious accounts of Sierra Leone's football clubs, his painstaking postmortems of political intrigues, and his self-extolling reports on how he had resolved some recent palaver, left me cold. I saw him now as his elder brother had always seen him: frittering away his life playing draughts near the market, distractedly moving from job to job and place to place, failing to take care of his children's education or the welfare of his wives. He, in turn, found me exasperatingly introverted and unfriendly, and accused me of cheating him out of royalties from *The Kuranko* when it appeared in 1977, and transferring my affections and loyalty to his elder brother.

Nowadays I do not castigate myself. I think it is always easier to judge ourselves or others harshly than it is to understand what goes awry in human relationships. Judgments are a substitute for empirical understanding, though they always masquerade as genuine thought.

---

6. Noah's scheme floundered. Toward the end of the wet season the rice shortage became so critical that kin and neighbors begged Noah to lend them rice from his store. I enjoyed the irony: that my loan had gone to feed the needy, and that Noah would probably not be able to collect many of the debts because his debtors were kinsmen or too poor to repay them. When Noah assured me that his debtors were all honest, and that he would still profit from his investment, I protested: "But you've lost the capital with which you wanted to go into business." Noah shrugged and said, "Don't make it seem so hopeless, Mike."

Judging others gives a spurious moral legitimacy to an estrangement whose cause has neither been fully explored or accepted.

It is not possible to connect with every other human being. Sometimes the common ground is negligible or nonexistent. At other times it is established momentarily, then lost. Rarely does one discover in this life the intimacy, depth, and constancy that we call friendship and love. Under such circumstances, the notion of universal brotherhood would seem to be an absurd ideal. But even more absurd is the morality that blames us for our inability to realize its precepts everywhere, all the time, and condemns us categorically whenever we fail to wholly transcend our history.

First Contact

No one who sees Bob Connolly's and Robin Anderson's film First Contact can fail to be moved by the dramatic images of New Guinea highlanders seeing whites for the first time. But what exactly is it that touches us? What experiences of our own find expression in these images of others?

I saw First Contact not long before leaving Australia for the United States, and sequences from the film came back to me with hallucinatory vividness during my first few months in Indiana. The film persuaded me that *culture contact* is a misnomer. Intercultural relations cannot be reduced to categorical antinomies such as West/East, modern/premodern, us/them. What Robert Hughes calls "the shock of the new" is most immediately experienced not as a conflict of worldviews but as a traumatic rift within the field of consciousness and intersubjectivity that challenges almost all one's ontological certainties (cf. Nandy 1988, xvii).

Confronted with the unprecedented and strange, one's taken-for-granted routines of existence are suddenly nullified. Ambiguity and uncertainty prevail. To cope with such an existential crisis, human beings characteristically seek to restore to themselves some provisional certainty, some sense of being in control. People may make themselves over to the Other, taking refuge in mimicry or self-effacement to wipe out the embarrassment of difference. They may negate the Other in acts of projective paranoia and violence. Or they may deal with the strange by reimagining their relationship to it—reworking old myths or inventing new scenarios that provide a tentative basis for interaction. In these reimaginings one sees very clearly the way in which *alteritas* passes from being synonymous with Otherness and begins to take on, by virtue of its outlandish and novel nature, the trappings of transcendence. This transcendence may assume the form of an ethos centered on the idea of the "new man" (Burridge 1960). It may find expression in millenarian notions that a radical break from the past will usher in a new moral dispensation (Feil 1983, 94). Or it may simply encourage individuals to abandon ties and obligations to their local moral worlds.

But rather than cementing estrangement, culture contact always entails, in some measure, for each party, stratagems of reconfiguring the horizons of their own humanity. To describe this process as one of westernization or globalization is as empirically naive as describing the field of intersubjectivity in terms of the identity of the people within it. The intersubjective face of the colonial encounter is the face of Janus: neither good nor evil, neither black nor white.

There is inevitably a reflexive dimension to this train of thought, as I shall show. Though every anthropological encounter begins in strangeness and separation, that gap is gradually, though seldom utterly, closed. Some part of the ethnographer's own life experience always forms the basis for approaching the other, just as the other must see something of himself or herself in the ethnographer's actions, reactions, and comportment. Though there can never be complete overlap and agreement between the subuniverses of self and other, there must be *some* recognition of common identity if any kind of interaction—self-interested *or* otherwise—is to proceed.

SIXTY-SIX YEARS AGO the New Guinea highlands were still unexplored; most Europeans thought they were also uninhabited. In 1930 an Australian adventurer, Michael Leahy, organized a gold-prospecting expedition into the Highlands. Innoculated against typhoid, armed with rifles and gelignite, Leahy and his mate, Michael Dwyer, set off in May with fifteen native bearers. Leahy also took movie and still cameras to make a film record of his journey. It is from this footage, shot by Leahy and his companions on various expeditions between 1930 and 1934, that Bob Connolly and Robin Anderson made their film. They also used footage of their own: interviews with New Guinea highlanders who witnessed the traumatic events of fifty years ago; men who saw the destructive power of the Leahy's weapons; women who bore the white men's children.

Here is how Kirupano Eza'e, of Seigu village in the eastern highlands, recalled his experiences:

> I was so terrified, I could not think properly, and I cried uncontrollably. My father pulled me along by the hand and we hid be-

hind some tall kunai grass. Then he stood up and peeped out at
the white men.

Once they had gone, the people sat down and developed stories. They knew nothing of white-skinned men. We had not
seen far places. We knew only this side of the mountains. And
we thought we were the only living people. We believed that
when a person died, his skin changed to white and he went
over the boundary to "that place"—the place of the dead. So
when the strangers came we said: "Ah, these men do not belong to the earth. Let's not kill them—they are our relatives.
Those who have died before have turned white and come back.
(Connolly and Anderson 1987, 6)

Here is an account from Onguglo Komugl, of Kerowagi township in
Chimbu province:

We heard the white men were in Waugla people's country. We
couldn't go and see them because we were enemies of those
people. But we were very keen to meet them. We were anxious
that night and we couldn't sleep at all. We met them early next
morning—there were many of them, advancing in a line. All
dressed in white. At first we thought they were our enemies,
coming with new made shields. They came down to the river—
there'd been heavy rain and it was flooding—and as they
crossed the river all of us gathered around them. We were howl-
ing and shouting in excitement! And we were saying—these
are our dead people, come back! (Ibid., 7–8)

These recollections convey something of the stunned amazement, panic,
and shock you see on people's faces in the film. The trauma of first contact
is at once visceral and conceptual. People shit themselves in terror, weep
uncontrollably, talk wildly, throw themselves to the ground, and collide
with one another in a struggle to keep their distance. Intellectual efforts
are made to place the strangers in the scheme of things. Are they enemies,
the dead come back to life, or avenging spirits?

Gopie Ataiamelaho, of Gama Village near Goroka, recalls his thoughts
at the time:

We had experienced the presence of dead people before, but
we'd never actually seen them in their physical form. We knew
of their presence, by hearing them whistle, or hearing their
voices singing. That's how we knew the dead were present.
Other times we would feel the dead around us when someone

was sick, and one of the ritual experts was performing ceremonies over him. Sometimes then we would feel the presence of the dead. (Ibid., 35–36)[7]

Gopie was convinced the black carriers were dead clansmen. He recognized one of them as his late cousin Ulaline because he had a finger missing, just like Ulaline, and his speech mannerisms and expressions were identical. But he could only guess who the white men were:

> I asked myself: who were these people? They must be somebody from the heavens. Have they come to kill us or what? We wondered if this could be the end of us, and it gave us a feeling of sorrow. We said: "We must not touch them!" We were terribly frightened. (Connolly and Anderson 1987, 38)

Others argued that the white men were not the ancestral dead but mythical demiurges. In the Asaro area it was rumored that they were spirits who controlled the lightning. Among the Migaru Page Daribi people on the southern fringes of the highlands it was conjectured that Souw, a mythical giant, was returning to settle old scores.

According to the Daribi, human existence had once been untroubled by adultery, theft, sorcery, murder, and death. But this idyllic state had come to an end with the curse of Souw. The mythical crisis involved a widow and two girls—Yaro, who was light-skinned, and Karoba, who had dark skin—and a forest bird whose call signaled the presence of a snake in the bush.

As long as the widow accompanied the girls into the bush when the bird called, all was well. But one day the girls went into the bush alone and were accosted by a long snakelike object rising from a ravine. It was the penis of Souw, a giant light-skinned man who was also Yaro's father. Souw began to have sex with Karoba, who cried out in fear. Ashamed and angry, Souw withdrew his penis and went away downriver, spelling out his curse as he went. "You will have trouble, you will die, you will kill other men, you will work sorcery!" So saying, he bequeathed to humankind the evils of theft, adultery, fighting, sorcery, and death. Later, Yaro followed her father into exile and became the ancestress of all light-skinned peoples,

---

7. Gopie's account is reminiscent of an Etoro man's memory of the first European (Jack Hides) to enter his country: we "thought they were like people you see in a dream; "these must be spirit people (*kesame*) coming openly, in plain sight"" (Schieffelin 1991, 74).

while Karoba remained behind and became the ancestress of all dark-skinned peoples (Wagner 1967, 39–41; 1986, 60–61).

When Leahy and Dwyer, both tall men, appeared among the Daribi, people thought that a reincarnation of Souw had come back to wreak further vengeance. Like Souw, Leahy and Dwyer were fair-skinned. And like Souw, who had been able to slough off his skin like a snake and so remain immortal, each of the white men appeared to have a second skin that he could remove and discard at will (Connolly and Anderson 1987, 39).

TWO THINGS STRUCK ME about these reactions. First was the way people tended to etherealize the strangers. Otherness was experienced as a lack of substantiality: "Like people you see in a dream" (Schieffelin 1991, 74). It was as if the white man's anomalous place in the indigenous world bestowed a kind of unreality on them, such that they are thought to lack true bodiliness. People denied that the men from heaven defecated. Women wondered whether the strangers had penises.

Then curiosity overcame fear. Kirupano Eza'e again:

> One of the people hid, and watched them [the white men] going to excrete. He came back and said, "Those men from heaven went to excrete over there." When they had left many men went to take a look. When they saw that it smelt bad, they said, "Their skin might be different, but their shit smells bad like ours." (Ibid., 44)

Here is another man's comments on the strangers' sexuality:

> When they had their bath, we used to peep at them and that's when we found out we were wrong. In fact they were just the same as all us men. . . .When we saw them using the soap in the river, and we saw all the foam that was on their bodies, we thought it was the pus coming from a dead person's skin, like the milky part from the rotten flesh. Our minds were in turmoil when we saw such things! (Ibid., 46)

Clearly, intersubjectivity cannot be reduced to cognition. Schutz's notion of empathic identification understates the embodied character of intersubjectivity—the manner in which the subject recognizes the subjectivity of the other through shared bodily appearance and function. "Interchangeability of standpoints" and "congruency of relevances" (Schutz 1973, 10–12) are thus predicated on a sense of corporeal similitude. Only on such grounds can incorporative acts of exchange and social intercourse proceed. When it is empirically confirmed that the white men eat, drink, piss, shit, and have sex like other human beings, people abandon the view that the strangers are spirit beings, but now the burden of doubt falls back upon the doubter. People call their own identity into question. They make invidious comparisons between themselves and the white men. While it is terrible enough to be intimidated by a god, it is even more terrible to be intimidated by men—to recognize their weapons and trade goods as human artifacts, yet be powerless to possess or comprehend them. The humiliation is overwhelming. The illusion that one's own world is *the* world is shattered. Rumors circulate that the sky is about to fall, that the end of the world is at hand. And this is, in effect, true because in a single moment one has seen that the boundary between mythical and contemporary realms is less stable than one thought, that the world is more immense than one imagined, and infinitely more complicated. But perhaps the most poignant of all the speculations that begin to take hold is the view that the disturbed order of the world is a result of some ancestral error, or something one has done wrong—a reflection of some essential moral inadequacy. This theme runs through the myth of Souw's curse. It is also present in people's rationalizations of why the white men shot and killed people in many highland villages.

This from Seriate, of Goropa village:

> We thought they were spirits not real people, so we weren't
> afraid of them. We stood there and they killed our men. Now
> we saw what power they had and feared them! They killed
> many of our men and we buried them, putting two or three in
> the one grave. They killed us but it was our fault. They were
> people and we thought them to be spirits. (Ibid., 72–73)

Out of the harrowing experiences of first contact, novel interpretations of the world quickly emerge. But the theme of self-derogation remains constant, even before white missionaries and traders promulgate their own perfidious myths of native inferiority.

In the Southern Madang district, people recast the Book of Genesis to make it more consistent with their experience. God makes heaven and earth. He then creates Adam and Eve and gives them abundant cargo—tinned meat, steel tools, rice, tobacco, matches. But when Adam and Eve break God's taboo against sexual intercourse, God takes everything back. Cain's murder of Abel completes the fall from divine grace. In due course, however, Noah redeems mankind through his goodness and obedience, and God returns the cargo to Noah as a pledge of his goodwill toward humanity. Noah's sons, Shem and Japheth, follow their father's example and so continue to be blessed with cargo. They become the ancestors of white men. But Noah's third son, Ham, is stupid: he witnesses his father's nakedness and for his sin is deprived of cargo and sent to New Guinea, where he becomes the ancestor of the blacks (Lawrence 1964, 75–78).

In Tangu, a primal myth is reworked to explain why white men seem to have greater mastery over the world than blacks. The myth relates how a woman warns her family against killing a particular fish, the *ramatzka.* When the youngest ignores her and kills the fish, the earth trembles and the sea rises up, inundating deep valleys and dividing younger brother from elder brother.

The younger brother (Tuman) becomes the ancestor of the blacks, and a loser. His elder brother (Ambwerk), ancestor of the whites, gets all the luck. As a Tangu informant put it, "*Ambwerk* had paper. *Tuman* had yams and other tubers. Now, if it had been the other way about (if *Ambwerk,* not *Tuman,* had shot the *ramatzka*) you white skinned people would have had yams, and we black skinned people would have had paper and all the other good things" (Burridge 1960, 164–67).

How can one understand the alacrity with which New Guinea people deploy these myths of ancestral error and paradise lost, disparaging and blaming themselves for the cosmic dispensation that gave whites so many advantages and left them without?

I want to approach this question by a somewhat tortuous, biographical route. (Caveat: I ask my American friends to appreciate that what I chronicle in the following pages is a far cry from the kind of account I would now render, having lived for eight years in the U.S. It is to be read as testimony to the kinds of distorted and parodic views that a stranger inevitably brings to any overwhelmingly new world).

I HAD COME TO AMERICA RELUCTANTLY. Even before leaving Australia I knew how deeply I would miss my daughter and my friends in the antipodes. On my last evening in Sydney a group of us sat under the pergola in a friend's garden, drinking wine. The conversation was stilted. It was as if I was already becoming a shade. For several nights I had been troubled by dreams of the Midwestern landscapes where I was heading: glacial moraines, deciduous woodlands, and dead cornfields. Now, as I stared into my wine, I remembered my daughter in Canberra, my last glimpse of her in the rearview mirror of my taxi, driving away. She was wearing a black dress, crossing the road from the Civic Twin cinemas to the Turkish restaurant, already going about her life without me. I breathed in the scent of jacaranda and lilac, the salty cinder smell of the harbor, fearful that in leaving these things behind I would lose all sense of who I was.

When I arrived in Los Angeles I could no longer give myself one good reason why I had left Australia. I felt exactly as I was described on my immigration papers—a nonresident alien.

The airport made me think of Umberto Eco's *Travels in Hyperreality*. Duane Hanson couples everywhere—fatsos with bland faces and dishwater eyes, just back from Acapulco, heading home to Des Moines. Airport officials reeled off pat answers to my questions in an automatic speech that sounded as if it was produced by a silicon chip rather than a human larynx. Along the thoroughfare at terminal 7 I was stopped in my tracks by a Joan Collins lookalike—massed peroxide hair, overtanned skin, false eyelashes, forced smile. Propped on high heels, she was smoking a Sobranie in a gold cigarette holder and talking to a young corporate executive with a masonite briefcase, also groomed to kill. Their studied manners and cool gestures were like frozen frames from the video world of their fantasy lives, vignettes of human frailty masquerading as masterfulness and stardom. I took refuge in a bookshop. There was a special bookstand advertising the week's best-sellers: *Effective listening: hearing what people say and making it work for you . . . Executive essentials: the complete sourcebook for success . . . Alchemy of finance . . . Inside corporate innovation . . . Rich men, single women . . . CEO: corporate leadership in action . . . Unlimited power: the way to peak period achievement . . . Growing a business . . . The first time investor.*

I wandered on to a coffee bar. The girl behind the counter had purple glitter on her face and was dressed like a pumpkin. When I asked for an espresso she repeated a set phrase in an accent I couldn't comprehend. I ended up with a cardboard cup of something brown and undrinkable and a plastic stick to stir it with. Later, in the men's room I looked at myself in the mirror, half expecting to find that I too had been transformed into a Halloween monster.

There was a television set in every corner of the coffee bar. A quest was being launched for Miss Eye on L.A. As I was trying to work out the identity of Miss Eye, a toothless woman shuffled up to my table, smiled feebly, and handed me a card. It read: "Smile, deaf mute's alphabet, I sell this educational language card to help support 4 children, pay any price you wish, God bless you! I gave her a dollar and as she went on her way I turned my attention back to the TV—a bizarre mix of automobile commercials and human-interest stories about epileptics, rape victims, and cancer sufferers.

MY FIRST WEEKS IN THE MIDWEST increased my confusion. One thing I found difficult to come to terms with was the way people reacted to my name. Succumbing to an atavistic belief that a shared name betokens a shared identity, I found myself buying magazines that featured articles on the other Michael Jackson. It amused me to discover that while I had lost my identity and become a shadow of my former self when I left Australia, my famous namesake also felt "cut off from the rest of humanity," and likened himself to E.T. and the Elephant Man. While I felt like a complete nobody, he seemed to have crossed the boundaries between every imaginable category—male and female, white and black, child and adult, straight and gay, organic and plastic, person and machine, god and man—and reinvented himself as a kind of transcendent, cosmopolitan everybody.

Other trivial things undermined my sense of who I was, such as saying cupboard instead of closet, footpath instead of sidewalk, and pronouncing tomato in a way that made a shop assistant stare at me in incomprehension. A lot of my disorientation was ludicrous. Like the day I called a plumber to my apartment because the sink was blocked. The plumber came and pulled the plug out. I tried to explain that I'd never before seen an "In-Sink-Erator" and hadn't noticed that the plug had slipped into the plug hole. He gave me a sidelong look and asked me where I was from. I wanted to say "Papua New Guinea."

With the onset of winter I began to feel more and more dispirited. In the Siberian gloom I listened in disbelief as academics rattled off accounts of what they were writing, or exchanged views about deals, trade-offs, career timetables, ways to generate and package ideas. I felt I'd somehow taken a wrong turn and entered the world of corporate management. I'd seen the Mercury ads on television that played on peoples' anxieties about being comfortable and in control. Many of the academics I met seemed to drive the intellectual equivalents of Mercurys. As for me, I guess I was suffering from what was called a conflicted emotional agenda. I was consumed by self-doubt. I felt fraudulent. How long before I was rumbled and sacked? I disparaged myself continually, nursing my self-inflicted wounds like a humiliated circus animal, and nothing and no one could persuade me to do otherwise. I yearned to be returned to the wild, to be anonymous and in penury again. Seldom had I felt so keenly my kinship with the unemployed, the outcast, the dispossessed. But I was trapped, and the only way I could deal with my situation was to try and appease the authorities, to satisfy what I guessed were their demands, to accept every offer to give a seminar, attend a conference, teach a course. In this way I vaguely hoped to stave off the day when I would be held to account. But with every new commitment I took on, I felt more shackled and depressed. I watched people passing up and down the street, going about their business, and was puzzled by the sense of purpose they evidently possessed. I drifted through the days, watching myself from afar as my life was decided for me by circumstances beyond my control. I went along with everything others said, yet all the while experiencing that traveler's malaise that Malcolm Lowry speaks about in *Present State of Pompeii:*

> This pre-eminently, is where you don't belong. Is it some great ruin that brings upon you this migraine of alienation—and almost inescapably these days there seems a ruin of some kind involved—but it is also something that slips through the hands of your mind, as it were, and that, seen without seeing, you can make nothing of: and behind you, thousands of miles away, it is as if you could hear your own real life plunging to its doom (Lowry 1979, 177).

MY PURPOSE IN RECOUNTING these experiences is not to set my tears to music (to use Michel Tournier's wonderful phrase), but to access the first contact experiences of others.

We are accustomed to think of separation trauma as a loss. Someone we love or something to which we are deeply attached is suddenly taken away from us. We cry out against the injustice of it, as though we have been singled out as the victim of a perverse cosmic joke. We yearn for the loved one or the lost object as sometimes we long for our childhood. We live on in a void, an absence.

But it is also possible to suffer such experiences when brought face to face with something overwhelmingly new. It is not then a matter of mourning something absent but of cringing in the shadow of an incomprehensible presence. You see this clearly in the New Guinea highlanders' reactions to Leahy and Dwyer. People go into mourning, though it is not the ancestral dead they mourn but living people who were absent and have returned. The experience is too much to take. Staggered by the technological mastery that the strangers have at their command, people feel they have lost control over their own destiny. But this sense of loss is born of an unbearable discovery: the world is infinitely vaster and far more complex than one thought.

When people are intimidated and diminished by the strange, they often endow it with superior attributes. This happens to anthropologists during their first few weeks in the field. You can feel so lost, so dependent on the goodwill of the people around you, that to be given any sort of hospitality earns your undying gratitude. This is why anthropologists frequently romanticize friendships forged in the field and extol the moral integrity of "their" people. What is closer to the truth is that these so-called friends are simply individuals who happened to help the anthropologist salvage his self-esteem (La Barre 1972, 52).

To venerate another is, to some extent, to demean oneself. Missionaries often trade on this abjection, promising colonized and dispossessed peoples dignity in the eyes of God and salvation in the suffering of Christ, whose death and resurrection offer, for a time, hope of regaining the world one has lost. But the self-disparaging myths people invent in explanation of their plight do more than mirror the blighted views of the invader. They are one's means of buying time, striking bargains, wresting back control.

I HAD COLLECTED MANY self-deprecating first-contact stories over the years, the first during the course of my own fieldwork in northern Sierra Leone. Now, for the first time, I felt I understood them.

In the Kuranko village of Fasewoia, in the course of an aimless conversation one afternoon with a group of elders, I was abruptly asked if I considered the Kuranko to be my kinsmen. Mindful of the connotations of the Kuranko term *nakelinyorgonu* (literally, "mother-one-partners") I shook my head and said no. But the elders had used the term in a moral and tactical sense (Bloch 1971) to imply "fellow human beings." They reproached me. Was I not aware that Africans and Europeans had the same ancestral parents, and that our grandfathers were brothers?

According to the elders, the first people in the world were *bimba* Adama and *mama* Hawa—ancestor Adam and ancestress Eve. They had three sons. The eldest was the ancestor of the whites, the second the ancestor of the Arabs, and the third the ancestor of the blacks. The first two sons inherited book learning, but the last-born son—the ancestor of the blacks—inherited nothing, which is why Africans now send their children to school.

It surprised me that the old men should think of Africans as natively inferior to Europeans, and I asked them to explain why the last-born son failed to inherit the knowledge that is in books.

"If you uproot a groundnut," I was told, "and inspect the root, isn't it always the case that some of the nuts are bad and some good?"

The myth is widespread and old. Winwood Reade heard a version of it in northern Sierra Leone in the early 1870s:

> when God made the world He created a Black man and a white man. He offered to the black man his choice of two things: gold and a covered calabash. The black man took the gold, and the white man got the calabash in which a book was contained; and this book has made the white men powerful and wise, and the lords of the earth. (Reade 1873, 424)

Similar stories surface elsewhere in Africa, often immediately after first contact. In 1861 T. J. Hutchinson recorded this myth on the Gold Coast:

> it is believed that, when God made the world, He created one black man and woman, and a like pair of whites. The blacks being of course His favourites, He gave to them the choice of two articles placed before them—namely, a sealed-up box, and a sealed letter. In their avarice, they took the box, which they found to contain nothing but a few worthless metals; and therefore to the whites was left the letter, which told them everything—where to go, how to build ships, to make cloth, and guns, and powder, and rum. (Hutchinson 1861, 331)

A myth that Mary Kingsley heard in Cabinda is almost identical: God created all men black. Then He crossed over a great river and summoned everyone to follow him:

> and the wisest and the bravest and the best plunged into the great river and crossed it; and the water washed them white, so they were the ancestors of the white men. But the others were afraid too much, and said, "No, we are comfortable here; we have our dances, and our tom-toms, and plenty to eat—we won't risk it, we'll stay here"; and they remained in the old place, and from them come the black men. But to this day the white men come to the bank, on the other side of the river, and

call to the black men, saying, "Come, it is better over here."
(Kingsley 1897, 507–8)

On the Ivory Coast, in 1915, a Liberian priest recorded a myth in which God creates whites *before* blacks, which supposedly explains why Africans are less gifted than Europeans. The myth is still invoked by members of the syncretist Harrist sect, which flourishes on the Coast (Pomonti 1980, 14). In northern Gabon the Fang claim that Africans know less than Europeans because when God (Nzame) was imparting vital information to mankind, "Black man was inattentive and impatient." Other versions of the Fang myth focus on the African ancestor's irreverence when confronted with his father's nakedness—a motif which recalls the biblical story of Noah's sons as well as echoing a traditional Fang belief that the display of a father's nudity toward his son was "one of the powerful sanctions prevailing in that relationship" (Fernandez 1982, 70). Filial disrespect is also a leitmotif in Kaguru narratives from Tanzania that relate why blacks are morally and intellectually inferior to whites. One such narrative concerns twin children, one white and one black. The white child heeds his father's words, while the black child spurns them. On his deathbed, the father endows his white son with all he has but bequeaths his black son nothing (Beidelman 1963, 477).

Although many of these myths suggest biblical sources—particularly Genesis 9:18–27 (the story of Noah's sons and Ham's curse)—there is commonly an indigenous narrative that foreshadows them. Moreover, the myths often appear so soon after first contact that they cannot be explained as mere internalizations of European racial prejudices. Sometimes they are manifestly homemade, as in a Limba narrative from Sierra Leone that relates how Africans and Europeans were once brothers. That one brother became less advantaged than the other was a result of their father's favoritism. He wrote a book, containing instructions on how to make money, ships, and airplanes, intending to give it to his dark-skinned son. But his wife smuggled the book to her favorite son—the one with white skin. The dispossessed son ended up with a hoe and a basket of millet, rice, and groundnuts:

> You see us, the black people, we are left in suffering. The un-
> fairness of our birth makes us remain in suffering. That is why
> they want to send us to learn the writing of the Europeans. But
> our mother did not agree, she did not love us. She loved the
> white people. She gave him the book. . . .

Yesterday we were full brothers with them. We come from one descent, the same mother, the same father, but the unfairness of our birth, that is why we are different. We will not know what you know unless we learn from you. (Finnegan 1967, 263)

The notion that subsistence farming is a kind of inherited curse for some primodial disobedience is also a theme in Thonga mythology:

When Nwali created the first man, from whom both Whites and Blacks are descended, they were all naked. Gwambe slept with his sister, an act which had been forbidden, and she had a child. Since that time children are born; but this was not the intention of Nwali, who wished to create adult human beings only! The Gwambe (first ancestor) of the White people showed respect to his father, who was naked, whilst the Gwambe of the Blacks did not; hence the deterioration (*onhakala*) of the Blacks. "We were fools and have been deprived of everything, and Nwali said: You Blacks shall wear down your nails to the quick by digging the earth to find food!" (Junod 1927, 352)[8]

Finally, to establish that it is not only African agriculturalists who adopt these blighted views about themselves, consider the following story of the Kung bushmen:

Guthe first made all people the same. Then he divided them into different types of people. . . . Guthe first made the white men, and then the black ones, and with the pot scrapings he had left, he made the Bushman. (Heinz and Lee 1979, 117)

At first sight it is alarming to find African and Melanesian myths so similar to those promulgated by white racists—for example, the myth that blacks are the cursed descendants of Ham. But there are differences. In the first place, all the narratives I have cited emphasize an essential kinship between blacks and whites and hold out the hope of reconciling old disagreements and sharing the knowledge and wealth that was originally intended for all humanity. This intersubjective equality and complementarity between blacks and whites is alluded to in one of David Livingstone's

---

8. These kinds of myths were also carried to the New World. Black slaves told how God set down two bundles in a road and the black man took the biggest bundle, containing a pick, shovel, hoe, and plow, and was thereby condemned to a life of drudgery, while the white man took up the bundle containing pen and ink and so gained mastery (Hurston 1969, 101–2).

letters, written in 1847 in the region we now call Malawi. After comparing notes on Christian and African worldviews with a Bakwain rainmaker called Sechele, Livingston observed:

> They [the Bakwain] believed that as God had given the white man guns & other things whereby he excelled the black, so he had conferred the knowledge of rainmaking on them as one thing in which they might excel the white. It availed nothing when told that their rain medicines produced no visible effect. "Your medicines," said they, "product no visible effect either when you administer them, but they enter into the inward parts, do their work, and then the cure follows many days afterwards. In like manner our rain medicines enter into the clouds, heal them, and we have rain some time afterwards." (Livingstone 1961, 102–3)

In the second place, the African narratives serve quite different interests to those which give currency to European myths of racial superiority.

Consider the key images. The tellers of the tales invoke ancestral incest, filial impiety, murder, theft, cowardice, complacency, impatience, stupidity, and depravity to explain why blacks are less fortunate than whites. But it is facile to say that the myths simply reflect experience as wet clay paths bear the imprint of human feet. Rather than attempting to establish a people's degree of *commitment* to a belief, my interest is in the strategic *suspension* of disbelief. With myths, people actively work on the world, molding and reshaping it in terms of the exigencies of their everyday lives. These particular myths cannot be read as naive records of experience. Life would be *practically* unliveable if people were really stuck with these beliefs about themselves. The exaggeration verges on parody. Clearly there must be some method in the mythmakers' madness, some rhetorical strategy that the texts alone do not readily disclose. We need a context. We need to bring experiences of our own to bear upon these texts. We need to think of the mythmakers as actively complicit in their own destiny. We need to ask a pragmatic question: What do people gain by debasing themselves and demeaning their origins?

First of all, telling a story about one's experience effectively substitutes words for the world. Words are more accessible and manageable than the world. Thus the despair I felt when I first came to America was mitigated as soon as I was able to write about it. The same goes for the first contact myths, except that magical mastery of the world is achieved through speaking instead of writing.

Regardless of what one writes or recounts, the act of telling one's story transforms one's situation. One acts instead of being acted on. Rather than being a mere creature of fate, one connives in one's own destiny.

This is not to say that for a long time one doesn't suffer in silence, powerless to comprehend or do much except go along with things. In New Guinea and elsewhere people at first try to appease the strangers by imitating them. The strategy should be familiar to us all. When intimidated by the unknown we try to hide, to lose and efface ourselves, often conforming to what we guess the other expects of us rather than risk standing out and declaring who we really are. In New Guinea people collected scraps of the white men's toilet paper, tin lids, burnt matchsticks, and tea leaves. They traded food for trinkets they could wear. They donned the white men's clothes and imitated their writing.

It is reminiscent of Lévi-Strauss's experiences in central Brazil in 1938. When he encountered the Nambikwara, many natives had never seen a white man. Yet within days of Lévi-Strauss giving them pencils and paper, the Nambikwara were scribbling horizontal lines on paper in imitation of the ethnographer (Lévi-Strauss 1973, 296). As with the people of New Guinea, this was seen as a way of entering into the world of the other and in due course gaining access to European goods.[9]

The trouble with this strategy is that one quickly looks a fool. No material advantage follows from aping the strangers. Instead of bringing oneself closer to them, one is dismayed to find that one is merely confirming in their eyes one's essential otherness. There is, however, one way out of this impasse—to decide to play the fool, to make one's imitations of white men into parodies, to embrace the role into which one has been cast but in such a way that it will subvert the entire scenario. Automatic mimeticism becomes a performative strategy.

There's an old saying: "If you want to defeat your enemy, sing his song." Quite simply, it is easier to put oneself down than to put on airs, easier to fulfill another person's worst expectations than live up to their impossible demands. So the most important thing about the first contact narratives is their irony.

The way of irony—protecting oneself by never declaring one's motives, singing the stranger's song in one's own key—is like guerilla war. It is the strategy of the oppressed. To borrow Marx's vivid image, one forces the frozen circumstances to dance by singing to them their own melody

9. On comparable magical attitudes to literacy in New Guinea, see Meggitt 1968.

(*Man muss diese versteinerten Verhältnisse dadurch zum Tanzen zwingen, dass man ihnen ihre eigene Melodie vorsingt;* Marx 1953, 311).

Some anthropologists interpret public displays of helplessness and ineptitude as ways of eliciting sympathy from white bosses, much as a child throws a tantrum to get a parent's attention. But putting oneself down is not only a way of abnegating control; it can be a stratagem for regaining it. To recount one's story as comedy rather than tragedy is a triumph of disengagement: the original hurtful experience is rendered harmless. But to laugh at oneself implies a distancing from subjectivity such that one reconstitutes oneself, in effect, as an object. But this object, though superficially like the object constituted by the other, is a product of one's *own* subjectivity, oneself in disguise, as it were, and therefore subverts the power of the other to define one's identity on one's behalf. Self-disparagement and self-mocking can work as a preemptive strategy, undercutting the power of an oppressor to put one down. At the same time, in so far as conforming to the stereotypes of one's oppressor is flattering to him, this ruse provides a means for pursuing one's own ulterior purposes. A South Carolina slave in the 1840s explained such oppositional practices as follows:

> us slaves watch the white folks' parties when the guests danced a minuet and then paraded in a grand march. Then we'd do it too, but we used to mock' em, every step. Sometimes the white folks noticed it but they seemed to like it. I guess they thought we couldn't dance any better. (Pierson 1976, 166–80).

Another African-American put it this way:

> The white man is always trying to know into somebody else's business. All right, I'll set something outside the door of my mind for him to play with and handle. He can read my writing but he sho' can't read my mind. I'll put this play toy in his hand, and he will seize it and go away. Then I'll say my say and sing my song. (Hurston 1969, 18–19)

Assays

The Women Who Became the Pleiades

The myth is well known throughout the central and western desert areas of Australia.[1] In a Yankuntjatjara version of the myth, two virgin sisters traveled from the north, fleeing the incestuous attentions of a man called Nyiru. Journeying south and then west from Uluru (Ayers Rock) with their dogs, the women came to a place known as Waliny (or Walinja), where they found water, native figs, and other food-bearing plants. There they built a windbreak from brushwood and grass and made camp. Nyiru tracked the sisters to Waliny, where he underwent circumcision. He now sought to have sex with the sisters, and despite being attacked by their dogs, managed to penetrate one of them. The sisters now fled Waliny, only to be overtaken once again by Nyiru, who, despite the dogs, impregnated one of the women. Nyiru's son, Jula, was born of this union. After further travels the sisters went into the ground at a place called Akandjudula, on the margins of Yankuntjatjara country. There they subsequently climbed into the sky, where they now appear in the early mornings of late autumn and "walk" across the sky as the Pleiades.

In time the windbreaks that the sisters and Nyiru made at Waliny were metamorphosed into granite domes and rock shelters, and it is here, until

---

1. Among the Warlpiri the women who became the Pleiades were also in flight from a sexually indefatigable "cicada dreaming man" (Meggitt 1966, 146).

recently, that Yankuntjatjara men and their Pitjantjatjara and Ngatjatjara countrymen sequestered and instructed neophyptes, retouched the painted figures, and performed ceremonies for dingo[2] and honey ant.

The Waliny rock shelter (described by Tindale in 1959 as "possibly one of the most spectacular ones in Australia") was surveyed by missionaries and anthropologists as early as 1888–90, but its isolation protected it until 1970.[3] Indeed, in his 1959 account of the site and its associated myths, Tindale was careful not to describe its exact location "pending official decision as to action to protect it from unauthorized visitors and vandalism" (1959, 325). However, in 1970 it was decided that Waliny, like Altamira and Lascaux in Europe, should be developed as an on-site tourist museum. Plans for development included a kiosk, air conditioning, artificial lighting, and photographic displays. It was assumed that the ancient paintings had no sacred significance to any contemporary aboriginals, and that local people would be well compensated by tourist dollars, employment, and the gift of a four-wheel-drive vehicle.

As rumors spread of the proposed development, traditional owners, living mostly at Aparawatatja, became increasingly concerned. But the developers found a more attentive audience among younger matrilineal claimants at Amata.

Dissension centered on control of the tourist traffic, tourist dollars, and a promised Toyota. As arguments between patrilineal and matrilineal factions became more and more heated, a group of senior men under the leadership of Kayipipi moved to Waliny with their wives and families and set up camp.

Kayipipi's nickname was "Cheeky Billy," on account of his forthright manner; he was known as a man who did not give ground on matters of the law. Faced with increasing pressure and dissent, and with the developers now threatening to allocate the Toyota to another community, Kayipipi made his decision. One morning he scrounged some ochre, charcoal, and ash and went alone to the big cave where he set to work obliterating the sacred motifs. Some he overlaid with red ochre, others he covered with concentric circles.

2. The close association of the star sisters with their dogs is also recognized in the coincidence between the autumn rising of the Pleiades low in the eastern sky, which marks the new year, and the season when dingos give birth to their young.

3. Waliny was first surveyed by John Carruthers in 1888–90. Subsequent surveys were carried out by J. R. B. Love and W. B. MacDougall in 1941–45, N. Tindale in 1957, and C. P. Mountford and G. Lawton in 1969 (Wallace 1977, 67–68).

Soon revolted by his task, he stumbled from the cave and vomited. Later, he returned to complete what he had begun. Together with other senior custodians of the site, he worked for a day and a half. When the men's ochres were exhausted, they used children's crayons.

In PHYL AND NOEL WALLACE'S 1977 account of this preemptive destruction of the Waliny site by its traditional owners, Kayipipi is described in heroic terms. His very essence was of this place. His body and the body of the earth were one. His decision to destroy the site rather than allow it to be destroyed by whites was a noble act of integrity, a way of keeping faith with his ancestors and the law.

One can, however, understand this event without having recourse to the language of heroism, romanticism, exoticism, and cultural nostalgia. As Fred Myers has observed, a sacred site should not be seen as a "special kind of property." Rather, it is an expression of the autonomy of those who look after or "hold" the country and "run" its business (1988, 52). Through concerted activity at a sacred site, a group of people literally bring their identity into being, incorporating and objectifying themselves by reference to events that took place there in the past.

In the case of the Waliny site, however, it is important to note that Yankuntjatjara control over it had been eroded long before the vexed question of its use as a tourist museum arose. In 1914 a harsh drought had driven the Yankuntjatjara from the northern reaches of their country, and Pitjantjatjara people displaced them (Tindale 1959, 325–26). Still, it is possible that even if Yankuntjatjara people *had* sustained a continuous ceremonial relationship with the Waliny site, the destruction of its sacred paintings by its patrilineal owners was compatible with the preservation of the social integrity of the living and of their Dreaming. As Fred Myers notes, it is not a place or piece of property per se that has value; rather, the autonomy and "relatedness" of those who hold the place or property in their care. In a telling anecdote Myers relates how a Toyota was burned and destroyed by Pintupi when it threatened the integrity of the community who "shared" it (Myers 1988). Material things are replaceable. Sacred motifs and myths are recoverable through dreams. And land, though given away, may be borne in mind as a focus of identity. What is *not* replaceable or recoverable are the existential rights people have over their own destinies. This is the ultimate value. And in this sense we may suppose that Kayipipi's actions were *existentially* imperative as a way of expressing and preserving the ultimate Yankuntjatjara value: control over their own Dreaming, their own history, and their own fate.

In *At Home in the World* (1995, 137–55) I describe how a group of Warlpiri people reacted to the accidental destruction of a sacred site. This site was associated with an all-important *ngarrka* ("initiated man") Dreaming, and the desert walnut tree that some white miners had knocked down when bulldozing a detour around an impassable stretch of the Tanami road was the life essence (*pirlirrpa*) of a Dreaming ancestor. To understand the outrage and grief precipitated by this event, it is necessary to understand Warlpiri notions of the sacred (*tarruku*).

The sacred is a synonym for power. It conjures a sense of intensely constrained force, holding at once the capacity to generate life—if the protocols of intersubjective engagement with it are respected—*and* the capacity to destroy life if its taboos are infringed. Like the powers of the wild that the Kuranko regard with such ambivalence, the powers associated with aboriginal sacred sites have the potential both to create and destroy ("poison"). Everything depends on how people approach a site, address the ancestral spirits associated with the place, and perform ceremony there.

Sacred power is thus regarded as both inherent and as a product of human activity. The labor theory of value may be invoked here. For Warlpiri, the value of any site is given to it cumulatively through the vital and concentrated activity of those who hold that place in their care. This implies *social* value, since caring for a site or performing ceremony at the site involves creating and affirming *relationships* among those who call the site "father" (those patrilineally related it), those who have "drunk the breast milk of that place" (those matrilineally related to it), and contemporaries and countrymen on whom have been bestowed honorary rights of ritual affiliation. A site thus assumes an ethical and economic value proportional to the social value placed on the networks of people who perennially perform the ritual work of reembodying and reanimating—in narrative, song, painting, and dancing—the vital essence of the place. In the absence of this activity, a site does not cease to possess value; rather, its value lapses into latency. If the site is rarely visited and ceremony never performed there, this latency and silence may take on negative connotations. The site may be seen almost solely as a place of the dead, an object of sorrow and loss, a subject of fear. In other words the intersubjective relation between people and country loses its vitality in the same way that a body wastes away through lack of activity or the bonds of kinship fall into abeyance when people lose touch with one another.

An important point must be made here regarding the social nature of memory. For Warlpiri, memory is never merely a cognitive process, the past recollected in tranquility. Remembering is social. It entails concerted, concentrated, embodied interaction with kinsmen, affines, and countrymen to recreate modes of intersubjectivity that encompass both the living and the dead.

It is not uncommon for aboriginal people returning to a sacred site after some time away to weep as they come in sight of it, and to address the place with affection, anger, or words of explanation. Such "acting out" suggests that the places people call "proper dear ones" entail feelings of bereavement and loss. They are where forebears brought into being a world that one is, in one's own turn, obliged to sustain. And at these places, the ancestors, exhausted after their travels and their labors, returned to the earth to rest. In this sense, one informant told me, sacred sites may be compared with whiteman's war memorials.

The Warlpiri notion of the sacred reflects, then, the labor and life-sustaining activity that has been centered on a certain place since time immemorial. The sacred connotes the depth and density of human experience at the places people have been conceived and born, have camped, and, most compellingly, passed away. The compression of experience at *times* of intensified activity—particularly birth and death—gets translated into a sense that the *places* where these things occurred have deep significance. The meaning thus given to a place through focused activity and intense experience comes to be regarded as actually residing in the place itself. In other words, when subjectivity is lent to an object through concerted labor, the object itself becomes a subject (cf. Munn 1970). This is not a metaphorical construction in the sense that a place is consciously and deliberately compared to a person; the fusion is accomplished preconceptually in exactly the same way that a bereaved person feels that the object of his grief and desire—his dead beloved—lives on as a shade who mourns *him* and desires to remain with him in the land of the living. In other words, the projection of one's own feelings of loss onto the other—the lost object—is often consummated without the mediation of conceptual thought.

In the case of the Warlpiri site, the destroyed desert walnut tree had embodied the spirit of a person. Those who inherited this person's name and held the site in trust participated in this essence. Existentially, self and other, person and tree, were one and the same. To call the tree the Dreaming spirit (*yuwirnng*i) of the ancestral person was a *post facto* conceptualization of an intersubjective relationship *that was already in place.*

Most of the people with whom I spoke about the felled tree spoke of their relationship with it in kinship terms. This was why, in seeking compensation from the mining company, it was impossible to put a price on the site. One simply could not convert social or affective bonds into material or monetary terms. The value of the place expressed the value of the *relationships* that had been forged among those who were *kirda* (patrilineal custodians) and *kurdungurlu* (matrikin) for that place. The white miners who destroyed the tree had, therefore, destroyed the vital embodiment of a relationship between the living and the dead. They had, as Warlpiri, put it, killed the spirit of a person. This was why people were filled with grief and anger. But the miners had also denigrated the integrity and rights of the people who identified themselves through the tree and through the myths and ceremony that belonged to that place. Mourning the loss of the tree as a lost kinsman thus implicated a mourning for the loss of that which encapsulated the integrity, autonomy, and vitality of the living. Accordingly, compensation was sought less to restore the site than to restore respect for the controlling rights of the traditional owners. Payback was not simply a matter of settling a score; it was a way of making good an existential loss, a way of redressing an imbalance in Warlpiri dealings with whites. After years of having their destinies decided by a succession of white welfare administrators and distant government officials who invoked a liberal vocabulary of aboriginal self-determination and development only to decide themselves the terms on which these changes would occur—years in which the Warlpiri had avoided confrontation and kept their own counsel—they now stood up and demanded that whites recognize Warlpiri rights over their own country and their own lives.

In contemporary Australia, such demands are grounded in two hundred years of polarization and estrangement between blacks and whites. From the earliest years of settlement, white Australians perpetuated the legal fiction that the continent had been an empty land—*terra nullius*—at the time of settlement. The corollary was that aboriginal consciousness had also been vacant—useless, undeveloped, infantile, primitive, devoid of reason.

As William James noted, the ego may establish itself in reality "either by negating or embracing" (1950, 313). While most people seek some form of coexistence, some seek obsessively to entrench and retract themselves from the Other, which they construe as a "region of which they cannot securely possess." Continues James, "People who don't resemble them, or who treat them with indifference, people over whom they gain no influence, are people on whose existence, however meritorious it may intrinsically be, they look with chill negation, if not positive hate. Who will not be mine I will exclude from existence altogether; that is, as far as I can make it so, such people shall be as if they were not" (312–13). The devaluation of the humanity of another is thus a function of a disjunction willfully wrought within the field of human intersubjectivity. Even an inert material object acquires value when one commits energy and time to working on it. But in the absence of direct contact or dialogue, human beings are reduced, vis-à-vis one another, to the status of things. Accordingly, relationships become constructed in terms of statistics or as I-It rather than I-Thou. In Australia, Marcia Langton notes, most whites have so little direct social contact with aboriginal people that they readily succumb to cultural icons of aboriginality based on self-perpetuating fictions that are never tested against reality (1993, 32–36). The result is an ever-increasing dissonance between conceptual representations and lived realities that inhibits intersubjective recognition.

If mutuality and affinity are proportional to the work that goes into closing the gap between self and other, enmity is the by-product of nullifying relatedness through negative labor. Racism is subtractive. Interaction and dialogue between self and other are replaced by communicational bars. And in the absence of any interplay between self and other, the terms become equally and oppositionally essentialized—fetishized debris of a systematically atomized social universe.

It is against this process that existential anthropology speaks.

Losing the Straight Way

Any outsider who goes to live in a Warlpiri settlement is given a skin name. This gesture of inclusion places one in a social relationship with Warlpiri, and may, if its entailments are taken seriously, constitute grounds for downplaying the nominal difference between *yapa* and *kardiya*—people of aboriginal and nonaboriginal descent. But there is an *essential* difference that can never be effaced by this *nominal* identification, for a skin name evokes intersubjective connections with country—in particular, Dreaming sites that an outsider has no part of. The same is true of individual names. Less openly spoken than skin names, and taken out of circulation for a generation after a person dies, these names may also be bestowed on a trusted stranger as a token of deep identification, but the *place* associated with the name can never be shared.

Warlpiri identity, one might say, is never skin deep, never a one-generational matter. A person's being participates in the being of significant others, and these include those who have passed on as well as the places associated with their past lives. Rather than a categorical summation of individual identity, a name therefore denotes a *relationship* between immediate and nonimmediate horizons of Being that the Warlpiri refer to as *palka* (presently embodied) and *lawa* (presently absent). This relationship implies a perpetual oscillation, as between day and night, remembering and forgetting, or waking and sleeping—all common Warlpiri metaphors for the interplay between the self-evidential, everyday, revealed world and the hermeneutically concealed world of the Dreaming. Just as the desert blooms after rain, so people forgather and disperse, things pass from plenty to scarcity, and human life waxes and wanes. Dancing, singing, storying, bestowing a name, visiting a sacred site, having a dream in which painted or dance motifs are disclosed are all, figuratively speaking, modes of giving birth—of bringing back into embodied being (*palka jarrimi*) that which was temporarily absent, latent, or hidden. They are ways of "drawing out" the Dreaming from pastness and potentiality, and realizing it as actively embodied presence. These modes of transformative activity are simultaneously "signs," "prints," "marks," or "traces" (*yirdi*) of the circumambient Dreaming *and* ways of reanimating it—energetically bodying it forth, recreating it, uttering it, and externalizing it. In a sense this movement is from quiescence to activity, and one sees this constantly in the way a hand, with a circular movement, clears the ground before it is inscribed with the markings of a story, in the way ground is brushed and cleared for ceremony (*parnpa* denotes *both* the cleared space *and* the ceremonial activity), in the way the human skin is oiled and prepared for ritual painting, and the way a swathe is cut from the scrub to create a business site. All such clearings are preparations for the advent of newly embodied expressions of the ever-latent law.

One of the principal ways in which this vital connection between the latent and the patent is sustained is through looking after the country that one is most intimately identified with. As Warlpiri see it, this is directly analagous to looking after one's kith and kin. But unless one actually retraces one's ancestors' journeys through the country to which one belongs, and unless one is able to sing the story that recounts this journey in its archetypical form, one's life is, in effect, cut off from the deeper matrix of being that sustains it.

This relationship between lifetime and dreamtime is one of synecdoche. Past and present are brought together. Biography and mythology are effectively fused. What happens in the one is seen to have repercussions in the other. Thus the concerted effort of people in bringing the Dreaming into Being is reciprocally linked to the force that the Dreaming has in human conception and growth. There is a perpetual interplay between the two domains. Women get impregnated by the vital essence (*kuruwarri*) strewn along ancestral traveling tracks, names are drawn out of the Dreaming after they have remained latent and unspoken for a generation, individual dreams recurrently reveal episodes or signs of the Dreaming (Dussart 1988, 247–48), ceremony fleshes out and conjures up ancestral events, and every journey through the desert that touches places that have ancestral significance effectively recalls those places and brings them back to life in the here and now. You see evidence of this in the way, when myths are told, people slip unwittingly and intermittently between first-person and third-person narrative, and autobiographical recollections merge with mythological referents.[4] In these ways, each person's lifetime retraces history (cf. Myers 1986, 68; Rumsey 1994, 121–22). "We follow the Dreaming," one informant told me, comparing this to the way one follows footprints or the spoor of an animal across country. In this sense of the word, *history* recovers the meaning that Herodotus gave to it: a kind of tracking or tracing of human lives over time. But the link between people and the Dreaming is entirely reciprocal since without the concerted effort of human beings in the here and now the Dreaming remains latent and moribund.

What then of someone for whom the intimate bond between biography and mythology has attenuated or slipped away? Someone who may have a mental map of his country but lacks any firsthand knowledge of it. Someone unsure of his place of conception and birth, his past, his patrimony, and even his name? Someone who cannot follow the ancestral tracks without getting lost? What story might such a person tell to locate and define himself?

I DID NOT KNOW Jangala well. Spending most of my time with an older generation of Warlpiri men, I went along with the way they distanced themselves from him. But he came to my camp from time to time, to ask how my research was going, and to set me right.

I was trying to identify the groups that had rightful claims to royalty

---

4. Bob Dixon noted the same process in Yidinyji. "The first stories I'd recorded from Moses had one peculiar characteristic: the narrator would set the scene for a few sentences, using third person pronouns, and would then take on the identity of the main character, telling the rest of the legend in the first person (1984: 243).

money from a gold mine at a place called the Granites. In the company of other middle-aged men, Jangala would boldly draw lines in the dirt to mark the boundaries of Warnayaka—the central area of the Tanami in which the gold mine was located. Sometimes the four "corners" of the block would be marked by sticks stuck in the ground, and I would be confidently told that all those born within the boundaries of the block had claims to royalty money, while Ngarliya people (by implication, people from Yuendumu) had none.

The older men did not disguise their contempt for what they clearly saw as a nonaboriginal picture of territoriality. "Don't you listen to them," Zack Jakamarra insisted. "They don't know. They fibbing. They never walked around that country. They sit here, this Lajamanu. Just because they talk well—."

Zack's picture of the Tanami could not have been different. Where the younger men inscribed boundaries, the older men drew circles in the sand as they recited ancestral travels, and connected these sites with lines to signify the traveling tracks. And when they spoke of belonging they referred not just to lines of descent but networks and skeins of relationship that bind different groups together in alliances through marriage (*jurdalja*), adoptive and cognatic kinship, and ritual affiliation. Apart from the people who called a place "father" (the *kirda,* or "traditional owners" of a site), many other people were implicated in any site, and these negotiated ties, variously called *ngurrara jinta, kuruwarri jinta,* or *warlalja* ("one mob"), made it impossible to define unequivocal and binding principles of identity and nonidentity, inclusion and exclusion.

Jangala must have realized that I was setting little store by what he was telling me. As if trying another tack, he turned up at my camp one day and started talking to me about his origins.

His mother, Napangardi, hailed from Yawurluwurlu, a yam Dreaming site. She had been promised to a certain Jampijinpa who already had many wives. One day, in a jealous rage, several other men killed this Jampijinpa near Paraluyu and took his wives. Napangardi now married the man who would become Jangala's father. But Jangala never knew his name. He knew only the names of his mother's parents, that his father was *kirda* for Pirtipi-rti, and that he had passed away at a place called Parntapurru.[5] As a boy

5. Though the names of the dead are put out of circulation for a generation, people often refer to them in terms of the places where the individuals died. Thus Parntapurru-wana (literally, Parntapurru-alongside) signifies the place Jangala's father passed away, and is a circumlocution for his name. As Jangala remarked, "We bin lose im, right along Parntapurru."

Jangala had been told he was conceived at Pirtipirti (Thomson's Rockhole), the evidence being his "crippled" arms and the lesions on his skin that replicated the wounds suffered by a Dreaming ancestor in a fight with an interloper there. He was born at Wardilyka, to the east of Pirtipirti.

I suspected that Jangala's story was a ruse for claiming a cut of the royalty money from the Granites on the dubious basis of his father being *kirda* for a place in the general geographical area and on the strength of his having been conceived in that same country. Insisting that people were wrong in saying his father came from Balgo or Mount Barkly, Jangala told me, "Lots of people are trying to push us away." Then he added, "Our mother's family came from Yawurluwurlu," as if to suggest this also gave him rights at the Granites.

Then he digressed again. Now he was at pains to point out how he was genealogically linked to an age-mate, Jupurrurla, a man who had considerable clout in Lajamanu and was already receiving royalty payments from the Granites. It was a confused story, the main point of which seemed to be to emphasize that Jupurrurla's father had affinal ties with Pirtipirti.

Finally, as if to clinch everything, Jangala assured me that no one was really *kirda* for the Granites. In the past, no one lived there. There wasn't enough water. People only went there to gather wild tobacco.

Next day I was sitting with Zack and some other older men in the shade of some snappy gums near the football oval. When I told Zack what Jangala had told me, Zack dismissed Jangala's stories out of hand. The truth was, Zack said, that Jangala's father came from Mount Barkly. Jangala had been born in the Pirtipirti area, but as for his father, "No name. He bin finish in the bush." Speaking of the Granites, Zack stressed that there were *kirda* for the place, there was water there, and people did camp there.

A few days later I found Jangala eating "damper" with his girlfriend at a windbreak of corrugated iron outside the *jilimi*. I told him Zack had cast serious doubt on his stories.

Jangala did not argue with this. He confessed he had spent a lot of time trying to find out who his father was and where his father's country was located. It had been Jupurrurla who had urged him to play up his matrilineal roots. Older men like Zack had told him he could not claim royalty money on that basis.

"It must be tough not to have a place you can call home," I said.

Sadly, he agreed. All his life he had been looking for his father.

"What of the father who grew you up?" I asked.

It was old blind Jampijinpa, gangling and gap-toothed, whom Jimmy

Jangala led about by the hand. When Jangala was still a small boy, Jampi-jinpa had married his mother, Napangardi, and gone with them to the Granites. Later on he lived in Yuendumu and, finally, Lajamanu, where he and his brother took the name of the *kardiya* boss for whom they worked there.

"But," said Jangala ruefully, "I cannot trace my descent to him or to my stepfather. It has to be your real father."

STORIES LINK PEOPLE TO PLACES and legitimate these links. "That's his story," people say of a person's country of origin, his *warringkiyi*. Without such stories the connection between one's own life and the larger matrix of Life itself is lost. Stories can also forge and create links, as Jangala knew when he tried to convince me of his rights to royalties from the Granites mine. But there is only one true story, one straight story, and without this master narrative, one is lost.

Possibly Jangala found some sense of wider belonging in the *kardiya* world, where he worked off and on for many years, first as a station hand, then as a language assistant on the Warlpiri dictionary project.[6] But in the eyes of older Warlpiri men, Jangala cut a pitiable figure, embodying no doubt the loss of connectiveness between people and country that they had witnessed in the course of their own lives. "*Wirrarpa*," the older men would say, using a word that tellingly connotes the pathos of isolation and be-reavement. For men like Zack, the worst of it was not that knowledge had been lost (for knowledge of the Dreaming was always theoretically re-coverable), but that knowledge had become abstract. When the younger men spoke of "country" it was not country of which they had firsthand knowledge, country where they had walked, camped, been born, done ceremony, and suffered. In this sense the loss of stories implied a loss or devaluation of direct experience, a transformation, in de Certeau's terms, of tour into map. As Zack put it, "Young people got no *walya* [ground]. They don't know this *walya*. They only got that book, that paper. We don't use maps. We got the country in our heads. . . . But these young people bin move away from their father's father's country. They never walk around their country. They bin sit here. This Lajamanu. But I bin walk around."

6. Sponsored by the Department of Education of the Northern Territory of Australia, the Australian Institute for Aboriginal Studies, the National Science Foundation (U.S.), and the Systems Development Foundation (U.S.).

Myths/Histories/Lives

No life is sufficient unto itself. A person is singular only in the sense in which astronomers use the term: a relative point in space and time where invisible forces become fleetingly visible (cf. Lévi-Strauss 1990, 625–26). Our lives belong to others as well as to ourselves. Just as the stars at night are set in imperceptible galaxies, so our lives flicker and fail in the dark streams of history, fate, and genealogy. One might say that we are each given three lives. First is our conscious incarnation, occupying most of the space between our birth and death. Second is our existence in the hearts and minds of others—a life that precedes the moment of our birth and extends beyond our death for as long as we are remembered. Finally there is our afterlife as a barely remembered name, a persona, an element in myth. And this existence begins with the death of the last person who knew us in life.

These moments in a person's destiny find expression in different kinds of stories. What begins as a body of raw experience, too humdrum or perhaps too painful to be told, becomes a narrative, and later takes on the lineaments of myth. In this metamorphosis of life into legend, the original figures fade and reform, and often end up carrying the burden of our preoccupations. As Michael Young notes in his brilliant study of the ways myth and life story are interleaved in Kalauna, "myth is reconstructed through lived experience which mediates culture; and culture is reconstructed through lived experience which mediates myth" (1983, 35).

My fieldwork in central Australia brought me to an existential understanding of the way subjectivity inevitably entails intersubjectivity, and vice versa. To come into one's own a person must also feel at home in the world. Paradoxically perhaps, one can only be one's own person to the extent that one belongs to a wider context than the self—family, clan, circle of friends, workplace, or imagined community. Being at home in the world implies, therefore, a dialectics of identity (Jackson 1977, 238). But this perpetual interplay between hermetic and open-ended, enstatic and ecstatic modes of subjective experience implies problems of feedback and control. These cybernetic adjustments between self and other cannot, however, be measured objectively. Rather they are consummated intersubjectively as a sense of balance between one's experience of the world as something alien, external, all-encompassing, and overbearing, and one's experience of having some place in the world, some say over its governance. Every human life drifts between two poles: the entirely egocentric and totalitarian ex-

treme of dominating others, and the masochistic extreme of self-abnega-
tion, inertia, and victimage. For most people, life is a struggle for the middle
ground where it is possible to realize one's power to make a difference in
the world, to call it one's own, though within the limits of the needs of
others, as well as the constraints of history and genealogy.

When in 1993 my wife, Francine, and I went to live with an aboriginal
family on an outstation in the rainforests of southeast Cape York, these
issues of home and belonging reclaimed my attention. The history of the
social world we entered was as tragic and traumatic as any in aboriginal
Australia: more than a hundred years of conquest and violent dispossession,
of racism and murder, of the brutal breakup of families, of dispersal and
deportation, enforced missionization, and the denial of basic civil rights
(Loos 1982; Broome 1982; Rosser 1985; Rowley 1972). Successive generations of aboriginal people had been drawn into a wider polity only to find
themselves diminished and disadvantaged within it. Their struggle to strike
a balance between a sense of their own ethnic solidarity and a sense of
place in the national community had been frustrated and often futile.

The traces of this history were everywhere apparent, not in physical relics
or ruins but in the lived forms of aboriginal sociality itself, particularly
where outsiders were involved. Story after story bore upon the vexed history of black-white relations, though it was clear that this categorical opposition merged with an older and deeper dialectic between self and other,
insider and stranger. The family with whom we lived was a case in point.
Although the O'Rourkes[7] had endured the mission years stoically, they had
been marginalized long before. Traditionally, a retaliatory and retributive
killing was demanded if an important man died and sorcery was suspected,
and the people living at Banabila—so-called because of the swift tidal cur-
rent that ran at the mouth of the Bloomfield River—had been the scapegoats. Deemed "the weakest and most friendless" Kuku-Yalanji group,
Roth, writing in 1907, noted of them: "one of this tribe is generally, as a
last resource, fixed upon as the culprit; the latter is enticed away on some
hunting expedition, for a corroboree, etc. and then mercilessly speared from
behind" (Roth 1907, 387; cf. 1910, 92).

Like many aboriginal people, the O'Rourkes sought isolation as a survival strategy. But segregationalist and assimilationist government policies
left them and others like them no place to hide. Forced into a Lutheran

---

7. I use pseudonyms for all the aboriginal families and individuals mentioned in the following pages.

mission in the 1970s, the tactic of physical retreat metamorphosed into social stratagems of withdrawal and subterfuge. Their long history of marginalization, incorporated as a habitual disposition toward guardedness and reticence, may explain why the O'Rourkes resisted being moved to the mission (they were almost the last to leave their land) and were the first to leave. Of all Kuku-Yalanji "mobs" in the late 1970s, the O'Rourkes were, according to Christopher Anderson, "one of the mission's least powerful and materially worst off" (1984, 385). Yet their isolation implied considerable solidarity. "The O'Rourkes, out in the scrub, sticking together," was the way a local Aboriginal councillor once described them to me.

ONE CANNOT BEGIN TO UNDERSTAND aboriginal experience of what *we* call history without understanding *their* conception of the past. As I had seen in central Australia, custom and law exist *in potentia*—as the Dreaming—but must be continually brought back into sentient being (*in presentia*) through concerted ritual activity. This perennial recovery of the past is often described metaphorically as a drawing out, waking up, growing up, and giving birth. A person's relation with the past is thus lived as a *social* relation with the forebear whose name he or she carries, as well as with the site with which that forebear is ever-presently associated. In so far as the vital energy of ancestral (past) events is embodied in the land, time is spatialized. In so far as the past is felt to continually reenter the present, time is synchronous. As Veena Das so aptly puts it, the present is constituted as a "spectral present rather than a point present" (1989, 324). Put another way, "there are not two worlds—the world of past happenings and the world of our present knowledge of those past events—there is only one world, and it is a world of present experience"(Oakeshott 1933: 108).

The implication is that we must understand time and space intersubjectively. Many aboriginal people express bafflement and dismay at the ease with which Europeans seem to turn their backs on the past—as if it were *outside* lived experience. As if by implication the injustices and grief that white settlers visited on aboriginal people were now over and done with, dead and buried. For aboriginal people, however, this "history" is reiterated and embodied in the very condition of their contemporary lives, which is why people so readily fuse accounts of their own experience and accounts of their forebears' experiences as if past and present were effectively one.

Although many scholars still tend to separate history and myth—the first supposedly made up of series and successions of events that have actually occurred, the second largely invented, reconstructed, or imagined—it is necessary to set aside or bracket out this kind of distinction if one is to understand aboriginal ways of narrating experience. Phenomenologically, any "cut" between historic and mythopoeic, objective event and interpreted event, is untenable. History is a mode of experience, a world of coexistent facts, in which the past is continually re-presented (Oakeshott 1933, 108–18).

The key to understanding this phenomenon is memory. As Maurice Halbwachs showed, individual memories, like dreams, are continually being reshaped and reconstructed in the course of a person's *social* engagement with others (Halbwachs 1980). This may occur in the context of dialogue as well as in the course of bodily and ritual interaction (Connerton 1989). In these processes personal memories become collectivized and historicized; they cease to be properties of individual minds and enter into intersubjectivity. As such, the line between immediate and interpreted experience effectively disappears.

Just as aboriginal people tend to gloss over the boundary between biography and myth, so too the line between the historical and the personal is rarely clear-cut.[8] Indeed, there is an onus on the living to actively integrate the past into the present (Rose 1992, 30). As Ronald Berndt observed of Western desert peoples, the existential and moral *actualization* of the received wisdom in myth is something the living must accomplish in the way they choose to live (Berndt 1979, 28). Just as this fusion of Dreamtime and lifetime is achieved through storying, so the past and present are continually collapsed in the stories with which people render accounts of their social and personal reality. One is reminded of the way many young Jewish people speak of *their* suffering during the Holocaust, or African-Americans speak of *their* enslavement, as if they themselves actually experienced events that took place before they were born.

The psychology of separation trauma helps us understand what hastens this fusion of personal and collective memory.

As in any other human society, an aboriginal child's primary orientation is to his or her immediate family and community. These constitute the significant others who mirror and affirm a child's developing sense of who

---

8. For instance, Basil Sansom notes an important structural continuity between classical Dreaming myths and new narratives that work historical and personal experience of travel and travail into the old site-and-track forms (1982, 120–22).

he or she is. In aboriginal Australia this positive identification was often negated by white prejudice and propaganda, which relentlessly emphasized that such modes of belonging were the stigmata of primitiveness and dependency and could only perpetuate a state of aboriginal fallenness, ignorance, ill health, and inferior being. In short, the very loci of people's ontological security—kin, land, language, ancestry—were systematically invalidated. And if the stigma of aboriginal origins were not enough, punishment was meted out in the form of assimilationist policies that permitted children to be taken from their birth parents and licensed police to physically remove aboriginal people from their land and incarcerate them on reserves, missions, and penal settlements.

Existentially, these subversive strategies, punitive measures, and criminalizing and stigmatizing procedures often had the very opposite effects to those that were intended. Rather than make aboriginal people ashamed of themselves and determined to break with tradition, they drove people back to their roots for security and survival. It was in this way that "the stolen generation" came to extol their aboriginality over the so-called golden opportunities they had been given by well-meaning white foster parents for whom traditional aboriginal society offered nothing but illiteracy and alienation. If mythology, land, and language were not available as a matrix in which to place oneself, history was. History became the ontological surrogate of mythology. And the white world was made the dialectical negation of aboriginality. In so far as it had denied blacks any place in it, any rights in it, any choices over its governance, blacks would now define themselves by turning that denial against those who had first used it. Reinventing white history was part of this oppositional process.[9]

In this sense the fusion of biographical and historical horizons is not merely a way of understanding one's situation; it is, more immediately, a strategy of actively coping with it. In translating *my* suffering into the suffering of my people, *I* is transformed into *we*. By the same token, the person who caused my suffering is stripped of his or her particular identity and transformed into an instance of *they,* or further depersonalized as *it.* This

---

9. Aboriginal accounts of such historical figures as Captain Cook and Ned Kelly blur the line between what we would distinguish as myth and history. Among older Kuku-Yalanji informants, Chris Anderson notes, Captain Cook is mythologized as "the archetypal European" (Anderson 1984, 336). In Yarralin stories, Captain James Cook is often conflated with Dr. Cecil Cook, protector of aborigines in the Northern Territory from 1927 to the late 1930s—"a persona of conquest, the quintessential immoral European . . . the archetype of lawlessness" (Rose 1992, 187, 199; see also Maddock 1988).

transformation of particular subjective experience into a universalized and transsubjective category enables one to grasp and control a situation one experienced first in solitude and powerlessness. It is always easier to bear personal suffering if one can experience it as something shared by many others. Through the sense of kinship born of this identification with fellow sufferers one is able to find common cause against a common foe.[10] The belittling sense of having been singled out and persecuted because of some failing in oneself yields to an empowering sense of being part of a collective tragedy, a shared trauma. No matter what the wound, it is easier to act as one of many who have been victims of a historical wrong than it is to act as the isolated and sole victim of a personal slight.

But another transformation is implicated here. For as long as a trauma-tized person feels isolated and alone, his or her suffering is experienced and dealt with intrapsychically. This may take the form of repression, self-blaming, self-loathing, self-abuse, and self-destruction. But solidarity with others in whom one recognizes one's own suffering tends to move the locus of these defenses from the intrapsychic to the intersubjective. First, even seemingly self-destructive behavior such as binge drinking and fighting comes to conform to complex rules of sociality (Collmann 1988). Second, one may appropriate the language with which one is vilified and derogated, and use it half-joking against oneself and one's own kind, so tearing it from the oppressor's grasp, asserting control over it, and nullifying its effects (Jackson 1995, 13; Carter 1991). Third, one may rework events that one suffered in impassivity and silence as shared narratives in which one plays the heroic role of trickster. Self-deprecating humor and parody tend to char-acterize this transformation from victimage to advantage. Consider, for in-stance, the following comments by an aboriginal woman on the subject of rape:

> white girls complain if they are raped. Our girls are ashamed of
> it. They prefer that no one knows because they're afraid to be
> ridiculed. Others laugh. I've talked to Aboriginal women
> who've been raped by whites, Greeks, Japanese, Chinese or
> whatever, and they just toss it off as a joke. A lot of these sto-
> ries come to us in pidgin English and it does sound funny. It
> turns out that's one way of covering up their shame, . . . by

10. Basil Sanson (1982) describes this national aboriginal sense of shared identity and relatedness, defined historically through a contrast with settler culture, as "the Aboriginal commonality."

laughing at it. The actual part of a rape, the horrible part, I've never heard that laughed about. But the tricks that lead up to it, the goings on. They talk about it in such a way that it belittles the man who did it. (Gilbert 1978, 20)

In her account of her journey by camel across the Western desert, Robyn Davidson writes of how her Pitjantjatjara traveling companion, Eddie, dealt with an incident in which a white tourist denigrated him by calling him "Jacky-Jacky" and "boy" and ordering him to "come and stand alonga camel" for a photograph. While Davidson was consumed by indignation and anger, Eddie "turned himself into a perfect parody of a ravingly dangerous idiot boong," playing the tourists' stereotypes back at them as burlesque. In this way he turned the tables on the tourists, making them the victims of their own ignorance. Laughing hysterically at the episode later, Davidson saw how bitterness and victimage could be averted through ludic action (1980, 182–84).

Richard Broome has written perceptively of this strategy of the trickster, the ways in which aboriginals mimicked European bosses, assigned them derisive nicknames, or used subterfuge as payback:

> The unhappy peanut farmer in the north saw his best peanuts disappear all day into the mouths of Aboriginal pickers. Aboriginal stockmen on a muster could kill a prime cow, enjoy the good beef and then disguise the carcase to look like a natural death or a dingo killing. Aboriginal boys were expert at spearing vegetables through the cat door of the station store, or at tunnelling under the floor to drain out the flour and sugar from the bags on the bottom row. Others sabotaged the bosses' equipment. One manager claimed that his "dumb" and "lazy" Aboriginal workers could not be trusted to apply even a few drops of oil periodically to the bore-water rigs and that 25 had blown up in two years at a cost of $5000 each. Strangely, the bore at the Aboriginal camp never broke down. (Broome 1982, 135)

Warlpiri informants described similar strategies to me, detailing how they used all manner of underhand methods—trickery, mimicry, theft, recalcitrance—to counter exploitation and prejudice (Jackson 1995, 96–100). And as many first-contact accounts testify, aboriginal people often told self-disparaging, mimetically inventive, and ludicrous stories about their own initial ignorance of whites as a way of dealing with their traumatic loss of control (Dawson 1981, 105–6).

Another mode of "oppositional practice," sometimes spoken of as a culture of resistance (Cowlishaw 1988), may arise from everyday coping strategies, though it should not be analytically conflated with or reduced to them.[11] Here the ethos of the "oppressor" is openly scorned, political activism appears, and nationalism takes hold. The vilified self is now projected onto a vilified other. Self-hatred becomes a hatred of another, self-blaming is replaced by a search for scapegoats. Instead of withdrawing into oneself, one now withdraws socially from the other, who has become the paradigmatic not-self who once categorized and classified oneself as an abhorred alien.

MY WIFE AND I QUICKLY DISCOVERED that our interactions with people in and around the aboriginal settlement of Wujal Wujal on the Bloomfield River could not be disengaged from these intersubjective strategies that synthesized Kuku-Yalanji cultural patterns and defensive behaviors born of the history of contact with white miners, pearlers, administrators, missionaries, tourists, and travelers.

Though our aboriginal hosts were not so unreasonable and embittered to expect us to single-handedly make good their loss of land, livelihood, and autonomy, we were culturally implicated in the world that had disempowered them. Moreover, because we had undertaken to help in the struggle to reclaim traditional land, our *raison d'être* was construed not in terms that we defined but in terms defined for us by our hosts. This definitional process reflected a deep-seated contrast between insiders and outsiders, itself embedded in an existential contrast between the world one knows and has some control over and the world one grasps and controls with far less certainty.

Anthropologists have documented in great detail the ways in which, throughout aboriginal Australia, the social contrast between in-group and out-group (initiates and noninitiates, locals and strangers, etc.) encompasses and implicates a range of analogous contrasts between the inside and outside of the body, restricted and nonrestricted knowledge, and sacred

11. In his brilliant study of peasant insurgency in colonial India, Ranajit Guha observes that "structures of defiance" are "operative in a weak and fragmentary manner even in everyday life and in individual and small-group resistance, but come into their own in the most emphatic and comprehensive fashion when those masses set about turning things upside down and the moderating rituals, cults and ideologies help no longer to maintain the contradictions between subaltern and superordinate at a non-antagonistic level" (1983, 12).

and profane objects, words, and places (Morphy 1991, 78–81; Keen 1994; Myers 1986, 48–62; Jackson 1995, 141). In southeast Cape York the social divide between insiders and outsiders is expressed in everyday life as a pattern of breaks or checks in communication and sharing. Though not always formalized as strict taboos, these discontinuities in exchange have a similar effect to boundary markers. In the first few months of our fieldwork, whenever Francine and I asked people questions we were rebuffed by the identical phrase "I dunno," or with impassivity and silence. John von Sturmer speaks of this aboriginal response to outsiders as "cultural deafness" (1981, 28). Even our request to be taught how to fish—as important for our livelihood as for theirs—was met with indifference. Was it too preposterous that whites should be dependent on *bama?* Was it impossible to believe that we preferred fresh fish to store-bought food? Was the idea of self-consciously teaching a person how to fish too absurd? Or was local knowledge of the sea and river something not to be imparted to outsiders?

All these rhetorical questions contained a grain of truth. But people kept their distance because this was their customary way of interacting with strangers. Rapport could never be hurried or assumed. And sharing information and resources was predicated on trust, which developed gradually, and could only be given by one's host. On the Bloomfield River, moreover, it was quickly borne home to us that food, money, knowledge, and resources were not as a rule distributed outside the family. As Anderson observed, different Kuku-Yalanji "mobs" have "little to do with each other socially" (1984, 375). Shopping, food sharing, and capital consumption are almost invariably concentrated within the "mob" (365–75). One consequence of this self-protectiveness and insularity is that most violence also occurs within the mob (378).[12]

As *jawun* (friends), my wife and I were placed in an anomalous position. Our association with the O'Rourkes made it very difficult to establish ties with other families. From the outset our hosts made it clear to us that our resources should not be shared with others and that our social circle should not extend beyond theirs. But in being incorporated into the family we also became part of the field of contradictions within it, obliged to share our resources—vehicle, knowledge, contacts, time, energy—with our hosts. The tensions and crises that were born of this two-way struggle for auton-

12. Generalizing about all Cape York Peninsular, Sharp observed, "I simply could find no society; I would have to describe it in terms of an ego-centered *set* of societies; no one individual was the center of a system of networks which overlapped isotypically with anyone else's" (Sharp 1968, 159, cited in Sutton and Rigsby 1979, 725; cf. Anderson, note 13 below).

omy and control, while personally trying, proved anthropologically illuminating, for they encapsulated a wider social history and *habitus.*

Clearing the Ground

Our campsite was in a bloodwood grove within hailing distance of the house that Fred, his wife, Amy, and several of Amy's siblings[13] had recently occupied on traditional land purchased for them through an Aboriginal and Torres Strait Island Commission (ATSIC) loan.

First day in the field I borrowed Fred's rake, cane knife, axe, and spade and grubbed skeins of roots, cut out stumps, leveled the ground, and pitched our tent. Then for two weeks I worked alongside Fred and his brother-in-law Benji, cutting, clearing, and finally mowing the long grass around the house with Big Bob, the heavy-duty motor mower I had brought up from Cairns at Fred's request.

While Amy's three brothers were steadfastly reticent, Fred was unnervingly deferential. Though I felt insecure and inept, Fred appeared to assume that I was in charge. When Big Bob broke down, it became clear that since I had bought the motor mower it was up to me to fix it. Though Fred had guessed that it had a four-stroke engine, not a two-stroke as I had assumed, he had said nothing when I mixed oil with the gasoline, causing the spark plug to gum up and the engine to fail. Now, as I struggled to clean the air intake, the air filter, and the spark plug, Fred and his brothers-in-law looked on impassively. My mechanical abilities a sham, my authority bogus, and the situation inescapable, I felt as Orwell described in *Burmese Days* when obliged to shoot a rogue elephant: damned if one did and damned if one didn't.

Feeling that one has been reduced to a parody of oneself is a common experience for cultural strangers. The less one's cultural habits, dispositions, and expectations fit the new milieu, the more they stand out and seem absurd. This exaggerated sense of social ineptitude was increased by Fred's and Benji's reluctance to occupy center stage, leaving it to me, as it were, to initiate actions and call the shots. Even if I had possessed the mechanical

13. The O'Rourkes were typical of Kuku-Yalanji "mobs"—a kindred crystallized about a group of siblings with their spouses and children (Anderson 1984, 382; 1988, 515), though atypical in that the focal figure in the family was a matriarch who had little power or influence beyond the family itself. Amy and her husband made almost daily contact—through visits and fishing expeditions—with Amy's siblings (and their children) not resident on the outstation. Moreover, Amy's infirm and elderly mother, who lived in the senior's home at Wujal Wujal, often came to the outstation on visits.

skills to repair Big Bob, I would have remained *socially* conspicuous and vulnerable, because this was a culture where keeping a low profile, maintaining obliqueness and indirection in communication, and avoiding initatives for which one might later be made to take the rap and thereby be shamed, were, I was beginning to learn, characteristic strategies of intersubjective engagement. Webb Keane calls this a strategic "separation of voice and agency" (1997, 140).

"Might be a good idea to make another heap away from that fruit tree," Fred said to me one day, subtly avoiding a direct order (which I might have taken amiss) yet obliquely referring to the fact that the last pile of leaves I had burned had damaged a nearby fruit tree.

So ubiquitous is this circumspective style of talking that von Sturmer advocates it as a "primary consideration" for cross-cultural conversation in aboriginal Australia:

> Partly it consists of not presenting oneself too forcefully and not linking oneself too closely with one's own ideas. If a topic is known to be touchy, apologise in advance: 'I don't know if I talk right way or wrong way. But can't be helped. I got job to talk about this thing. If I talk wrong way, well we might have to think different way . . . .' There should be an extensive use of conditionals: 'Might be', 'could be', 'might be some people talk/think that way . . .', and so on. Leave oneself an escape route: 'Might be I right or wrong . . .'. Do not talk loudly or aggressively (known as 'talking rough'). Do not interrupt another person when he/she is speaking, even when what they are saying is nonsense. (von Sturmer 1981, 29)

Initially, my wife and I were not free to renegotiate our status. We had to wait for the family to accord us fictive kinship or adopt us as friends. This rendered us liminal. Estranged from the image we had of ourselves, we found ourselves thrust into stereotypical roles that reflected a complex history of *bama*[14] experience with whites: an amalgam of moral rectitude and paternalism associated ostensibly with the values of missionaries, and a nononsense, uncouth ockerism (or "red-neckism") associated with dealings with locals. For instance, a few days after we had set up camp, the family gathered for a feast of green turtles cooked in an earth oven. But Fred did not deign to offer us any meat, assuming that whites did not like it. And when he confided that he and Amy had married a few years ago, though

---

14. *Bama* is the word used throughout southeast Cape York for an aboriginal person.

they'd lived together as man and wife for about nineteen years, I sensed that he assumed I would disapprove of such an unsanctified relationship.

Things came to a head on Christmas Day, three months into our field-work. The family had gathered at the outstation for the holiday, coming from as far afield as the related aboriginal settlements of Mossman and Hopevale. Billy, Amy's younger brother, was drunk. All morning he moved among us muttering about how strangers camped and fished on Weary Bay without any acknowledgment of the fact that it was his land, where he had been born and raised. Just before lunch Billy expressed irritation at Fran-cine, whom he had expected to drive to the mission to pick up his mother and aunt. Although it had already been arranged that someone else would fetch them, Billy began swearing at and castigating Francine.

Fred lost his temper. Amy too.

"You don't talk like that to *jawun* [friend]," Amy remonstrated. "She's our friend, she's helping us, she's not just anybody, she's not *bama,* she's *waybala.* You don't talk to *waybala* like that. You just stupid."

As Amy went on in this vein, Fred stepped up and hit Billy hard in the face. Then, backing away a little, he punched him again on the face and on the side of the head, cutting open one of his brother-in-law's ears. "You hurt Francine's feelings! You don't do that," he shouted. And belted Billy again.

Billy's sullen drinking mate, Richard, expressed no loyalty. "You're a dick head," he said, distancing himself from the whole affair.

As Fred backed off, Billy's sister, Jessie, thumped and upbraided him as well.

Both Francine and I felt responsible for precipating the fight, and we felt bad for Billy—the victim, the youngest son, at the bottom of the peck-ing order in the family. But I was also shocked to realize that we were still stereotyped as white bourgeoisie—set apart by a supposed refinement of sensibility, a concern for decorum and respectability.

As we were getting ready to eat, Billy drunkenly staggered back to the trestle table and took eight cans of soda. "What, yous having a party? Is it a funeral or something? Must be a funeral, someone died."

He blundered off down the track toward the gate as Fred hurled after him: "You bloody idiot. And I'll tell you that when you're sober too, you bloody idiot."

THE TERMS OF INTERSUBJECTIVE ENGAGEMENT shift subtly from culture to culture. On Cape York, as elsewhere in aboriginal Australia, grievances are aired and performed publicly. At the same time, fighting is an important aspect of sociality, a way of squaring accounts, getting satisfaction, and asserting autonomy (von Sturmer 1981, 18; Myers 1986, 161, 171). As a mode of negotiating a sense of existential parity between people, it is seldom anomic; on the contrary, it enables the rapid and effective settlement of grudges. As for empathy, it would be a mistake to see it, either, as an entirely spontaneous and subjective affair. Nor, once negotiated, can it be guaranteed to last. If enmity is short-lived, so too is empathy. Accordingly, intersubjective relations are continually modulated as circumstances change, and empathic and combative behavior are equally important modes of negotiating relative distance between self and other. At the same time, both empathy and enmity must be understood as cultural "acts" that are performed for practical and social purposes rather than simply expressed as a matter of private and emotional need.

In both performative modes, the exchange of words is often secondary or superfluous.

What broke down the cultural distance between Fred and myself was not some abstract attitude but a developing habit of working together and exchanging stories. But at no time would my fieldwork consist in questioning. At the outset I discovered that even the most trivial or casual inquiry smacked of prying, and undermined the need people had to feel in control of their relationship with us. So I learned to work with Fred and Benji in silence, cutting through entangled vines, grubbing out small palms, slashing grass, raking dead leaves, and burning stacks of debris in the evenings when the wind had died. When we laid off work and sat in the shade of the raintree to rest or slake our thirst, we told stories. But always, at first, stories about neutral subjects.

I told Fred about my experiences in West Africa and central Australia. In turn he told me how one could make a decoction of green ants (*yangka*) to cure colds and treat chest complaints, how one should watch out for death adders hidden under fallen bloodwood leaves, how roasted resin from ironwood roots could be worked into a black cement (like the spinifex resin used in central Australia) for fixing spearheads and woomera nocks. As I watched him mould the black tar and later shape a woomera with his penknife, he told me these were skills he learned from his father. I had a strong impression that in doing exactly what his father and "the old men" once did, Fred was resuscitating them in his memory—his kinship with them realized not as an abstract image but as a *relationship* based on the mimetic reenactment of a craft skill.

Indeed, a similarly embodied memory informs a lot of contemporary foraging; in walking where one's ancestors walked, fishing where they fished, camping where they camped, and treating ailments as they did (with wild plants, insects, and shellfish) one effectively reenters the past and reconnects with one's predecessors. This may explain why, though English is now used as much as Kuku-Yalanji in everyday life, *bama* always have recourse to the vernacular when hunting or pointing out bush tucker (*minya:* protein food, such as tree goannas, green turtle, and flying fox; *mayi:* vegetable food such as wild plums and bush cherries).

After a few days working together Fred began to recount something of his Lamalama roots. He grew up fearful of whites. His family used to hide from them, avoiding contact at all costs. As a small child walking the beaches of Princess Charlotte Bay with his family, foraging for turtle eggs, fishing, and camping, everyone would flee into the scrub when the police came. The police meant trouble—one's childen forcibly taken away or arbitrary arrests. That's why *bama* were so "shy," Fred told me. Withdrawal was the best tactic for keeping out of trouble.

When he was nine he was taken from his parents to work on a cattle station. The white station boss came to the *bama* camp one day and said he wanted the boy. If Fred's parents had refused they would have risked being deported to Palm Island along with children of mixed marriages and recalcitrants.

"Couldn't your parents have hidden you?" I asked.

"We weren't game to go and hide in the scrub. You couldn't go far anyway."

"What if you tried to run away?"

"Get beaten, taken back. Nowhere to go anyway."

When I asked Fred if he got homesick, he said he cried for his parents all the time.

"Was there any one you could turn to, to take care of you?"

"I tried," he said, and described an old aboriginal man who took him under his wing for a while. "It was a hard life," Fred said. "When I was young we couldn't leave the job on the station."

He saw his parents only once a year, at Christmas time. "But back then, in those days, we didn't think things could be different. *Bama* were "shy" of whites. Only now did he realize how unjust things were. "We had to work with bosses and that, you know, station owners. We had to. If we had to go anywhere we had to get permission from police. Sometimes they'd say yes. Sometimes they'd say no. We had to stay in the same place.

Always those bosses telling us what to do. They always had the upper hand. They'd use whips, fists, rifles, anything, and you couldn't hit back."

But one time Fred did.

His boss abused him for no good reason. "Then he banged me," Fred said, smashing his fist into his cupped hand to make the point. Fred did not retaliate immediately, but two days later approached the white boss and asked why he had punched him in the face, what he'd done to deserve that. The boss refused to explain, but threatened to sock Fred again. Fred pressed his question, readying himself for a fight. As soon as the boss threw a punch, Fred leaned to one side, then walloped the boss full in the face, bloodying his nose. As the two men wrestled on the ground, blood was everywhere.

Fred hesitated, pained at the recollection.

"You shouldn't settle arguments that way," he said. "I reckon it's wrong what I did."

He was taken to the police station at Laura and thrown into the lockup. He feared the worse. "But things were already changing then," he said. "We were getting our freedom. They let me go."

IT SOON BECAME CLEAR to me that Fred's deferential attitude implied neither respect for white authority nor expertise, but a need to avert confrontation and open disagreement. It was, as it were, a kind of avoidance behavior.

In southeast Cape York, avoidance and joking encapsulate contrasted poles of intersubjective life (Thomson 1935). In both cases, verbal and nonverbal modalities of behavior merge to register or mark degrees of social distance between specific categories of people. As John Haviland has demonstrated in his detailed studies of in-law languages among the Guugu-Yimidhirr, respectful and familiar speech styles imply social distinctions between classificatory and close kin, respectively, and between affinal and consanguineal kin, and involve two metaphorically distinctive modes of address: the first, "indirect" and "slow and soft"; the second "straight," "hard," "loud and rapid," "sharp, abrupt and peremptory" (Haviland 1979a; 1979b). These modes of interlocution entail intercorporeal and mimetic behaviors such that circumspection in speaking involves averting one's eyes and "turning away," by contrast with direct "face to face" encounters where one can speak and act with less constraint. Critical to understanding these distinctions between respectful avoidance and familiarity is "a tension between sexuality and its control" (Haviland 1979a, 378). Avoidance relations connote genealogical or geographical distance (a man formerly married from "far away," preferably a woman from another dialect area); joking connote consanguinity and propinquity. This is why avoidance and joking both allude to sexuality; in the first case, by studious obviation, in the second, by organized obscenity. By and large, the greater the social distance between people, the greater the focus on controls over speech and physical contact. The remote was "poison" or "dangerous" to the degree that one lacked confident control over it.

Although joking and avoidance (in both Guugu-Yimidhirr and Kuku-Yalanji) are less and less systematically implemented as socially appropriate behaviors between determinate categories of kin and affines, they remain important coping strategies, available for use in a variety of intersubjective situations. That is to say that the behaviors are not determined by the contexts to which they are *conventionally* tied, but may be used opportunistically as ways of dealing with any ambiguous or fraught situation. In Wujal Wujal as in Hopevale, avoidance is not only conceptualized as a rule, it is implemented and experienced intercorporeally. In approaching another group's camp, for example (and such wariness also obtains in approaching a sacred site), one is careful not to "sneak up," but to alert people to one's presence by feigning a cough, shuffling one's feet, or walking "in fits and starts" (cf. von Sturmer 1981, 15; Jackson 1995, 29, 37, 141). One must then sit on the margins of the other group, eyes averted or turned toward the ground, saying nothing, waiting for one's hosts to approach with food and thereby initiate social contact. It is considered "cheeky" to behave otherwise, which accounts for why *bama* take such exception to the direct gaze of white strangers, which they construe as aggressive "staring." In the same vein, *bama* will take offense if the beam of a stranger's car lights is shone into their camp or house, or strangers hail them in a shamefully loud voice in a public place. Driving at dusk near the Hann River, far from home, we once passed an ominous-looking Land Rover half-hidden in the scrub. Amy and her sister immediately ducked to avoid contact, but later broke into uncontrolled laughter as they reflected on their anxiety. The point is that direct contact is avoided with places and persons you do not know, and the same circumspection is expected of strangers. As for one's in-laws, "you have to be serious," one man told me. "You can't joke and mess about [*kuya-bungal*] with them." A generation ago, strict avoidance of eye contact, silence, physical separateness, and a ban on eating certain foods maintained this relationship of respect; sensory contact of any kind was considered shameful. Nowadays, however, only the relationship between son-in-law and mother-in-law is treated with such seriousness. Though his mother-in-law was disabled by a stroke, Fred avoided touching or speaking to her. One day, when the old woman lost her footing as she was climbing out of our vehicle, Fred impulsively grabbed her arm to prevent her from falling. Later he told me how unsettled he'd felt. The flat of his hand held a little way from his floating rib, he confessed: "It was not really right."

Since avoidance behaviors are not binding rules that are slavishly followed but coping strategies that may be implemented in a variety of situations, it is not surprising that they have changed their conventional locus with changing times. Consider patterns of in-law avoidance (*warrki*). As aboriginal sociopolitical horizons widened in the colonial period, whites supplanted in-laws as the paradigmatic strangers within, ambiguously placed between enemies and kinsmen. In a sense, *bama* have invoked and used the traditional form of in-law avoidance to deal with their ambiguous relationship with whites—a category of persons one can never trust, whose intentions one can never read, and whose behavior is often deprecatory and invasive. At the same time, the enforced concentration of people on missions and reserves has made it difficult to conform to traditional marriage rules. Social differentiation has become increasingly ambiguous because in-laws are also kin. And physical propinquity often makes avoidance well-nigh impossible. But the weakened adherence to rules of in-law avoidance should be seen, not as a loss of tradition, but as a strategic response to the changing social character and permeable social boundaries of the Kuku-Yalanji world.

Culture, in this view, is both raw material *and* finished product—a resource on which people draw in negotiating the stony ground of intersubjective life *and* a set of constraints that define the parameters of individual freedom. Deconstructing the macrocosmic language of social groups and social institutions into the microcosmic field of lived interpersonal relationships enables one to see that cultural forms enter into and figure in, rather than completely determine and delimit, the strategic field of social interaction and intersubjective experience. All too often anthropologists hypostatize and ontologize their analytical concepts, assuming them to actually inhere in and determine the course of the events they purport to explain. This denies or occludes indigenous ways of expressing and explaining experience, and fosters an exoticizing typological process whereby different societies are set apart in terms of social institutions that are accorded exaggerated and reified value—lineages in Africa, honor and shame in the Mediterranean, knowledge, belief, and art in aboriginal Australian (cf. Abu-Lughod 1993, 27; 1996, 274).

Kuku-Yalanji culture is less defined by exotically distinctive ceremonies, artifacts, myths, and beliefs than by strategic modes of coping that reflect both traditional norms and historical innovations. Indeed, I consider it wise to bracket out questions as to whether the coping strategies I outline in the following pages are "traditional" or "modern," "magical" or "political." What is at issue is not whence beliefs derive or what beliefs "mean" in any essentialistic or epistemological sense but what people do with their beliefs, what follows from their use. Meaning is therefore tied to changing existential situations that are only partly conditioned by cultural or historical precedents. Accordingly, one may understand the dialectics of identity not in purely cultural or political terms but in terms of an existential struggle for choice, control, presence, and ontological security. And ontological security may be threatened equally by cultural invasion, bureaucratic subversion, and *personal* forces that work against an individual's sense of integrity and well-being.

The Bag of Clothes

After several months in the field we had gone from being strangers (*ngarr-bal*) to being *jawun*. *Jawun* or *jawun-karra* may, in different contexts, connote anything from "friend/guest" (much like the term *stranger* in West Africa [Skinner 1963; Fortes 1975; cf. Simmel 1950]) to "countryman" (comparable to *walytja* [Pintupi] and *warlalja* [Warlpiri] in central Australia—"people who belong to the same place, to the same country" (Jackson 1995, 64–65), including actual and metaphorical "family," sharing common interests, and "whose daily lives are tied together" (Myers 1986:56). In the words of one Kuku-Yalanji man, *jawun* are "friends from other places." Living with a *bama* family one is expected to give ungrudgingly as a kinsman, yet as a stranger and sojourner one is kept at a distance. In being categorized and addressed as *jawun* we had lost the aura, authority, and foreignness of whites but had gained few of the advantages—as, say, affines do—of adoptive kinship. Though our three-and-a-half-year-old son, Joshua, a threat to no one, *was* called "brother," Francine and I, as *jawun,* were placed in a position where the O'Rourkes felt secure and in control.

As strangers we had no rights or claims over anyone, unlike kinship and affinity that may be invoked opportunistically to elicit acceptance, inclusion, and care. One often saw this at work with drunks. "Give me a cigarette, you my full uncle," a claimant would shout. Or, "You my cousin." In the *bama* view such tactical use of kinship terms averts the shame of asking. No one would stigmatize a kinsperson by refusing his or her request, even if it was made abusively and drunkenly. Invoking kinship was thus a way of safeguarding oneself, of soliciting respect, of avoiding humiliation. Kinship implies knownness. Being *jawun,* Francine and I could neither expect nor invoke such familial immunity.

IN EARLY NOVEMBER we headed north to attend a meeting on a remote out-station at which important issues connected with the Lakefield land claim were to be discussed. This was Fred's country, his land claim, though the whole family made the trip, Francine and I included.

We started late after a hectic morning driving Amy's mother home to Wujal Wujal, dropping Fred's puppy off at his brother's house, and smuggling Amy's niece, Sunday, away from the mission. Sunday's husband was on a bender, and, fearful for her children's safety, she had decided to take refuge in another community.

The last twenty miles was one of the worst roads I'd ever driven over, and by the time we pitched our tents that evening in a grove of mango and custard apple trees above a dry river bed everyone was bone-tired and irritable. Tensions were only exacerbated by the mosquitoes and sandflies, and the rotting fruit and cattle dung that littered the ground.

Amy and Jessie, Amy's sister, slumped into lethargy and homesickness. As Jessie complained that the ground was too hard under her tent, Amy bemoaned the absence of amenities. "They should bring us wood and water," she said, implying that the land council workers were not doing their job. "How we going to get *mayi* [food]?" And it was too hot, she said. There was no shade. Her feet were swollen and sore. Her mouth was stinging from the pineapple she'd eaten.

As I toiled with Fred to level the ground under Amy's tent, Fred kept up a running, scathing criticism of his wife and sister-in-law. "We not slaves," he said. "We slept on the ground in the *murri* camp. My mother worked hard. She didn't complain. Carried water, carried wood. We never just sat around waiting to be helped. We had it hard. We had to work all the time. No one carried our loads for us."

It was one of Fred's preoccupations, this contrast between hard and soft. When he came to live with Amy on an island in the middle of the Bloomfield River in 1975, they would walk the three miles along the beach from the river mouth at Plantation Creek and back without any difficulty. Now they depended on a truck. "Getting soft," Fred said. "Spoiled." Once he confided that he never went to the clinic at Wujal Wujal; he feared the nurses might send him to Cooktown Hospital in the ambulance, and he didn't want to appear "soft."

Now Fred was sharpening his contrast between the soft life of those who had grown up on the missions and the hard life of those who had lived on remote cattle stations. As he muttered on, Jessie sat inside her tent in tears, railing against the injustice of Fred's remarks. She was a stranger in that place, she said. Fred wasn't. It was his traditional land. Fred should be taking care of her because this was his country, these were his people. She wasn't at liberty to take initiatives. "I'm not an animal on four legs. I don't deserve to be treated like a dog."

Amy echoed her sister's complaint, though conspicuously avoided any direct confrontation with her husband.

That night, as I lay awake reflecting on the tensions of the day and how they all seemed to arise from loss and landlessness, an unearthly keening came through the darkness. Ascending and descending scales, a hoarse yet melodic line, a sound as if from sleep disturbed by nightmares, or possession. Fred's brother was convinced someone had died. But it was one of the older Lamalama men, voicing his emotions when his daughter, whom he had not seen for several years, turned up from a distant settlement.

This was the proper way of showing one's feelings, Fred explained. "Fair dinkum," he said, because the tears were real. And we talked for a while of what it was like seeing kinsmen again after many years apart, returning to land from which you had been physically deported, places you had not visited since childhood. "When I went back to our old camp at Lilyfield," Fred said, referring to the cattle station where he was taken to work as a nine-year-old boy, "there was nothing there, only wild pigs. And that made me feel real sad, you know. I left my country a long time ago."

ON THE DAY WE LEFT, rain was threatening and everyone was eager to get away. We broke camp early, packed, and said our good-byes. But Joshua, who'd been unwell, was asleep on a tarpaulin and Francine and I were loathe to wake him. So for half an hour everyone stood around waiting, while I, sweating, filthy and unaided, struggled to tie a tarp over the gear on the roofrack of the Toyota.

When we finally headed south, only Fred expressed his relief, joking loudly with his daughter and nephew. Amy sat stolidly, staring ahead. Jessie gave nothing away. And Billy gazed out the window, his face as inscrutable as a chunk of anthracite.

It was well after nightfall when we got back to the outstation and unloaded the vehicle. As I passed down the swags, bedding, eskies, bags of clothing, and fishing tackle, Billy moved them onto the veranda.

Then, as the last load was dumped, Amy raised a cry of alarm. Opening one of the black plastic garbage bags she found it full of garbage—the identical-looking garbage bags in which she'd put her clothes had been left behind.

She was beside herself with grief. "My blanket, my blanket," she wailed. "That not rubbish, that my blanket, I put it there by that mango tree."

She went indoors, crying remorselessly for her lost possessions, only to emerge again and rummage among the other bags and shine her flashlight into the cab of the Toyota.

Everyone else sat around.

"We in too much hurry," Fred said, setting the tone for the recriminations to follow. "I never like to hurry, always go slow so you don't forget things."

I took this as a reprimand. After all, I had supervised the loading of the vehicle. But Francine remembered asking Billy if the bags under the mango tree were rubbish and Billy saying yes. And I said I had been on the roofrack, with Billy passing things up to me, and therefore hadn't seen the bag of clothes.

Jessie, who quickly had made sure her belongings had not been mislaid, stood in the shadows, crowing over her good fortune not to have lost her gear, congratulating herself on the way she always wrapped her clothes in a carpetbag or tent bag when she traveled. It wasn't wise to use garbage bags.

Billy remained silent.

In this tense atmosphere Francine and I drove back to our camp, resolving to search for the missing clothes at the Hopevale rubbish dump, where all the trash from the land claim meeting had been taken. If we didn't find it there we'd give Amy a blanket and some sheets and reimburse her for her loss. If she pressed us we would return north in the morning and try and locate the garbage bag.

Next morning the storm seemed to have blown over. But then, as we drove from the outstation on our way to the mission to collect Amy's and Fred's pensions, Jessie asked, "Shouldn't we lock up?"

"We don't need to," Fred said. "We got nothing to steal."

It was a reference to his wallet, which had been cleaned out by a visitor from the mission a few days before.

"No blankets or clothes either, eh Fred?" I said.

Everyone laughed except Amy, who dourly repeated my remark in all seriousness, woefully adding "We got no blankets, nothing. We no need to lock up, eh?"

But the laughter had momentarily cleared the air and I hoped the incident had been put behind us.

"We all make mistakes," Fred observed. "We need a blow, too," he added. Princess Charlotte Bay was too far. The blanket could be replaced, and Francine's time was better spent preparing the application for ATSIC funds to repair the toilet block at the outstation.

But the clothes were not forgotten. Two days later Fred said he'd lost his truck key. It must have been in Amy's garbage bag, he said.

The key turned up later that day. But after telling us he'd found it, Fred noted that while we had been away his spare wheel had been taken. "We got to pay that telephone bill, too," he added. And I began to suspect that because we had been held responsible for the missing bag of clothes we were now obliged to make good other losses as well.

Fortunately, news reached us next day that Amy's bag of clothes had been retrieved from the Hopevale dump by someone astute enough to notice the bag did not contain garbage.

That same day Lew, an old friend of Fred's, who had been camping at the outstation, lit a fire that got out of control.

Lew didn't hang around. He left the outstation to avoid a confrontation.

Now all the anger that had been directed at us was turned against Lew. Jessie was all for kicking him off the outstation. Fred's face was clouded with anger as he complained about Lew not asking him for permission to burn off, informing no one when the fire got away from him. But we, at last, were off the hook. The deadlock in *our* relationship with the family had been broken by a more marginal, more dispensable individual, a third party onto whom tensions could now be displaced.

THESE EVENTS DISCLOSE a lot about people's relations with outsiders, whether these are locals from different "mobs," people from other settlements, or whites. And they also invite discussion of the role of avoidance and joking in coping with stress and resolving conflict.

Like many recurrent crises in contemporary Kuku-Yalanji life, crowdedness is a root cause. Feeling crowded out precipitates a crisis of control. No longer in charge of one's social situation, one feels imposed on, encroached on, and pushed. In a place where people customarily camped, hunted, and fished in small family groups, and where dense concentrations of people were only ever temporary, respect and autonomy alike were inextricably tied to control over social distance (cf. Reser 1979). Wujal Wujal is one of the most overcrowded aboriginal settlements in Australia. One informant remarked to ethnographer Christopher Anderson that there was so little room to move that one felt "like a crane standing on one leg on a little island." But crowdedness implicates time as well as space—something that was brought home to me whenever people spoke of the strictly imposed timetables of the mission regime. Fred's observation that he was being hurried away from the outstation—which is to say, pressed to pack up in *our* time rather than at his own pace—reflected a similar sense of subverted autonomy. The crises that periodically exploded under these kinds of space-time pressures involved a peremptory reassertion of social distance. During the Christmas fight Amy in effect demanded that Billy remain more distant from Francine as a mark of respect. Abused as "stupid" (that is, socially unskilled), Billy reacted by distancing himself from the outstation; he went and stayed with a sister elsewhere for several weeks. When Lew realized he had overstepped the mark and become a scapegoat, he hurriedly packed up and went away. And on several occasions when fights erupted, Amy and Fred went down to Weary Bay and set up camp there. One also observed this need for what Erving Goffman called "spacing" (1963) in fishing and foraging activities. Almost every evening we drove to Weary Bay or the mouth of the Bloomfield River to fish. The adults stood about fifty yards apart from one another, focused on their fishing, keeping their own counsel. The children played freely along the beach with the older ones exhorted intermittently with hoarse shouts to watch out for the younger ones. Amy once confided that this was the best time— when you could be calm and composed, when you could concentrate on what you were doing without unpredictable distractions and impinging demands.

In such instances, avoidance is a strategy for reestablishing respectful physical and social distance. Shame—the inverse of respect—is thus an expression of inappropriate proximity, incest being the most extreme example. But avoidance is not only a way of countermanding relations that have become too close for comfort; it is a preemptive way of averting confrontation. *Bama* habitually avoid initiating or being seen to initiate actions so that they will not bear the brunt of censure if things go wrong. If matters do get out of hand, the same habits of deflection and displacement come into play. People disclaim responsibility and disown their part in the event, often laying the blame on someone who is marginal or otherwise unable to respond. Even close members of the family will be scapegoated if they are absent. This constant diversion of attention away from oneself often appears to an outsider as a self-abnegating form of inertia or obduracy. But silence is a kind of self-immunization, a form of social camouflage. Thus Amy avoided a fight with Fred, even though she shared the hurt of her sister Jessie, by appearing not to hear what was going on. And keeping one's distance from a potentially explosive situation may also be accomplished by dumping on an outsider.

Scapegoating reflects subtle ground rules of family politics. Impasses in the power games within dyad relations are resolved by having recourse to a weaker third party. By blaming the most marginal adult in the "mob" (in this case, Billy, the single man and youngest son), the family core retains its solidarity and integrity. Yet Billy could "take" the rap and fight back in ways a child or disabled person could not, and it is important to emphasize that scapegoating in the part of Cape York of which I had experience does not run to victimizing or abusing dependent children.

The defensive search for self-closure thus extends to the family itself. Just as individuals who feel threatened become taciturn and withdrawn or move away, so an individual family tends to reestablish its integrity by avoiding and distancing itself from anyone who in its eyes constitutes a threat to it.

If avoidance tends to seal a person or family off from others, joking works against such insularity, such impermeable boundaries. Avoidance and joking are, in this sense, contrasted moments in a dialectic of closure and openness. If avoidance entails moving apart, joking enables people to come back together. Thus in endeavoring to make light of the loss of Amy's clothes—restructuring the event playfully as a shared story—Fred and I prevented the episode hardening into a permanent separation. In this sense, joking is forgiving and redemptive.

Ghosts

In the bloodwood groves and rainforests of southeast Cape York, people are surrounded by many ghosts—ghosts of the known dead; the unquiet ghosts of a violent history, ghosts with vengeance on their minds.

It is impossible to ignore this numberless and nebulous community of lost souls. They assume a life of their own. But most significantly, they reflect the extent to which everyday life is pervaded by the experience of interrelationship: an unflagging conversational concern for absent kin, and for the comings and goings of those to whom one is most attached.

In a seminal paper on Nukulaelae spirits, Niko Besnier observes that the unsystematic, capricious, and often heteroglossic world of ghosts poses not only a problem for those on whose lives they impinge; it constitutes a problem for traditional models of anthropological explanation with "their emphasis on structure and coherence" (Besnier 1996, 76). Elkin, writing in 1938, considered aboriginal thinking about spirits "confused" because it failed to be clear about the fate of the soul immediately after death (1943, 342). Yet such "inconsistency" accurately reflects the ambiguity of ghosts and memory alike.

The most commonly used term for ghosts or shades in Kuku-Yalanji is *dubu*.[15] While an anthropologist might admit that an after-image or memory survives the loss of a loved one, aboriginal people tend to project this after-image as a separate, independent, wandering soul. And where we might speak of the bereaved as experiencing ambivalence toward the dead—mourning and drawn to them at the same time as they feel abandoned and angered by them—aboriginal people attribute these mixed feelings to the shades themselves. This is why ghosts are felt to haunt and often hound the living; they are incensed by their isolation and ostracism. Putting the names of the dead out of circulation for a generation (*burri-kari*) and abandoning a house or camp one shared with the deceased are ways of distancing the living from the dead. But more pertinently they are ways of controlling the boundary between these domains. Thus shamanistic healers, who are better able than most to control interactions between human and spirit worlds, may tap ghostly powers for the social good. Avoidance, however, is the norm. This is why one is told never to leave water around a camp when one is away; thirsty ghosts may come and take over the place. In the same vein, ritual fumigation (*kunjirr*) of the possessions of the dead is imperative if one is not to be tormented by their spirit.[16]

---

15. Several other terms denote particular kinds of spirit or phases in the life history of spirits; *dajay* is the spirit of a person immediately after death, *binyu* the spirit of a person manifest as a shooting star, and *bayin* the spirit of a dead child (Oates 1993, 78–79).

16. This is why there was such outrage when a jail was built adjacent to the cemetery at Wujal Wujal. Isolated and confined, a person in a cell would be more than usually susceptible to the unpredictable shades that filled the graveyard.

As time passes and the dead become more imperfectly remembered, they become increasingly ambiguous. This is because ghosts merge vestigial memories of precursors and predecessors (past time) with images of the shadowy, minatory world of otherness that lies around one but eludes control—the *space* of the long dead, of strangers and enemies. Indeed, no longer solely made up of *persons* who have passed away, ghosts come to encapsulate *things* one feels one has lost—one's land, traditional livelihood, language, and culture. The sense of loss that pervades much of aboriginal Australia must be understood in existential as well as substantive terms, as a loss of balance and control over what are seen as the vital elements of one's sociocultural identity. One's deep sense of absence—of ghosts—is the measure of this existential loss. Accordingly, the relationship between people and the spirit world is fraught with the same problems that beset relations between aboriginal and nonaboriginal Australians. The question as to how a viable distance can be maintained between the living and the dead is at the same time a matter of how one can maintain some kind of control over one's relationships with strangers.

IT WAS A YEAR AFTER RACHEL'S husband's death, and people had driven from as far afield as Mossman and Hopevale for the "clothes burning." Late in the day we sat outside the house that Rachel and her family had vacated a year ago, speaking little, watching as logs were fed into the fire in the pit in the backyard.

Rachel was driven into the yard in a vehicle. Crying and wailing, she had to be helped from the car. A heavily built woman, made heavier by the burden of her resuscitated grief, she collapsed into a chair still crying, among the posessions she and her husband had once shared.

The house had already been "smoked," ritually fumigated. Now the boxes of clothes, bed linen, blankets, and kitchenware stacked around the fire were to be given the same treatment—held out over the flames and decontaminated of the spirit of their late owner. It is usually a sister's son of the deceased who "burns" the clothes, but Parker Jones felt too unsteady on his feet to stand close to the pit, and Fred was asked to stand in for him. "He was related," I was told, "but not too close."

Benji—who had been drinking and was therefore less inhibited than usual—explained what was happening. "*Bama* way," he told me. "Now the *dubu* won't torment anyone. You won't hear voices at night, you'll be able to sleep, you won't have accidents." As for Rachel, "she free now,"

Benji added with some embarrassment, bemused by the idea of the old woman remarrying.

It was often like this. People only opened up and told me about customary ways of doing things when they were drunk. The Lutherans had worked long and hard to disparage and deny Kuku-Yalanji beliefs, and *bama* were only too acutely aware of white skepticism. Fred had a habit of joking to me about local beliefs: a way of distancing himself from them in case I judged them absurd. One afternoon when the sky over the range became grey and ominous, Fred commented, "Might rain soon." Then, turning to Amy, he added "Better tell that storm to wait until we get the tent up." I took this remark as a concession to my supposed inability to believe that by burning grass tree and ironwood bark Amy could ward off storms.

It was the same with ghosts, and it was a long time before Fred talked to me about them with any seriousness. When he did, he studiously avoided the first person, as if to save face in the event of my scoffing at his admissions.

"*Bama* really believe in ghosts," he said as we drove back to the outstation from Wujal the night of the clothes burning.

Next evening, fishing at the boat ramp, Fred raised the subject again, this time providing a more specific context. Speaking of a couple from Hopevale who were related to Amy and had been staying at the outstation, Fred said, "Jimmy's gone away. Karen's scared to sleep in the house on her own."

Karen was Jimmy's wife.

"Why is that?" I asked.

"*Dubu.*"

Fred called a young bloke over to where we were sitting.

"*Bama* really believe in ghosts, eh?" he asked the younger man, but snorting, as if disclaiming the idea.

The young man nodded.

"It's easy to become frightened in an empty house or a deserted camp," I said, and explained how I disliked being alone in our house in Bloomington, Indiana. How the woodwork creaked at night. "No one likes being alone, cut off from their loved ones," I added. "I think this is why people are afraid of the dark, afraid of ghosts."

Though I did not want to explain away the fear of ghosts by claiming that it was a projection of separation anxiety, Fred seemed to appreciate my willingness to find some common ground. Whereas on other occasions he had been critical of people who were afraid to be on their own, boasting that he and Amy were never scared when at the outstation by themselves, he now yielded a little. He told me of lights he had seen. How these lights were evidence that the spirits of the dead were all around us.[17] And he explained that *dubu* shy away from groups of people, only haunting and harassing people when they are alone.

A critical issue arises here. In the first years of life a child's sense of self is so dependent on the mother's familiar presence that her absence or loss may be experienced as a "narcissistic trauma," as severe as the loss of a part of the child's body (Bowlby 1975, 443). Many psychological anthropologists have argued that the same degree of separation anxiety obtains among adults in small-scale non-Western societies, particularly on occasions when a person is alone, in darkness, or outside his or her home community (Levy 1973, 151–53). Trepidation over ghosts is a projective expression of this anxiety and, as Fred's comments make clear, is connected to the intensity with which people identify with others. William James observed that "the great source of terror in infancy is solitude" (cited in Bowlby 1975, 448), but the same is true of any society in which adult subjectivity or selfhood is not systematically separated from the field of social relations in the form of iconic individualism, privacy, and personality. The fear of ghosts is, therefore, not an index of undeveloped or weak egos but of the positive value placed on intersubjective existence.

THE NEXT TIME the subject of ghosts was broached was when one of Amy's relatives, Cynthia, came back from Mossman with Fred after a funeral. Cynthia related how a light, which she called "the eye of the dead," had followed them as they drove over the Rex range. When Fred accelerated, the light did too, keeping pace with the Toyota. "Bright, eh?" Cynthia exclaimed. "Really bright."

"What do you think it was?" I asked.

"Might be that dead man they buried yesterday at Mossman," Cynthia said.

ANOTHER INCIDENT: one night Jessie woke to find the electric torch turned on. "How come it was turned on? No one left it on," Jessie said. And she

---

17. In Kuku-Yalanji thought, ghosts of the newly-dead manifest and move about as fireflies, travelling back to the country where they were born.

explained how she had removed the batteries, hoping the torch would not turn on again, but spent a restless and sleepless night. In the morning there was a phone call from Mossman. A relative had died.

SOME WEEKS LATER Fred told me more about these lights. Not long ago, camped on the beach at Weary Bay, he and Amy saw what looked like the beam of a torch among the trees a hundred yards away. Shortly thereafter, news reached them that a relative had died.

Fred said he believed in such portents though he knew whites did not take them seriously. He was fascinated with UFOs. As a young man of seventeen or eighteen, he had been keeping a night watch over some cattle that had been corralled during the day when he saw what may have been a meteor in the sky (my interpretation), a blue light ascending. Not long after this, news reached him that a close relative had died.

AS THESE ANECDOTES MAKE CLEAR, ghosts are not only traces of the past, they are auguries of the immediate future. Recurrent reminders of what has already passed away, they also presage imminent loss. As such, ghosts embody an unflagging sense that the world wears away, that one's autonomy is forever being undermined, that the border between one's own tentative yet seemingly stable world and the ever-encroaching wider world can never be safeguarded. All one can do is stick together (ghosts don't trouble people in company), asserting the solidarity of family in the face of the forces that mass against it. But there is a difference between losses that one can accept as in the nature of things, such as the death of the elderly, and losses that are seen as avoidable because they are the result of human agency. In such losses there is inevitably a sense of outrage and of injustice.

Seldom did I experience this more keenly than when we accompanied the family on a trip to Wyal-Wyal to visit Frank Roper, an old *waybul* (white fellow) who was said to have in his possession a set of photos taken a hundred years ago that depicted the aboriginal people—Amy's forebears, in fact—who lived near the cane fields that flourished there at the time.

Frank Roper fancied himself as a local historian. It turned out that his photos had been copied from Walter Roth's ethnographies and from the Oxley Library, in Brisbane. One, dated 1876, showed about fifty "natives" in a bloodwood clearing. The men and boys were standing, some with woomeras and spears, all with overlapped hands covering their genitals.

The women, with their babies, sat at the men's feet. A plurality of isola-
tions, to use Sartre's phrase, a group of persons constituted not in any social
relationship with one another but solely through an artificial relationship
with the alien cameraman under whose orders they have lined up (Sartre
1982, 256). Now Frank assumed that commanding role, showing us the
photos one at a time, employing them to illustrate his laborious and ama-
teurish account of the region. He spoke as though Amy, Jessie, and Benji
were bereft of any local knowledge. As Francine and I cringed, he rattled
off mispronounced place names, explained traditional patterns of dispute
settlement, speculated on the fate of the original "pygmy inhabitants" of
the cape, and described an alleged engraving of a European sailing ship
on Mt. Peter Botte. He spoke of aboriginals in the past tense. At the mercy
of Frank's imagination, these noble savages could not protest his botched
history, any more than Amy, Jessie, and Benji could object to his dismissal
of contemporary aboriginals as less deserving of our respect because they
had "lost their traditional culture."

These days culture is frequently invoked as an essentialized and divisive
notion. Not only does it work, as in Frank's case, to invalidate the human
aspirations to social justice of contemporary aboriginals on the grounds
that they have lost their true cultural identity, it militates against the recognition of the humanity we share, and the human rights to which we have
a common entitlement.

Frank was unstoppable. An autodidact with a captive audience, he
showed off his "finds"—his photos, his books by missionaries about the
old days—and presented us with further invalidations of aboriginal life.

"Corroboree is not an abo—[he stumbled as if aware the word might
have racist overtones]—rigine word at all. White men made it up. Prob'ly
from corroborate. I think you'll find I'm right on that."

Later he pronounced that he was "not much good on names." Never
forgot a face, but had no memory for names.

He had been raised at Mossman. Many of his childhood playmates had
been aboriginal. One boy in particular, his closest friend.

Years after leaving Mossman, Frank ran into an aboriginal bloke who
addressed him as Ropey. Frank racked his brains, trying to remember who
the man was.

For two years Frank would see this bloke around town, and be greeted
as Ropey. Frank would greet him back, but "without a clue who he was."

"It took two years for the penny to drop. It was my old mate. So next
time I saw him I asked him why he never told me who he was."

"I didn't want to tell you," the other said. "I wanted you to remember who I was by yourself."

THE MORE WE LOOK PAST one another, and the greater the distance we allow to intervene between one another, the more our relationships come to resemble the relationship of the living to the dead. Ghostliness is a metaphor of separateness, which is why, perhaps, in the past, whites were sometimes likened to ghosts. Not just because aboriginal people thought they were the dead returned but because, like the dead, they occupied a powerful niche at the edge of one's immediate horizons, refractory, unpredictable, and seemingly indifferent to the protocols of human mutuality.

As we headed away from Frank's house with the hills in mist, I glanced back in the rearview mirror once and saw Amy's face, clouded and morose. "My *bubu*" (my country), she said quietly.

That evening we drove to the northern end of Weary Bay to forage for *darkay* (mud clams) and *bulkiji* (pipis). It was the same location as in one of Frank's photos—Plantation Creek (Balabay) running out onto the open beach, Rattlesnake Point (Marbaymba) in the distance, some young aboriginal men clustered around a dinghy that had been dragged up from the surf.

I asked everyone what they had thought of the photos.

"Sad," Jessie said.

"Why?"

"Because they are all dead. It's long ago, and they have all passed away."

An Etiology of Storms

In most cultures people assume a cutoff point between a world they count as theirs and a world they consider other. This cut between self and not-self may be expressed in terms of a contrast between kinsman and enemy, culture and nature, or being and non-being, but however made, its existential implications tend to be similar, for lines of distinction inevitably entail questions as to how one negotiates, controls, and crosses them. This is the anthropological paradox of taboo that, as Edmund Leach, Mary Douglas, and Victor Turner have argued, demarcates and separates only to heighten anxiety and increase interest in the possibility of annulling or suspending the line between opposed categories. The classical figure of Hermes, with its clustered connotations of mixed or garbled messages, distrust, confusion, and deceit, encapsulates the same paradox (Brown 1969; Kermode

1979). Borders are defined not only by the markers or barriers that prohibit transgression but by the messages and traffic that surreptitiously find a way across them.

Consider the linkages and lines of communication between the natural and the social world. Being able to decipher these correspondences is vital to life and livelihood—a way of gaining insight into the workings of one's world as well as controlling it. Living on the Bloomfield River was like living in the Tanami desert; one was continually astonished by the habitual and studied care with which people "read" the surfaces of their environment for clues as to deeper meanings. Each evening, as we came down to Weary Bay to fish, the family would silently inspect the sea for signs of mullet jumping, stingray basking, or schools of herring. It was the same wherever we went. The rainforest was constantly and quietly observed for the telltale spoors of deadly snakes or for *minya* or *mayi,* the discovery of which never failed to excite and mobilize people.

Other more conceptually formal correspondences abounded: when the hammer bird is heard (in the cold months), mullet are plentiful; when the bean-tree (*Castonaspermum australe*) flowers, scrub fowl are in season; a kookaburra laughing in the early morning presages a death; a man fighting for no good reason signifies that his wife is pregnant.

Often these indicative correspondences and sympathetic equations have, as their corollaries, strict embargos. When the flesh of the parcel apple is pink (in October), it is the season to catch stingrays. This is because the liver of the stingray is also pink at this time (and at its tastiest), and is added to meat to make it more palatable. But eating stingrays in the squally premonsoonal months of October and November is prohibited: it is said to encourage destructive storms.

Indeed, so many taboos are rationalized in this way that the connection between storms and sociality compels close attention. *Bama* are no more preoccupied by the weather than most urban and suburban Westerners. But while weather signifies little more for us than the unpredictability of nature or the volatility of our political and economic climate, *bama* make it a root metaphor for the unpredictability of persons' behavior.

In particular, cyclones and monsoonal storms are likened to the tempers and persuasions of people who are enemies. A hundred years ago Roth reported that in many parts of northern Queensland, thunder and lightning were means of sorcery, and people sometimes called on these resources to drive white settlers from their land (Roth 1897, 168;1903, 8). On southeast Cape York this identification of devastating weather with human ill will is still so deep that climate is one of the prevailing and most potent metaphors of intersubjectivity. Nature, in this sense, can never be entirely divorced from culture. The dynamic of a storm system is the dynamic of interpersonal life; one is the objective correlative of the other.

AS THE FIRST THUNDERSTORM of the wet season approached, the sky turned indigo and the wind suddenly veered and picked up. There was a rattle of dry leaves, and dry leaves falling, followed by the crumpling sound of thunder like heavy furniture being moved around in an upstairs room.[18] But though the storm only threatened and the thunder remained far off, its presence was deeply felt and discussed in detail. Fred confirmed that his daughter Estelle had seen a frilled lizard on a palm frond the day before— an augury of storms. Others painstakingly analyzed the course of the storm, speaking of where the thunder came from, discussing its exact sound, and commenting on which storms in the past it most resembled. Indeed, the character of the storm was unpacked like the character of a person. Far from being a generic phenomenon, storms had to be discussed in all their idiosyncratic detail in order to second-guess their intentions, to divine their moods, to read their minds.

Though storms are the personification of enemies and enmity, they are connected, more immediately, with the taboo between son-in-law and mother-in-law. Storms that come dangerously close are seen as infringing the strict prohibition on physical contact between these two social categories. In this sense the social boundary between kin and affines is compared to and assimilated to other contrasts—kinsmen versus outsiders, *bama* versus whites.

Techniques of monitoring and controlling this boundary exploit this set of analogous contrasts. One morning I watched Billy knotting hanks of grass that he piled up with ironwood bark (*jujabala*) and logs of grass tree (*nganjirr*) before setting fire to it "to keep away the thunderstorm [*jarramali*]." I asked him to explain.

"The storm smells it," Billy said, "and goes away. There's a story about that. Old people told us."

When I asked Billy if he could tell me the story he said nothing. "How

---

18. Kuku-Yalanji has exact terms for the rustling noise of wind in dead or dry leaves (*yanja*) and for the distant rumbling of thunder in the weeks before the wet season breaks (*kubun-kubun*).

does it work?" I asked. Since *bama* regularly burn logs and tufts of grass tree (*Xanthorrhoea arborea*) to keep mosquitos away—and mosquitos come with the rain—I thought the explanation might lie here. But Billy explained that the grass tree and the other things he was burning were related to the storms as son-in-law is related to mother-in-law. As the storm approaches it smells its son-in-law and so changes its course to avoid that place.[19]

This logic of avoidance is based on a deep correspondence postulated between social and natural relationships. But this cuts two ways. While it is used magically as a technique for warding off storms, it can also be used discursively as an explanation for misfortune.

One afternoon, following several days of heavy thunderstorms and torrential rain, Francine and I dropped in to visit Amy's sister Gloria, in a nearby settlement. We found everyone huddled behind closed doors, listening for the approaching storm.

What caused this anxiety? Why had not Gloria lit fires of grass tree as others did to keep the storm at bay?

One possible answer is that thunder and lightning are means of sorcery. Storms are the agents of revenge, malice, and anger. People's fear of storms is thus a measure of the trepidation with which they view outsiders. Fred spoke of an aboriginal man from Kowanyama who came to Wujal some time ago. Since it was widely believed that people from southwest Cape York were able to control storms for the purposes of sorcery, it was rumored and suspected that he was a "burri-burri man" (sorcerer). Often, however, the fear of outsiders is less specific, and simply expresses one's distrust of anyone who hails from a world of which one has no confident knowledge and over which one has no real means of control.

Another explanation of the disquiet in Gloria's house rests on the alleged link between thunder and lightning and retributive justice. To infringe any taboo—not only the prohibition between son-in-law and mother-in-law—is to lay oneself open to the retributive anger of storms. Cyclones, for instance, may be the outcome of transgressing a "story place" or breaking food taboos.

Francine and I did not find out whether the people in Gloria's house had violated any such taboo or feared this kind of natural justice. But our conversation proved edifying. Mention was made of a particular species

---

19. Wild grape (*kangka*) vines are also burned to fend off storms; this particular species of vine (*kalal*) is also said to be the mother-in-law of thunderstorms.

of hallucinogenic mushroom that glowed in the dark. Large ones could be used to light one's way at night. The hippies used to eat it, we were told: it made you dizzy, it blew your mind. There were many things like this that one should not eat, just as there were categories of persons one should avoid. Contact with any of these prohibited things made one vulnerable to storms.[20] Ecology and climate were thus vitally connected to the social order; violent storms were the expression of transgression.

Thunderstorms are not only associated with malevolent or uncontrolled outside influence, they are metaphors—as with us—for turbulent and troubled states of mind. Thus the phrase *jarramali bajaku* (literally, "exceedingly stormy") is used of persons who readily lose self-control, railing and shouting for no good reason, going berserk. But though storminess here denotes the kind of unrestrained and tempestuous behavior associated with drug use and drunkenness, it remains closely tied to the notion of social equilibrium. Keeping *oneself* under control is synonymous with *social* order. Thus Amy and Fred, like many other older people, extolled the virtues of life away from the crowdedness, drunkenness, rancor, and mayhem of the mission. Living in small groups on traditional land, minding one's own business and staying away from trouble created both inner peace and a viable family life. This is why Amy and Fred decamped to the beach whenever there were too many people and too much tension at the outstation. It was the social equivalent of the way people in the past moved camp periodically "to give the place a rest, to let it get clean."

Jarramali Bajaku

I had met Billy my first day in the field. He was standing barefoot by a thudding boat on the beach at Weary Bay, his trousers rolled, a knife in his hand. Coarse-featured, reticent, and single-minded, he was dragging a green turtle from the dinghy so it could be butchered in the shallows. I watched as he gutted the turtle, letting the long coils of its innards wash away with the surf, carefully cutting free the slabs of green, fatty meat from the carapace, neither giving nor taking orders. Later, at the outstation,

---

20. In the past far more than now, as Anderson notes, highly developed food restrictions were intimately connected with patterns of social avoidance and circumspection between opposite-sex siblings and affines. For instance, giving or accepting food from an opposite-sex sibling connoted incest, and for a man to even mention oyster (*marbu*) in his sister's hearing was prohibited, since the word was a near homonym of *mabu* (vagina). See Anderson 1984, 118–22 for a detailed account of comparable prohibitions.

he cut firewood, dug an earth oven, built a fire, laid the stones, and cooked the turtle meat, which the women had wrapped in foil parcels. He was a man apart. The last person along the beach when we went fishing. Frequently heading into the bush alone, pig shooting. He had never married. At the outstation he shouldered the burden of the heavy work: cutting firewood, building fires, fetching water, washing dishes, setting up and dismantling tents. (Francine once observed that if you are not married, and have no family of your own, you are destined to remain the little brother forever.) When he was not working he sat for hours staring into the scrub, seldom talking.

On paydays it was different. Billy dressed in a white shirt and clean trousers and headed off to the mission to pick up his pay. Then he got drunk. He would turn up late at night, waking us with his coarse invective and shouting.

One afternoon I met him on the road. Blind drunk, his feet rose and fell as if the ground was sinking beneath him. Usually taciturn, he now commanded the world.

"You right?" he shouted at me.

"I'm fine," I said, struggling to adjust to this new persona. "How about you?"

"You right, Michael?" he shouted again, as if he had not heard me.

He got me to hold a crumpled ten-dollar bill and torn dole form while he unbuttoned and unzipped his trousers. Then he concealed a fifty dollar note in the back pocket of his undershorts—insurance against being fleeced while in a drunken coma. After clumsily zipping and buttoning his trousers he urged me to walk along with him. Rolling like a sodden log in heavy surf, grinding his teeth with a sound that reminded me of the creaking timbers of a wooden ship, he eventually blundered off into the bush.

"I might get lost Michael," he sang out at me. "You might have to come and find me."

Later I passed him on the track to our camp, beyond conversation, haranguing the bloodwoods and the spirits associated with that place: "Don't you know who I am? I'm Billy O'Rourke!"

It was similar with other heavy, habitual drinkers. Like Michael Stallybrass, who would stand in the middle of the main street at Wujal railing at invisible antagonists. One day he put his VB beer bottle on the road, then squared up and challenged it to fight. It was a way of showing people you were a force to be reckoned with, that you were someone.

One time Francine overheard poignant snatches of one of Billy's blistering tirades. He was boasting that the coast from Cape Tribulation to Cowie (Kaway) and on to Weary Bay (Jajikal, literally, "Pandanus") was his country. His improvised song about its natural abundance and its loss translates as follows:

> Where's my country,
> Jajikal, where is it?
> The place where there's lots of fish.
> The strangers come here,
> They don't know.
> I was a child here.
> The strangers don't know.
> They don't know.

It was a constant refrain of his when he was drunk, this lack of recognition and respect. And whites were often blamed. "Tourists bring sickness," Billy once told me, invoking a physical metaphor for existential loss.

All human beings desire to live, and have a pretext for living. Life is a repudiation of death. But being is never merely the absence of nothingness. What constitutes health, respect, dignity, recognition, and self-worth—these words that figure so prominently in the Western humanistic tradition—is a sense that one's life is to a significant extent within one's own grasp and control rather than continually eclipsed, invaded, violated, and invalidated by others. In this existential view the critical thing is that one has a social world beyond oneself that sustains rather than erodes one's sense of mattering, of being able to make a positive difference to the way the world is. A human life is a field of vital energy. But this energy must find expression in one's ability to control and balance the relationship between oneself and one's wider world. Sometimes, as with us all, Billy lost this balance, and respect. He vented his anger at the landscape, invoking a spiritualized lifeworld where he was recognized. When he walked into a fight and had his face smashed in, I used to think he invited this violence as a last-ditch expression of freedom:embracing the brute force of a world that overlooked or belittled him.

Though such last-ditch, magical modalities of control appear masochistic, pathetic, self-defeating, and even suicidal to outsiders, they often remain the only places where life goes on, where a surrogate sociality is contrived, and where the necessary illusions of Being are conjured. Sartre's phenomenology of the emotions is relevant here. When people are blocked from using *socially* reasonable means of achieving ontological security or salvaging self-respect, they will often have recourse to their emotions and bodies as surrogate means of saving face or managing their situation. Unable to flee an assailant, a person may faint; unable to win an argument, a person may resort to verbally abusing his opponent. In these instances the emotions are not mere by-products of consciousness but vital means of transforming it. When our paths become difficult and our ways are barred, writes Sartre, invoking a universal image of intersubjectivity, we still must act. "So we try to change the world, that is, to live as if the connection between things and their potentialities were not ruled by deterministic processes but by magic" (Sartre 1948, 58–59). This is not a game, Sartre notes, because we commit ourselves to magical activity as though it were as much a matter of life and death as rational action. Nor is it reflective; it is a mode of action that arises unselfconsciousnessly whenever our words fall on deaf ears, our actions prove inefficacious, our intentions are misconstrued, and our desires are frustrated.

However, it is never the individual body pure and simple that is involved in magical action, for in all societies the image of the body tends to coalesce three overlapping domains: personal body, communal body, and body of the land. Metaphorical correspondences between these domains not only imply their conceptual and functional unity, they predicate the possibility that action in any one domain will have repercussions in the other (Jackson 1989, chap. 9). This possibility is realized whenever rituals are carried out in one accessible or manageable domain in order to transform the state of another inaccessible or disturbed domain that is considered analogically linked to it (149). Exploiting the metaphorical links between different bodily domains is thus a way of bringing control back to a part of the world where control has been lost. When such culturally sanctioned measures fail, a person can always fall back on his or her ability to manipulate mood, emotion, and consciousness. And at the end of the road there is always the "final freedom" of which Camus spoke—the freedom to take one's own life.

The near and the local are where one gains control over wider and more remote horizons. To pile grass tree and ironwood bark onto a fire is an immediate and magical way of turning the tables on the minatory forces that threaten to throw one off balance and annul one's identity. I have seen academics retreat from the world in the same way, acting within the microcosm of a department or committee as if their very existence depended on their decisions being implemented and their views affirmed (cf. Bailey 1983). In effect, by reducing the global world to the scale of the individual's own local world, the unnerving gulf between macrocosm and micocosm is magically closed (Devereux 1980, 204).

Storying

There is something foreign and forbidding about a landscape that has not been named. But in giving a name to a hill, a ridge, a bay, we bring it, an external object, into our own immediate experience. Naming is a sign that we, who have language, are able to incorporate things that lack a language for themselves into *our* world. In this way we go some way toward closing the gap between subjectivity and objectivity.

A place name is also a trace of a story, the story about how the name came to be given. In telling and retelling this story we recover and reinforce our sense that stories can overcome the antinomy between human and extrahuman worlds. This sense of a nominal and narrative connectiveness between our inner lives and the abiding but external life of the land is as important to our humanity as is our sense of connectedness with other people. Links with place constitute one of our first and most intimate metaphors for intersubjectivity since before the events that make up our lives are construed as occurring sequentially in time, they are experienced as embodied and located in space. *Home* is a word we use for this accumulating fund of personal stories and events that become synonymous with the places where they occur. Places become the objective correlatives of our inner lives. Home is the word we use for the place that is richest in this compost of remembered events unfolding over several generations in the same location.

ON SOUTHEAST CAPE YORK, as in central Australia, every journey that Francine and I undertook with aboriginal people precipitated stories. Fred would point out the bridge where Cecil's father drove into the river and was killed, the crossing where someone else narrowly escaped death, the place where his old Hillman car caught fire, the stretch of road where he and Amy only just made it through before a flash flood washed the road away.

The road always involved what Merleau-Ponty calls an "interleaving" of objective landscape and bodily subjectivity (1968, 137–38). Memories of previous travels through the land were consummated in an ever-present sense of being part of it—inhabiting and haunting it. But this experience cuts two ways. The road unravels a train of memories, a tracing of past events. But every journey accrues new events and new associations that become grafted onto the old so that what has been is always being supplemented and fleshed out in the here and now. "The remembering makes it now," Tim O'Brien observes. "That's what stories are for. Stories are for joining the past to the future" (O'Brien 1990, 40). This is why Fred greeted Cecil's father as we passed the place where he had passed away.

I often remarked this in the way people slipped into and out of the first person when reciting myths, unself-consciously intermingling reminiscences of their own experiences at certain places with ancestral events of which they had no immediate experience. In this way, traveling any track or road tends to mediate connections between immediate and nonimmediate lives and set in motion a process that effectively fuses embodied and immediate experience with the etherealized and nonimmediate world that lies about it as pure potentiality. A person's singular subjectivity is thus merged with the more abstract leitmotifs of *cultural* life: land, language, and the law.

Elizabeth Povinelli provides a telling example of this topology of Being in her study of the Belyuen community of the Cox Peninsula:

> On a road to and from the Belyuen community is a spot where
> a particularly horrific car collision occurred in the late sixties.
> When driving by, people typically wave and "remember" the
> story of what happened there, although everyone knows the inci-
> dents already: how a long-standing intergroup dispute prompted
> a sorcery-initiated car wreck, who died, what relationship the de-
> ceased had with the passers-by. Depending upon the speaker's
> linguistic abilities, people call out to the site in Batjemal, Emi,
> or Belyuen English. One day in 1989, I was driving with five
> older and a few younger women and children down this road.
> As we passed the site, an older woman saw the young man
> who had died in the accident sitting, and then disappearing,
> next to the tree where it had happened. We stopped and looked
> at the tracks that this *nyoitj* made in the dirt and then returned
> to the community to see why this *nyoitj* had "come out." (Povi-
> nelli 1993, 163).

Nyoitj, Povinelli explains, is "the self embodied at a site" (162). To see such a spirit suggests that one's consciousness has shifted from idiosyncratic person to ancestral personage, the latter being associated with the body of a place. In this shift from the immediate world of lived particulars to the less immediate cultural plane of reality, human being comes to be embedded in the Being of the world. And it is storytelling that effects this transformation and creates this embeddedness, connecting people to country, connecting particular experience to shared parameters of meaning.

On Cape York the focus shifts somewhat. In this more sedentary environment, "story places" (*yirmbal,* in Kuku-Yalanji) are not always patronymically identified, and "Dreaming tracks" are less significant in defining who belongs where (cf. Sutton 1988, 255). But in both regions stories articulate people's notions of who they are and where they belong, as well as providing models for going beyond exclusiveness and difference.

In April 1994 Francine and I made a trip to a notable Kuku-Yalanji "story place" with two Aboriginal friends, Henry and Eileen Simpson. The place was known as Kijanka (literally, "moon place"), and to get there we had to negotiate a narrow clay road that climbed steeply from the coast, then rose and fell, twisted and turned across bushed plateaus and valleys where a hundred years ago immigrant miners transformed the landscape in their search for alluvial tin.

We left the vehicle and walked the last half-mile to the falls. Through the trees, ferns, and outcrops of rain-tarnished granite I glimpsed the deep pool above the falls known as Karrulbul. At this point Henry gestured that we should fall back and let Eileen and Francine walk on ahead.

This was a "woman's place," Henry confided. Men and women could not approach it together, though the story was known by both sexes and belonged to all Kuku-Yalanji people.

Henry's account of the moon story began in much the same way as the narrative recorded in about 1930 by Ursula McConnel. According to this narrative, in the beginning there were no women in the world.[21] The men who inhabited the camp at Kijanka went out hunting every day, but there were no women to dig yams, find grubs in dead wood, or wash and grind zamia nuts.

One day, when the other men left to go hunting, Kija (the moon) and his brother-in-law remained behind in camp. As his brother-in-law slept, Kija attempted to have intercourse with various boulders, which he first shaped and incised with female sexual features. Dissatisfied with the riverstones, Kija fell on and speared his brother-in-law as he slept. He then

21. The myth is not unique. Roth reports that among the Tully River aboriginals, men and women originally sprang out of a local river but were sexually undifferentiated. On the Proserpine River, aboriginal informants told Roth that the moon made the first man and woman, respectively, out of stone and box tree wood (1903, 16)

took the body to a rock pool at the foot of the falls where he eviscerated and cleaned it, then smoked and dried it. Having severed the penis and testicles, he cut a vagina (the discarded parts became stones), and proceeded to copulate with the transformed and feminized corpse. That same afternoon, an infant girl was born.

When the other hunters returned and discovered that their brother-in-law had been killed, they attempted to spear the moon in vengeance, but Kija fled downstream as far as Kaway, where he ascended into the sky. As for the "woman" he had made, she turned to stone on the hill above the falls.

Henry led me to the rocky bluff overlooking the river, pointing out the petrified lawyer-cane bridge that once crossed the crest of the falls, then other stones—remnants of the hunters' camp, and, on the north side of a hill above the falls, the woman the moon made from the body of his brother-in-law. The moon is associated with women, Henry explained, because women's Menstrual periods coincide with the lunar cycle. "The moon made everything," he remarked. By creating the first woman the moon brought reproductive fertility into the world. For this reason the Kija story was "the *bama* Adam and Eve story." Without the moon, life could not be reproduced. The moon was a perpetual image of life's waxing and waning.

When we left the falls, and it was quiet again among the trees, Henry asked me if *waybala* (white people) possessed such stories.[22]

"Like Adam and Eve?" I asked, since Henry had already drawn the comparison.

Henry seemed dissatisfied, as if I was short-changing him. I was reminded of the view, widespread among indigenous peoples everywhere in the early years of conquest and colonization, that whites withheld deep knowledge and "cargo" from native peoples, and possessed a powerful master narrative that they kept to themselves—the key to material wealth and technological superiority.

Rather than invoke the Bible again I told Henry that there was another corpus of *waybala* stories that were not, strictly speaking religious but were used to make sense of many cultural and natural phenomena, including the rivalry between fathers and sons and the origin of storms.

---

22. Chris Anderson also alludes to this notion of two worldviews or laws encapsulated in separate master narratives. In 1977 his informant Bob Yerrie remarked, "Everybody got story, eh? *Waybala, bama, Nganjinga* ['our'] law, might be good law, I don't know. Belong to *bama*. I don't know what belong to *waybul*. Might be *waybul* gotta law . . . different law" (Anderson 1984, 337).

As I outlined the Greek myths, Henry listened patiently. But it wasn't until I described Zeus that we found common ground.

Henry at once regaled me with stories of storms.

Many years ago, he said, a white rancher, exasperated at *bama* spearing his cattle, rode up to a river encampment of *bama* and shot a young girl dead. Seeking revenge, the girl's father went to the rancher's place as thunder. The rancher shot at the thunder but again and again his bullets passed harmlessly through its body. Then, with a single lightning bolt, the thunder speared the white rancher.

Hardly pausing, Henry recounted another story of revenge.

It happened at a time when his grandfather lived at Shipton's Flat. One of the old man's sons was killed at Thompson's Creek (Dikarr). The old man severed his son's leg from the knee to the groin, wrapped it in bark and took it home with him. The leg would help him dream and divine the identity of the murderer. Not long after, a cyclone killed the murderer and the old man had his revenge.

In Henry's third story lightning also figured as an agent of retributive justice. There was a certain man who "messed with many girls," getting them pregnant, causing trouble. Lightning sought him out, coming from afar as he was driving a tractor in a Mossman cane field. "Bang! he dead, just like that."

Possibly Henry expected me to corroborate his stories by relating some Zeus-like narrative from my own cultural repertoire. But what could I say? His stories of antagonism and revenge had touched on what were perhaps unreconcilable differences.

I belonged to a world where metanarratives such as the moon story no longer bestowed legitimacy or justified actions. Nor did rules of scientific method, correspondence to the facts, and consensus within a professional or scientific community determine what was true and false. In a postpositivist, postmodern age such modes of determining ethnographic truth were under seige (Lyotard 1984), and even the myths of humanism—that all men were created equal, or that resources should be distributed "from each according to his abilities, to each according to his needs"—were outrageous forms of wishful thinking when one considered the terrible history that colonized people had endured.

But this is to see difference solely in epistemological terms. In fact, ethnographic understanding is a product of interaction and dialogue, and accordingly contains the possibility of going beyond the merely local or personal, to afford glimpses into a wider world of shared existential quandaries and imaginative strategies. Henry's need was, in a sense, the same as mine: to establish what *bama* and *waybala* held in common, and why, in the past, though *bama* had conceded so much to whites, there had been so little respect given in return.

The moon story was a kind of allegory of a reality we both sought. Most obviously, it is concerned with the ways in which a world at once static and turned in on itself enters time by entering into reciprocal relations with others. Thus the world of men becomes a world of men *and* women, and begins both to reproduce itself and establish the basis of exchange between wife-giving and wife-receiving moieties. The rules that reinforce this recip-rocal order, such as the rule of brother-in-law avoidance, are enunciated. As Ursula McConnel observed, the world is transformed from one based on identity to one based on difference (1931, 22). This implies the creation of sociality itself, since the difference that emerges in the myth between Dabu and Wallar moieties—named respectively for black-bodied and yel-low-bodied species of bees—is overcome or mediated by prescriptive mar-riages between them.

That this marriage rule no longer carries much weight is lamented by older people like Henry, along with the lack of respect for elders, indiffer-ence to avoidance rules, and the taboo (*warrki*) against close contact with one's sister, sister-in-law, mother-in-law, and brother-in-law. To some ex-tent, the moon story has lost its legitimating power.

But the potential of the story to remind us of the basis of human sociality, and the ways in which the very telling of a story itself brings that sociality into being, were realized during my excursion to the falls with Henry. The trip established some basic trust between us, and although Henry knew I was skeptical about the intrinsic truth of the moon story, he had seen that I would not deride it as mere superstition.

It is neither, therefore, a question of whether stories mirror the world as it "really" is, nor of what meanings inhere in any given narrative. It isn't even a question of how stories are performed or enacted. What matters most are the truth effects of telling stories, the empathy they generate, the exchange of experience they enable, and the social bonds they mediate. Stressing that a story is "true" undoubtedly increases its use value, as I discovered among the Warlpiri where stories had to be *junga*—straight and true—in the sense that they conformed to the *jukurrpa*, the Dreaming, the law. But one had to listen to the stories, to hear them well, to be able to repeat them in one's own turn and thereby hold the Dreaming exactly as one received it. For Warlpiri, as for most nonliterate people, this was the quintessence of knowing. So, as Jennifer Biddle has perceptively observed, the truth of stories emerges from a *relationship* between teller and listener: in the social bond they forge between the generations or those who come to share in them (Biddle 1991). Stories are, in this sense, continually "salvaged," continually brought back into being, their value stemming not only from the ancestral realm to which they constantly refer but from the immediate intersubjective lifeworld they sustain. By listening keenly to Henry's stories, a bond was affirmed. The question as to whether I believed *bama* notions of spiritual agency and story places did not arise. What counted most imperatively was the respect I showed for the teller of the tale simply by listening and comparing notes without any striving to subvert his discourse with my own vocabulary, to drown out his voice with my own, to translate his views into mine. A direct analogy can be drawn with commensality. In sharing food with a stranger, the unappealing appearance or unappetizing taste of the food should not be focal. What matters—what is most "expedient," to use James's pragmatist terminology—is that the food is given and received (just as one's words are heard and heeded) rather than judged according to some extracontextual personal or moral standard. It is same with people. Kuku-Yalanji generalize and moralize about each another far less than we do, often commenting that a certain behavior is in that person's nature but rarely expressing a desire or demand for that nature to be changed. This is particularly true of children, whose physical and emotional demands are accepted tolerantly and seldom judged as evidence of an incorrigible nature or bad parenting (cf. Hamilton 1981, 128–29). In other words, right and wrong are seen pragmatically rather than epistemologically. The social implications of behavior are given primacy over its intrinsic truth.

A FEW NIGHTS AFTER OUR TRIP to Kijanka I sat with Henry on his porch at Wujal. For a while we exchanged small talk. Henry complained about his son's mates, drinking all night and keeping him awake. He said that if ever he got his land back he would move there to gain greater peace and quiet.

After a while I turned the talk to something Henry had told me at Buru about strangers, how, in the old days, strangers had to keep their distance.

"Strangers smell different," Henry said, and offered an anecdote to explain what he meant.

Many years ago a tin prospector asked Henry if he might go to Henry's country to look for tin deposits. Henry gave him the go-ahead, but when the prospector went up into the hills, snakes appeared in his path wherever he turned.

Henry decided to accompany him. They crossed a stream. Immediately there were snakes everywhere. The stranger was alarmed but Henry wrenched a leafy branch from a tree and drew it under his armpit, imparting the smell of his sweat to the foliage. When he threw the branch down, the snakes vanished. It is one's body odor that identifies you as belonging to the place.

Same on the coast, Henry said. Sea snakes will swim along with their heads raised out of the water when they smell a stranger in the vicinity.

I was struck by the fact that smell was prioritized as a metaphor for difference rather than appearance, skin color, or behavior. In the Western world difference is almost everywhere decided on the basis of visible distinction, and different tastes, different body odors, or different behaviors adduced in support of the visual metaphor (see Stoller 1989; Howes 1991; Classen 1993). At the same time, Henry's allusion to smell reminded me of the extent to which the human sense of self and other is not always dependent on cognitive or conceptual identifications but rather on the immediate experiences of sight, smell, touch, voice, and taste. The loss or absence of a loved one often brings this home: it is the smell of the other's body, the sound of her or his voice, and things associated with the other's life—a piece of music, an article of clothing, a shared place—that define the quintessence of the absent individual.

I asked Henry if sea people and land people had different smells.

Henry nodded. Sea people (*jalunji,* literally, "of the sea") have a fishy smell (*bikarr*); they carry the odor of saltwater and sea fish. Land people (*ngalkalji,* literally, "away from or outside the sea") have a strong smell, though it is not as strong as the smell of strangers. Henry explained that the strong odor came from eating marsupial meat.

As I pressed Henry to tell me more I learned that different families have different smells, and that a woman loses her smell and acquires the smell of her husband's people when she marries. The same goes for children; if they are "grown up" in an adopted family they will lose the distinctive smell of their natal family. So smell reflects the food one shares with others, as well as physical propinquity. Smell was a metaphor for group identity. This is why if you trespass on a story place your smell betrays you as an interloper, and the beings associated with that place "poison" you.

"Same with strangers or *waybul,*" Henry said. "*Waybala* smelled like the slime of an eel, old people said. Blacks like smoked meat or fish, the smoke from fires. *Waybala* smell different, but they smell like *bama* after they bin live with us for a while."

"What about me?" I asked.

"You smell like *bama*," Henry said.

Fugue

In the rainforest life teemed and amazed. In the course of a day and a night myriad lives came into being and were extinguished. The mantle of our lantern was a spurious moon, the graveyard for hundreds of thousands of gnats, crickets, and flying ants. Not a day passed without the life cycle of some new species consummating itself before our eyes. Along the path, lines of processionary caterpillars inched forward; when one fell behind, the whole column came to a halt until it caught up. Our clearing was filled with butterflies feeding on wallaby dung and fallen fruit, then mating and vanishing. Fragments of wings like pieces of blue cathedral glass lay on the ground, picked at by the breeze, the last vestiges of their bodies eaten by ants.

The vitality of this physical environment was matched by the volatility of the social world into which we were increasingly drawn.

TENSION HAD BEEN BUILDING for weeks. When a fugitive who'd been living in and around the mission for several months took a shotgun and blew Beryl's husband's brains out because, as people later said, "he did not like Bob's glasses," Beryl, Fred's sister, together with her six grandchildren, came and camped at the outstation. Not long after, Fred's niece turned up from Mossman with her white boyfriend, Dave, and their two kids. Amy and Fred, while hospitable enough, resented these intrusions. Fred mumbled about Dave's history of trouble with the law, and derided his bombastic stories of scamming and scavenging, his empty promises to repair Fred's truck. Nor could he tolerate the way Dave walked into his camp at will, "talking freely" with him, "cutting in" on conversations that were none of his business. "*Bama* way," Fred said, "father-in-law and son-in-law don't sit together like that. Dave should have more respect."

As for Amy, she withdrew into Jobian silence.

The last straw was when Amy's nephew, Terry, and his wife, who had been talking for some time of moving away from the mission, arrived at the outstation and began clearing a campsite not far from where Francine and I had pitched our tent. Exhaustion, sleeplessness, mosquitoes, Joshua's ill health, and the grueling conditions of life in the rainforest were already telling on us. Like Amy and Fred, we were close to breaking point.

But there was neither escape or respite. After Fred's truck broke down and Cecil's vehicle went up in flames as a result of a faulty fuel line, our vehicle became the family's sole means of transport. With Francine and I under pressure to ferry people to and from the mission (for welfare payments, provisioning, and family visits), as well as to and from the beach every day for fishing and foraging, it was inevitable that our vehicle would be at the center of the breaking storm.

Terry complained that there were "too many people at the farm." One day he told Amy, "Beryl and those white fellas don't belong here. We got no room." In Terry's opinion it was a case of their mob against *jawun* and outsiders, a category that included in-laws *and* anthropologists. Things came to a head one day when, on a trip to the mission, our vehicle was so overcrowded that we had to leave Terry and Sunday behind. That night, as we were getting Joshua off to sleep, Sunday came down the track to our camp and demanded we drive to a nearby township, where Terry was drinking with some mates.

Sunday was not going to be put off. Joshua's ill health and our exhaustion were no excuse. "It's not me," Sunday said, passing the buck. "Terry wants yous to get him."

Perhaps an hour passed after Sunday slouched off muttering imprecations before Terry showed up. He was dead drunk. Sensible of how violent he became when he had been drinking, Sunday fled with the baby, leaving their son asleep in the house. Amy, Fred, Dave, and his wife had already gone looking for Terry along the road.

Enraged at finding the house in darkness, Terry came up the track and demanded that we take him in search of the others. I said we were too tired and refused his request.

Boiling with anger, Terry stumbled off. His voice became louder and louder as he went away through the darkness. "You fuckin' help other people all right," he shouted, "but what about we?"

Then we heard his son crying as he was rudely roused from sleep.

Minutes later Terry passed through our camp again, carrying his son on his shoulders. Now he was hurling abuse at Fred. "Fred not fuckin' boss for this place. My father is. Fred not from here. This not his land!" And then I heard him on the road, fifty yards away through the fanpalms and bloodwoods, as he encountered Fred driving back from the township. I heard the exchange of abuse through the trees, then Terry's torch hurled onto the clay road.

In the early hours of the morning Francine woke me. She'd been unable to sleep for the drunken shouting along the road. Now someone was forcing his way through the scrub toward our camp. She thought it might be Terry.

I dressed and went outside. It was only Alfie, a young man from the mission whom we vaguely knew. Drunk and disoriented, he was carrying a knife to fend off vengeful ghosts. I led him down the track to the house where Fred found him a mattress and blanket.

In the morning Terry's parents left for Mossman to escape the fighting and the abuse. As for Sunday, she made it to Hopevale, where she took refuge with her family and had a restraining order made out against her husband. It wasn't the first time, Fred explained.

Fred and Amy urged us not to take Terry too seriously. "Terry got no right to kick you out," Fred said. And he rehearsed his old theme: how he disliked people whose behavior underwent radical transformation under the influence of drink. Terry exemplified this. Self-effacing and deferential when sober, he became a foul-mouthed, crazed bully when drunk.

Fred often advised me to humor drunks and avoid criticizing them to their face. You had to be careful lest they take the shame to heart and kill themselves in a fit of deep remorse. A case in point was Peter—soft-spoken, tall, pleasant-looking—who had been emotionally vulnerable since his mother's death a year ago. One night Peter got drunk and tried to swim the Bloomfield. Another time he tried to hang himself from the bell tower at the mission. You had to be careful with Peter, Fred said. But Fred was in no mood for sympathy where Terry was concerned. "I don't like shy people," he said. "Terry wouldn't be so cocky if he wasn't drunk." On top of everything, Terry was a coward, according to Fred, always picking on drunker or weaker opponents to fight.

After a while we fell to talking about Alfie, who we'd thought was Terry coming to do us some harm. Embellishing the story of the night and picturing Alfie crashing through the undergrowth with his knife at the ready, we found in laughter some relief from our fears and frayed nerves.

Four days passed before Terry came back from his bender. Dark and disgruntled, deeply miserable, utterly alone, he sat clumped outside the house sharpening a spear.

None of us wanted him to feel shame. None of us wanted to antagonize him.

He had gone to Hopevale, he said, and brought Sunday back. She was now at the mission.

All of us knew how many times Sunday had warned Terry that if he didn't desist from hanging out with the single men and getting drunk, she'd clear out. Now, apparently, she'd delivered her ultimatum: either he quit drinking or she'd divorce him, and the restraining order backed her up.

Two weeks later we drove to Cooktown, where Terry was obliged to appear before the police. In the five hours that Terry was inside in the police station, being cautioned about the implications of breaking a good-behavior bond, we waited in the park with Sunday. Sunday made no bones about who would be to blame if Terry were taken into custody. "It's not my fault," she said. "I didn't tell im to drink in the first place. It's his fault."

She paused. *The familiar distancing disclaimer,* I thought. *The abnegation of responsibility, the masking of one's own disquieting emotions.* Then she ventured, as if her own anxiety had finally got the better of her: "He little bit frightened."

AFTER THE TRIP TO COOKTOWN we experienced a few days of comparative calm. Then the storm broke again, precipitated by the same elements as before: too few resources and too many people. And behind this crisis, too, was the tension between Fred's world and Amy's—those who belonged there and those who had married in.

One evening Fred announced that when he went up to Lakefield for the next land claim hearing he was going to take the telephone key so no one could use the telephone in his absence. He was fed up with shouldering the burden of the phone and electricity bills; he wanted to save his money to repair his truck. Amy, however, was against this. What if her baby grand-daughter fell ill; Terry and Sunday would need to phone the clinic at the mission.

Piqued, Fred called Amy a *myall.* Hurt and incensed, she stalked off.

Minutes later Fred came to our camp and related what had happened. Amy was wandering along the road, he said. Probably heading to her sister's place for kinship and consolation. Could we go and get her?

It wasn't necessary. Amy soon returned to the house. Distressed and declaiming about her dead son, killed because of grog, she enumerated all her losses. The family dispersed. The land given up. And as for Fred's land claim, "I not goin' up to that bloody Port Stewart again. I went up when

I was young. But all the nieces and nephews married now." As for the telephone, she would fix that once and for all.

As she threatened to smash it with an axe and sever the cable with a kitchen knife, Fred struggled to restrain her, warning her that she was in peril of electrocuting herself.

It was, I thought, Amy's desperate bid to cut all ties with the outside world, to distance herself absolutely from the grog and the strangers who had destroyed the only world that mattered to her: her family, her land. Later, one of Beryl's granddaughters told us that Amy had been upset because she had caught no fish for several days. This also rang true. Because even the resources of the sea were under threat now from white fishermen who camped on Weary Bay without asking permission, crowding *bama* out.

The bitterness simmered for days. Amy's sister accused Fred of "taking over." "You not boss for this place," she said. "Amy, she the boss. She got to stand up and stick up for herself."

Then Jessie turned her invective against Francine, accusing her of playing the family false.

"We don't understand a friggin' thing," Terry muttered, referring to land-rights legislation, which, though vital for the aboriginal future, was beyond the comprehension of most *bama* and largely controlled by white lawyers, anthropologists, and outside experts.

THE NEXT DAY, news reached me—on the telephone, which was thankfully still working—that my father had died. I immediately began preparing for a trip back to New Zealand for his funeral.

Leaving the field at this time helped me get things into perspective. Customarily, an ethnographer does not recount in much reflexive depth or detail the circumstances of his or her life in the field. Too anecdotal for some, too self-centered for others, such accounts are rarely seen as illuminating the kind of sociocultural realities that it is an anthropologist's task to record. But I knew that no adequate account of the social world in which my wife and I had lived for a year could be rendered without disclosing our places within it. This is not to say that my anthropological goals were merely reflexive; the events in which I had participated helped me understand the dynamics of the aboriginal lifeworld itself. Nevertheless, I was convinced that my capability as an anthropologist and human being to work out a *modus vivendi* with people like Fred and Amy was the critical measure of the worth of my anthropological understanding of their experience and their society. If intercultural coexistence *were* possible, it would have to be realized and sustained in the intersubjective space of our everyday lives.

TWO AND A HALF YEARS would pass before my wife and I returned to Cape York. When we came back it seemed that only a day had elapsed. We set up camp on the beach at Jajikal, a stone's throw from where the O'Rourkes were encamped, and in the following days exchanged family news, went fishing, and discussed progress with land claims as if our time were as uninterrupted as the surf that surged and withdrew on the sand.

But one thing *had* changed. People now addressed us as *jawun* with unalloyed friendliness, openness, and trust. And we felt far less pressured than in the past. If asked to provide food and cigarettes, or give money, we found it easy to meet our obligations yet draw the line, declaring that our own resources were limited. And people would accept this, turning away with embarrassed giggles. Fred and Amy urged us to return for good; they needed us there. We said we would think about it. *Bama*-way, we wanted to leave every possibility open.

HERE/NOW

Where Thought Belongs

From its inception as a science, anthropology has steered an erratic course between particularistic, ethnographic aims and more comprehensive, universalistic ambitions. To a large extent anthropology's discursive oscillation between these extremes is a function of social distance: the deeper one becomes involved in the lifeworld of the people with whom one lives and works, the more hesitant one is to use the existential complexity of that particular lifeworld as a basis for generalizations about humankind.[1] Participation in the quotidian life of any social microcosm—be it family, village, profession, or ethnic group—makes detachment and disinterestedness difficult. This is why the great universalizing moments in the history of anthropology are, ironically, marked by a distancing of the intellectual from the world. Life is replaced by libraries and the infinite variety of experience is exchanged for the finitude of documented data. What passes for scientific objectivity at such times is often a retreat from the world seeking its own justification.

1. Bourdieu speaks of the paradoxically dual character of the intellectual who, until recently, embodied a desire to do pure research *and* be politically and effectively *engagé*. However, this antinomy has now been replaced by another, in which the intellectual struggles to maintain his or her voice in the face of state indifference or nonnegotiable corporate demands (Bourdieu 1992b).

Is it then possible to reconcile social engagement with the goal of universal understanding?

The problem is one of disentangling the notion of the universal from the notion of privileged position. Of reinventing a concept of the universal that draws us into rather than estranges us from the lifeworld. This implies that thought should be seen as a critical element of our quotidian existence and not as a means of transcendence. In Adorno's words, we "reject the illusion . . . that the power of thought is sufficient to grasp the totality of the real" (1977–78, 120).

Of course, anthropologists have not been alone in making far-reaching claims on the strength of particular, superficial, and fleeting experience of the world. The archaeological impulse that drives all epistemology—digging down through the midden of the phenomenal world to uncover foundations, essences, and first causes—is as deeply embedded in anthropology as in philosophy. Not content simply to describe in depth and detail the shifting interface between fugitive phenomena and their own interpretive persuasions, thinkers have traditionally sought some superior justification for their quest for meaning. As Sartre notes (1983; cf. Le Goff 1993), the rise of the intellectual accompanies the rise of the bourgeoisie, which, as a class, feels compelled to affirm itself in terms of a global conception of the world. This elevating demand has been accomplished by extolling analytical reason, the means whereby a totalizing and unitary vision of the universe could be confidently promulgated. Since no one human being can achieve such omniscience, the intellectual has been, from the outset, someone who strays outside the boundaries of his or her particular specialization, someone whose claims to global understanding are as spurious as they are excessive.

Most human beings fall into thinking that the values of their particular world apply equally, if not obviously, to all others. Egocentricity and ethnocentricity are universal human failings. But surely, intellectual humanism and scientific rationality are exceptions to the rule? Surely the intellectual or scientist *can* overcome the prejudices and limitations of his or her own background and grasp the world of others as it appears to them?

We know this is seldom the case, no matter how well intentioned we are and how hard we work to control the bias of our own upbringing, our own historical and cultural take on things. Moreover, as Sartre notes, the intellectual's humanist egalitarianism is always hollow, for by virtue of being "the possessor of an unjustified privilege," he or she is "living proof that all men are not equal" (1983, 239–40). Paul Feyerabend puts the matter even more bluntly. Taking Husserl to task for proposing that philosophers "are functionaries of humanity," Feyerabend avers that it is a "phenomenal conceit" to imagine that any single individual can have sufficient knowledge of all races, cultures, and civilizations to be able to speak of "the true being of humanity." What does Husserl know of the "true being" of the Nuer? he asks (1987, 274). The same criticism may be leveled at Kantian notions of universal maxims on the grounds that these uncritically project the values of the European bourgeoisie onto the rest of the world (MacIntyre 1984, 221).

In so far as anthropology espouses universalizing aims, it struggles against its own origins in the imperious discourse of colonialism (Herzfeld 1987, 13). Like myths of transcendence, the humanistic tradition of universals all too often rests on an assumption of cultural and intellectual superiority that comes dangerously close to the mystique of fascism (Lefebvre 1991, 130–31).

Given the intrinsic Eurocentricism of anthropology, one may ask what is the possibility of a science of humanity—of a genuine anthropology—in a pluralistic world? Is there any worldly justification for the anthropological project, or are its gestures toward a universal moral language simply the glib and condescending projections of *our* conscience-stricken ideals onto Third World peoples whose voices, cries, and contrary views go largely unheard?

One way of approaching these questions is to remind ourselves that a common metadiscourse or universally shared notion of humanity is, *in practice,* seldom a necessary precondition for social interaction (cf. Feyerabend 1974, 274–75). In practical life what matters is not that we possess an impregnable understanding of the human condition but that we are able to utilize points of view, rules of thumb, and *modus operandi* that help us enter into more mutually fulfilling relationships with others. To this end assumed universals and notions of common humanity may, in practice, prove to be no more efficacious than assumptions of radical difference. In no society is amity a simple function of common identity. On the contrary, sameness is often less compelling than difference, and shared language or worldview is nowhere a guarantee of empathy and intimacy.

Ironically, the strongest argument for cultural universals begins not with assumptions of sameness but with issues of difference. Rather than pose abstract questions about how we can have *knowledge* of others as a prior condition for interaction or understanding, we begin with the obvious fact that people *do* interact despite cultural and linguistic differences.

At this point it is useful to explore some widely shared metaphors of intersubjectivity—the notion that human relationships are like nets, chains, many-stranded ropes, knotted cords, strings, or paths. For the Yoruba of Nigeria and the European gypsies, life is likened to a journey along a road (Drewal 1992, 26, 33; Fontesca 1995, 4–5). Among the Maya, the "root *b'eh* 'road' has far-reaching associations," including the notions of a person's lot, life projects, and daily preoccupations (Hanks 1990, 310–13). Throughout West Africa relationships within both the social body and the visceral body are likened to paths and roads (Bisilliat 1976, 555–78; Jackson 1989, 145–46). In Melanesia roads are images of enduring social relationships, as well as of the exchanges that sustain those relationships (Nihill 1986, 5, 125–31). And in aboriginal Australia tracks embody the vital essence of journeying ancestors, and thence the wherewithal of social relations (Tamisari 1997; Munn 1973, 173). All such metaphors convey a sense of interpersonal relations as entailing a dynamic of contending *and* converging intentionalities. Though Hegel saw intersubjectivity as a "life and death struggle" for recognition (Hegel 1971, 171–72), it may be more useful to construe the dialectic of self and other not as a struggle for survival but as a struggle to adjust opposing interests, imperatives, and identifications. This struggle is inescapable. It defines the human condition. And it involves material possessions and ideologies as much as intangible and intuited attributes. As interminable as the dialectic that Lévi-Strauss discerned in the unconscious structure of myth, it consists in unending dialogue, negotiation, exchange, and bargain—sympathetic *and* antagonistic—in which individuals and groups strive for equity and balance between things that they consider rightfully theirs and things that they deem to belong to others. Stasis is never achieved. Inequivalences of talents, resources, interests, and felt needs militate against it. And in the same way that the incommensurability of things and persons in systems of exchange makes ongoing exchange inevitable (Sahlins 1965), so ontological insecurity drives people relentlessly to recover and sustain their sense of Being in the face of forces that threaten to reduce them to nothingness.

Nothingness may be taken to mean both *being* and *having* nothing. Though material impoverishment does not necessarily imply a dearth of social and spiritual resources, and wealth never guarantees personal fulfillment, it would be wrong to explore any human situation without also exploring economic and political conditions.

On southeast Cape York one confronted the world in a nutshell: too many people, too few resources to go around.

John Berger (1985, 264) speaks of this as "the crisis of utopianism." Thirty years from now the world's population will have doubled. With the prospect of diminished per-capita economic growth in the capitalist world and increasingly frustrated aspirations among the underprivileged at home and abroad, the no-man's land between the haves and have-nots may well become a battleground. In such desperate times humanistic appeals for a just apportionment of resources or an end to cruelty (Rorty 1989, 141–88) become equally absurd. Orwell's prediction—that in the twentieth century human equality would become "technically possible"—will not sustain us in the twenty-first. The hope that socialism might guarantee a fair distribution of wealth among all classes and all nations has been challenged, as *Animal Farm* anticipated, by entrenched greed and privilege. The goal of universal literacy is, in poor countries, simply unaffordable (Illich 1973, 89–101). And the humanist ethos, espoused by so many for so long, of liberty, equality, and fraternity, is something to which fewer and fewer people in the well-heeled nations of the world bother to pay lip service.

We live in a world where the wealth of 358 individuals is greater than the combined annual incomes of 45 percent of the world's people (United Nations Development Program 1996). As the gap between rich and poor widens, it is perfectly possible that the rich will strive to secure their possessions against the barbarians at the gate. Already the walls are going up. Migrants become scapegoated. Dark images circulate of a demonized underclass. Prisons are built apace. At the same time, sentimental stories appear exhorting the underprivileged not to abandon the American Dream. Everyone can make it if they try. But hearts harden against the needy and the poor. Affirmative action is brought to an end. Aid programs are axed. Humanitarian assistance to "basket cases" like Bangladesh and the Sudan is deemed to be a waste of valuable resources. People speak of overdosing on images of genocide and Third World famine. And all around us, in their "struggle" to maintain profitability, corporations "rationalize" their operations by laying off thousands of workers each week.

If theoretical knowledge is to be rejoined with practical action, and anthropology is to remain a humanism, where does one go from here?

In the first place, ethnography testifies to the fact that it is not only possible but liberating and illuminating to cross the boundaries between different cultures. In a world that cares and communicates less—despite all that's said about the global village—anthropology continues to be, in Ivan Illich's memorable phrase "a tool for conviviality." In the second place, ethnography has yet to fulfill its potential as a powerful way of decentering and demystifying Western perspectives on the world, helping us question our own cultural assumptions, enabling us to see ourselves as others see us.

But this unsettling of habitual points of view is empty unless it is taken into the real world and tested in the course of our everyday lives. This is the thrust of Sartre's observation that "the only way the intellectual can really distance himself from the official ideology decreed from above is *by placing himself alongside those whose very existence contradicts it*" (Sartre 1983, 256; emphasis added).

Edward Said has recently argued in the same vein. The task of the intellectual, he writes, is to "universalize" the crisis of his or her own culture—the Holocaust for the Jews, colonization for aboriginals, partition and exile for the Kurds and Palestinians—"to give greater human scope to what a particular race or nation suffered, to associate that experience with the sufferings of others" (1994, 44). He continues: "It is inadequate only to affirm that a people was dispossessed, oppressed or slaughtered, denied its rights and its political existence, without at the same time doing what Fanon did during the Algerian war, affiliating those horrors with the similar afflictions of other people. This does not at all mean a loss in historical specificity, but rather it guards against the possibility that a lesson learned about oppression in one place will be forgotten or violated in another place or time."

Said goes on to suggest that the intellectual can speak for all humankind, not in terms of a claim to be objective, neutral, or omniscient (which is an epistemological pretension) but in terms of a commitment to ally himself or herself with the oppressed and unrepresented (which is an ethical and political commitment). The intellectual's *raison d'être* is "to represent all those people and issues that are routinely forgotten or swept under the rug. The intellectual does so *on the basis of universal principles: that all human beings are entitled to expect decent standards of behavior concerning freedom and justice from worldly powers or nations, and that deliberate or inadvertent violations of these standards need to be testified and fought against courageously*" (11–12; emphasis added).

But we need to be cautious here. On the one hand, Said invokes Adorno-like arguments against identity thinking: the intellectual is a kind of outlaw-hero "whose whole being is staked on a critical sense, a sense of being unwilling to accept easy formulas, or ready-made clichés, or the smooth, ever-so-accommodating confirmations of what the powerful or conventional have to say, and what they do" (23). But on the other hand he advocates the intellectual's uncritical embrace of the "weak and unrepresented."

I share Bourdieu's view that rather than simply *standing with* the oppressed in a possibly vainglorious gesture of solidarity, the intellectual must seek a critical *understanding* of the condition of oppression itself (Bourdieu

1996, 22). As with Sartre before him, Said's revolutionary romanticism occasionally gets the better of him, and persons and categories of persons are spuriously equated. Adorno's point was that we should at all costs avoid the kind of liberal shorthand that opposes collectivities as either oppressors or oppressed. The task of the intellectual is not to speak for abstractions— cultures, categories, or doctrines—but to disclose the truth of existence. And existence, as Sartre explained, cannot be reduced to essences, any more than it can be cleansed, as Adorno reminded us, of ambiguity. Oppression and freedom, creation and destruction, good and evil, are mutually entailed and inextricably entangled in *all* human situations, and modes of knowing or acting that assume that intersubjectivity is otherwise are equally dangerous. This is why the intellectual must both testify *through engagement* to the way things are *and* keep an open mind—striving to demystify, deconstruct, and defuse the words with which we try to capture, arrest, and control the confusing dialectics of identity while at the same time repudiating the fetishization of vocabulary that leads us to overlook or forget the transitive, abundant, outlandish, and mutable character of experience. No one person or group can be said to possess the moral high ground by virtue of either pain or privilege. Neither suffering nor reason confer superiority. One can only speak of a perennial struggle to affirm one's right to live in a world one calls one's own without invalidating the same right of others.

As I review my experience of fieldwork in Africa and Australia I have to say that stronger than any sense of distinctive or determinant cultural identities has been the force of things held in common. Not the commonplace truths that all people marry, raise children, and suffer loss, but the existential truth that I believe holds good for all humankind: that people need to have some say in the world into which they are thrown, that they must in some measure choose their own lives and feel that they have a right to be here, to be free to make a difference, to be loved and affirmed, to be more than piano keys, ciphers, names, at the mercy of the gods, of oppressive laws, of impersonal injunctions, or mere fate. Like Arthur Kleinman, I expect the anthropological project to be an exploration of the human condition, and not simply of the cultural conditioning of our humanity. "That which is at stake for men and women is constrained by shared human conditions, and, at the same time, it is elaborated by the particularities of local life worlds and individuals. Thus, *human conditions supercede the dichotomy between 'universal' and 'particular' forms of living*" (Kleinman 1995, 273; emphasis added).

The focus on intersubjectivity helps us overcome the sterile, essentializing, either-or habit of categorizing experience in terms of purportedly sub-stantial, immutable, and opposed states of being such as self versus other, local versus global, West versus East, North versus South. By shifting our focus to the mutable field of intersubjective experience, such antinomies come to be seen not as reflecting the world as it is unto itself but the world as we represent it to ourselves the better to inhabit it with some sense of knowledge and control. And it brings the locus of our human responsibility back home, to the particular lifeworlds we inhabit, the particular fields of intersubjectivity of which we are a part. In these intersubjective fields iden-tity and essence may provide a useful currency but they should never be allowed to possess absolute value.

An Island in the Stream

Desmond approached me one day outside the mission store where I was waiting for the family to complete its shopping. A wiry, weather-beaten man in bare feet and a cheap plastic raincoat. Part aboriginal, the fingers of his right hand were conspicuously missing. I guessed him to be about sixty, his hair as grey and unkempt as my own. He wanted to know if I could give him a lift to Cooktown sometime. He was living on an island in the river. He knew Fred. Anytime I was going to Cooktown, he'd be grateful for the ride.

He spoke with ingratiatingly good manners, as if wise to the ways of middle-class whites, and was practiced in asking favors.

When I went to Cooktown a couple of days later, Desmond came along. My daughter Heidi drove. My small son, Joshua, sat between us in the front seat. But it was Desmond who did all the talking. Leaning forward from the back of the vehicle, he ear-bashed us all the way from the outsta-tion to Black Mountain.

He hailed from Toowoomba, born of an aboriginal father and nonaborigi-nal mother. When still a boy, his mother banished him from the house for assaulting his elder brother. For years then he moved from one foster family to another. As for his adult life, it had comprised a similar litany of radically disconnected episodes in different places that made it hard for one to be-lieve all this had happened to the same person. He'd been a crane driver on the Sydney waterfront for several years. A decade married and living near Centennial Park. But his children disappointed him. "I looked them up once but didn't think much of them, and moved on." He spent two years as a Buddhist monk in Thailand (as proof, he rattled off the five noble truths in Pali). Then he had a stint at university studying psychology, followed by five years nursing his ailing father at Tennant Creek in the Northern Territory until the old man died in his son's arms. Desmond was at pains to impress Heidi and me with his filial piety. Though *he'd* been abandoned as a boy, he made sure there was always beer in his father's fridge, $500 in the top drawer of his dressing table, packets of tobacco.

He came to the Daintree with the Greenies to protest the bulldozing of a road through the rainforest. But when he learned that the local aboriginal people actually wanted the road to go through, he changed his mind. He lived at Wujal Wujal for a while, then moved to his island in the river. "I owe nothing and own nothing," he said. And as if to underscore this he spoke of a German girlfriend he once had. "Very beautiful she was. One day I asked her if she was happy. She told me she was content. So I told her to bugger off and find someone who would make her happy. I was mistaken. I didn't realize then that contentment transcends happiness."

At the end of a very long day I helped Desmond tote his supplies and coconut seedlings down the track to the river. It was low tide, and as he waded across to his island, unperturbed by crocodiles, he shouted an invitation that we should come and see him over the weekend.

That Sunday Francine, Heidi, Joshua, and I stood on the riverbank opposite his island. "Ahoy there, Desmond!"

Joshua echoed my words.

Desmond's voice came back out of the paperbarks and scrub. "Is that Joshua I hear?"

Shoving his aluminium dinghy into the water, he stood unsteadily at the stern and, with a long green bamboo pole, by turns punted and steered the dinghy toward us.

On the island we followed him through the shade of the paperbarks as he talked of the scrub hens he'd heard "chortling and yodeling in the blimmin' night" and the tree that had fallen in a recent storm. "Heard it too, cracking apart and crashing down, couple of nights ago."

"So how are you surviving up there?" he asked, meaning at the mission. "I wouldn't live with all that shouting and bawling. They're starving for identity. They'll do anything to get you to notice them."

"They?" I queried.

He ignored the question and expatiated on how important initiation was for a person's self-development, how it put paid to childish attachments and childlike behavior such as tantrums, attention seeking, and shouting fits. "You learn to express yourself like an adult. Dancing. Performing ceremony. Commanding, not demanding, attention. Using your intelligence. Exercising self-control. Discipline, restraint. That's what the law was all about. But here they're black trash, just like you have white trash."

I was taken aback by the derision in his voice, his sudden irascibility. But I agreed with what he said about initiation, about the need to get away from one's home place in order to confront the wider world.

"Not confront!" he retorted angrily. "That's white man's talk. Aboriginality isn't about identity. It's about this!" And he jutted his chin at the surrounding trees. "All this, around us. Being one with this."

I heard him out, just as I had on the road to Cooktown. His pastiche of ethnography, psychology, and Buddhism. His opinions as vehement and as blunt as an ultimatum.

"I'll tell you about the Dreaming. *My* Dreaming. I don't have a Dreaming. Not something out there. It's all in here!" He touched his fist to his chest. "I am not the dreamer, I am the dreamt."

We were now sitting on the mown buffalo grass near his hut. Francine was preoccupied by Joshua. I was listening as patiently as I could as Desmond went on about how idyllic it was on "his" island. "Look," he said, pointing to the tall grass growing along the shore. "I've left those big tufts of guinea grass so that they throw shadows at night. They're people. They judge me. If I'm doing all right here, they approve. If I'm not, they say so."

I felt his loneliness. His desperate need to be regarded as wise and at one with the world.

As Desmond began rolling a cigarette from his packet of Drum tobacco, Heidi asked if he'd prefer a tailor-made.

"I would. I'd love one."

Heidi tossed her pack of blue Winfields and a cigarette lighter onto the ground between them. Desmond had to lean forward to pick them up.

It was as if this was the cue he'd been waiting for. "Don't throw things at me!" he snapped. "Don't treat me like a dog! Don't make me take them. If you meant to give them you should have got up and put them in my hand. Then I would have received them gladly. In Thailand you'd be killed for such rudeness."

Heidi was stunned. She said nothing. I was on the verge of getting up and walking away.

"Do you know what I say to those people up at that mission?" Desmond asked suddenly. "I say to them, 'Name me one white person who's ever done anything for you?'"

"We're whites," I said.

"Well, you might be okay, I don't know. You might have an ulterior motive for being here, I don't know."

He paused, then brought the flat of his hand down hard on a pat of dried horse dung in the stubble, as if to clinch his argument. "See this?" he said, dividing the pat of dung into quarters before moving them slightly apart with his fingerless hand. "Tectonic plates, right? Whites say every race sprang from separate seeds. Dinosaurs. Trees. People. But we didn't migrate here! We didn't come from Africa! We were born with this land! We were seeded here from the beginning! We didn't come from somewhere else like you did!"

DESMOND'S CONCEPTION of belonging to the land—which he expressed variously as a form of umbilical attachment, a manifestation of the Dreaming, and a kind of Buddhistic pantheism—nowadays permeates the discourse of indigenous peoples in the antipodes. In Aotearoa/New Zealand Maori intellectuals and activists drum home the point that they are *tangata whenua* (people of the land), while other migrants are invaders and interlopers who have imposed their way of life on indigenous culture by fraud and force. Spiritual affinity for and identification with the land give legitimacy to the claim that prior settlement implies primary rights. The argument is frequently shored up by a series of racial and cultural antinomies that have labyrinthine legal, moral, political, and religious repercussions. Thus the difference between black and white is assimilated to the difference between prior and successive, sacred and profane, spiritual and material, *communitas* and selfishness, right and wrong, deep and superficial, and so on.

Generally speaking, the more marginal a person feels, the more likely it is that he or she will be attracted to this kind of essentializing and foundational discourse of identity, self-definition, and transpersonal belonging. Ontological insecurity and political weakness promote a search for an invincible category—an ur-culture, nation, parent, or cosmos—to which one can assimilate oneself, in which one may be reborn, to which one can say that one unequivocally belongs. Marginalized peoples, like orphaned or unloved individuals, tend to have recourse to such categorical retreats and ideological iconicities (cf. Herzfeld 1997, 57–73, 139). Indeed, identity thinking becomes a *modus vivendi,* and so, in the antipodes, essentializing leitmotifs such as aboriginality and Maoritanga give beleaguered individuals a spurious *though wholly imperative* sense of mass and solidarity that bolsters and augments their flagging, imperiled, or confused sense of self.

But while iconic exaggeration undeniably has strategic value for marginalized peoples, it is a serious mistake for anthropologists to try to imitate the language of the oppressed on the assumption that this goes some way toward making good the losses that colonized peoples have suffered at European hands. Not only is such empathy spurious—because few anthropologists are ever doomed to the dire and marginal situations one finds in Third World societies—but it abnegates the anthropologist's responsibility to work *from within his or her own situation* to create greater equity and social justice.

Liisa Malkki has recently argued that by having recourse to an essentializing rhetoric of difference and distinction, European historians, anthropologists, and colonial administrators in central Africa inadvertently reified and promulgated a divisive language of ethnic fundamentalism and pseudospeciation that contributed to the Rwandan tragedy in the 1990s (1995, 14). Arguably, therefore, the justification and integrity of anthropology might be said to lie in its capacity to use historicist and cross-cultural perspectives to critique the kind of identity thinking that reduces the multitude of human voices to one voice and the ambiguity of meaning to one meaning. Critical to this project would be the recognition of the intimate link between language and location, voice and belonging.

Conquest and colonization have everywhere involved the dispossession of the two things most vital to indigenous peoples' livelihood and integrity: land and language. It was no accident that the colonizer sought to steal the voice of the colonized at the same time that he alienated their lands. Since, in indigenous as in classical societies, *logos* (speech) was the breath of life, and the word *was* flesh (see Onians 1951, 67–69), the abrogation of native languages negated the native's very existence. In Lakota terms, if one's language is "thrown away" one is oneself extinguished (Momoday 1996, 382). Quite simply, the denial of speech served to cripple a mode of intersubjectivity that simultaneously embraced relationships between self and other, community and country. At the same time, obliged to fall back on the language of the oppressor and usurper, native people lost their footing in the world they had been driven to embrace—hesitant in their intelligence, uncertain in their relations to their ancestors, halting shadows of an invasive other.

If we are to do more than pay lip service to the many voices of humankind, we would be wise to proceed from the concrete to the abstract rather than the other way around. In its manifest lack of immediacy, abstraction has always lent itself to tyranny: a facile ironing out of difference in the name of administrative order (cf. Berger 1985, 266–67; Adorno 1973,

20). It is interesting in this regard how wary so many preliterate peoples are about converting opinions, based on particular experience, into general truths, and how suspicious they are of abstraction (Jackson 1995, 165). Such is certainly the case, in my experience, in aboriginal Australia, which may explain why racism—by definition a matter of abstract and monopolistic generalities—is something of which aboriginal people can but rarely be accused. Thus while many whites in central Australia and Cape York readily sought to edify me with essentializing and generalizing accounts of aboriginal people, informing me that "they" had an aversion to paying petrol and phone bills, that "they" did not like hot curries, and that if "they" got all the land they were claiming they wouldn't know how to look after it or what to do with it, aboriginal people, by contrast, generally used concrete anecdotes to contextualize and provisionalize their views. Take Fred's story, for instance, of the white fella at Wyalla who accused him of taking water from a tap near the airstrip without permission. Fred retorted that he had taken no water; anyone who knew him would know he would never take anything without asking.

"I just listen," Fred told me. Though insulted, he kept his own counsel, suppressed his anger. "But next time I see that bloke," Fred added, "I'll say something. I'll tell him *waybul* don't like *bama* getting back their land."

Ironically, behind most sweeping generalizations lie specific, repressed, and unresolved *personal* conflicts, and this holds true of everyday life and ethnography alike. Though generalizations, like value judgments, purport to offer glimpses into some timeless and transcendent truth, they are usually defenses against impotence, magical ways of conjuring an illusion of knowledge, compensatory strategies for coping with a sense of deep inadequacy in the face of the complexity and contradictoriness of lived experience. Though it is inevitable that many people will always categorize themselves as black and white, colonizer and colonized, male and female, oppressor and victim, traditional and modern, the goal of anthropology is to deconstruct such categorical oppositions by bringing home to us the various reasons they are invoked, the various uses they serve, and the complexity of the lived experience they mask.

To be sure, the history of the Western encounter with non-Western peoples has been, generally speaking, an outrageous history of broken promises and bad faith; of pillage, theft, rape, chicanery, and intolerance. But such deformations and distortions in the field of human intersubjectivity are incipient in *every* interpersonal encounter in which the presence of the other is denigrated or denied. The subject-object split contains the seeds of human destructiveness. When *either* a racist *or* a revolutionary acts against an abstract entity such as "Niggers" or "The Government," "The Oppressor," or simply "Them," he is so estranged from the reality of intersubjective existence that he thinks no person will be harmed by his violent assault against the "object" of his hate. Though children lie mangled and lifeless in the rubble of the public building he has bombed, though a man is strung from a tree in a country lane, though a mother is raped and murdered in some butcher's yard, all that he knows is that his abstraction has been served, his objective has been met, his god has been appeased. And he will even declare that he had no grievance against anyone personally.

The fight against abstraction and reification is a fight against the forgetfulness that is the ground of the possibility of such acts. For without the radical splitting of person from Principle, being from Being, local from Global, existence from Idea, *I* cannot even begin to imagine the Other except as myself.

However, as Frantz Fanon has shown, in any violent situation an oppressor's gains come at a price, for in denying humanity to others he does violence to his own humanity and will often bear the psychological scars of this for as long as he lives (Fanon 1968). From this it does not follow that the humanity of the victim is the greater for his or her pain and suffering. Indeed, when one shifts one's focus from the macropolitical sphere of militant nationalism and explores the micropolitical sphere of hearth and home—R. D. Laing's "politics of the family"—the relationship between dominance and subordination becomes very complex.[2] People's struggles for national liberation often entail increased intolerance for the claims of other minorities, and gender inequalities and domestic violence may in fact be exacerbated. Moreover, as Ranajit Guha has shown, dominance is, in any event, never simply a matter of one class unanimously imposing its will on another; collaboration and consent are as dialectically entailed as resistance and opposition (Guha 1989, 229–32).

For these reasons I find myself less and less interested in catalogs and chronicles of man's inhumanity to man, for we are all capable of dehumanizing acts, than in specific accounts of the ways in which a sense of humanity finds expression under even the most heinous and demoralizing conditions. I think of a Lakota man, filled with vindictive rage as he recollected

---

2. Consider for example the way Desmond moved the burden of his preoccupations around, retrospectively mythologizing and ennobling his father in order to displace his resentments onto people he called "black trash" and "white trash."

his people's history of persecution and betrayal. Prepared to kill whites and then be killed, he descended from a night alone on a hill, with the morning star and a sliver of the moon in the dawn sky, and knew that he wanted to live, so that, instead of yielding to anger and further destructiveness, he determined to devote every remaining day of his life to the work of forgiveness (from the documentary film *The West*). And I think of Wole Soyinka, imprisoned during the Nigerian civil war, who, when finally freed, affirmed love, and in that affirmation knew that his "adversaries had lost the conflict." Or Sidney Rittenberg, after nine years in solitary confinement during the Chinese cultural revolution, declaring that "they" had drawn a "circle that shut me out; but I and love drew a circle that included them, and we won" (from a documentary film).

That which saves one from nothingness is the realization that when one's power to act on the world is rendered utterly ineffectual, one is not *oneself* thereby reduced to nothingness. In the face of the loss of the power to do, one still retains the power to undo, for action is never merely a matter of making a material difference to the way things are; it includes *the work of the imagination* whereby reality is continually rethought and reconstrued. For Hannah Arendt the crucial expressions of this redressive and redemptive power of thought are forgiveness and the promise. To forgive and to give one's word are ways of acknowledging, in the most generous sense imaginable, that one's own fate is in the hands of others; not as a felt fear for one's life but as an act of faith in the possibility that people may grant one another the freedom to surpass the point at which their relationships have come to nothing. Forgiving is never necessarily a forgetting, though many traumatized individuals endeavor to forget that which they cannot forgive. Nor is the focus of forgiving on one's oppressor; rather, it is on the conditions under which one's own life, and the lives of those to whom one is most closely bound, can be released from the oppressor's grasp. Unlike revenge, punishment, or repressed memory, which tend to reenact and perpetuate the original trespass, enslaving one to it forever, forgiveness conserves a memory of the original outrage while releasing one from it.[3] It is in this sense that forgiveness redeems one's life and refuses the oppressor the power to determine it:

> The possible redemption from the predicament of irreversibility—of being unable to undo what one has done though one

3. The original meaning of *aphienai* is "dismiss" or "release" rather than forgive (Arendt 1958, 240).

did not, and could not, have known what he was doing—is the faculty of forgiving. The remedy for unpredictability, for the chaotic uncertainty of the future, is contained in the faculty to make and keep promises. The two faculties belong together in so far as one of them, forgiving, serves to undo the deeds of the past, whose "sins" hang like Damocles' sword over every new generation; and the other, binding oneself through promises, serves to set up in the ocean of uncertainty, which the future is by definition, islands of security without which not even continuity, let alone durability of any kind, would be possible in the relationships between men.

Without being forgiven, released from the consequences of what we have done, our capacity to act would, as it were, be confined to one single deed from which we could never recover; we would remain the victims of its consequences forever, not unlike the sorcerer's apprentice who lacked the magical formula to break the spell. Without being bound to the fulfilment of promises, we would never be able to keep our identities; we would be condemned to wander helplessly and without direction in the darkness of each man's lonely heart, caught in its contradictions and equivocalities—a darkness which only the light shed over the public realm through the presence of others, who confirm the identity between the one who promises and the one who fulfils, can dispel. Both faculties, therefore, depend on plurality, on the presence and acting of others, for no one can forgive himself and no one can feel bound by a promise made only to himself; forgiving and promising enacted in solitude or isolation remain without reality and can signify no more than a role played before one's self. (Arendt 1958, 237)

This idea of redemption informs the project of existential anthropology. Rather than taking up a standpoint removed from the world in which we live, an existential anthropology seeks to move us toward new understandings of our possibilities of acting not on but *within* the world. At issue always is whether anthropology can help us make some difference to the way we relate to one another in the real world. Though anthropological understanding will always remain an "indigent and distorted" image of the world, its displaced perspectives offer us the possibility of taking us out of ourselves, and, in rendering the quotidian exotic and the strange familiar, creating moments of doubt in and critical reflection on our relationships with others. Writes Adorno, "To gain such perspectives without valleity or violence, entirely from felt contact with its objects—this alone is the task of thought" (1974, 247).

In this redemptive sense the universal connotes not a transcendent viewpoint but simply the perennial possibility that human beings can move beyond their local or particular identifications through broadened horizons of intersubjective engagement. Consider, for instance, those for whom history has rendered identity meaningless. In contemporary Britain, people of "mixed race" (the very term is a pleonasm) are fast becoming the rule rather than the exception. Sebastian Naidoo, whose father is South African Indian and whose mother is white and British is not untypical of this exasperated generation. Presented with questionnaires that require one to specify one's ethnic identity, Sebastian sometimes checks "Indian," sometimes "Other," but once "I just scrawled 'human' over the whole lot. I wanted to make fun of their questions and show them how arbitrary their racial categories were" (Younge 1997, 23). The same problem of identity thinking arises in cross-cultural marriages. Of one such marriage—between a Romanian-born Jew and a Hindu—the Indian wife commented, "I don't see cultural differences; I can only see him." Another British-born woman married to an Australian-born Chinese husband spoke in a similar vein: "In day-to-day life we tend to think that 'my perspective is my perspective,' it has nothing to do with race or culture. I hope our children will be interested in both cultures and get the best of both worlds" (Freeman 1997, 11).

Another way of getting beyond identity thinking is suggested by the novelist Edmund White. In a perceptive essay in which he contrasts his experience of living in the United States and in France, White observes that while Americans emphasize a "politics of identity," foregrounding and focusing their particular affiliations, local communities, and special interests, the French extol the virtues of centrism. "In France there is no Jewish novel, no black novel, no gay novel; Jews, blacks and gays, of course, write about their lives, but they would be offended if they were discussed with regard to their religion, ethnicity or gender" (White 1993, 127). White's observations compare with James Baldwin's account of why he left America for France: "I wanted to prevent myself from becoming *merely* a Negro; or, even merely a Negro writer. I wanted to find out in what way the *specialness* of my experience could be made to connect me with other people instead of dividing me from them (Baldwin 1961:17).

For an anthropologist confronted by the language of categorical difference and identity both in the field and back home, these comments open a window onto what Lila Abu-Lughod calls "tactical humanism" and Tzvetan

Todorov calls "critical humanism," where a concern for the human condition is not precluded by our belonging to any particular historical or cultural situation. It is not that anthropologists must give up on the traditional task of studying local worlds in detail and depth; rather that notions like culture, gender, and ethnicity are construed as the *particular* contexts and ways in which people *live* their humanity and not its irreducible essence.

THROUGHOUT THIS BOOK I have thought it wise to avoid the issue of how universals may be isolated and defined in ways that transcend particular ethnographic and historical contexts, partly because so many alleged "universals"—such as the Oedipus complex and the incest taboo—have been taken out of their biogenetic, cultural, and intersubjective contexts and treated atomistically, partly because many so-called universals prove on close examination to be disguised "homegrown particulars" (Wiredu 1996, 2). As Bourdieu notes, invoking the universal is the commonest strategy for enjoining obedience, commanding respect, and legitimating one's own *particular* worldview (Bourdieu 1992a).

Still, the question remains: Is the only true human universal the need for human universals?

In a sense the problem is one of how we understand the relation between our notions of subject as an "organizing idea"—culture, society, biology, history, and so forth—and of subject as an "intentional person." What exactly is the relationship between interpretation, ratiocination, theory, and worldview, on the one hand, and lived experience, existence, practice, and lifeworld, on the other?

In *Allegories of the Wilderness* (1982a) I explored a variety of ethical dilemmas that arise in the course of everyday Kuranko social life—rivalry between half-siblings, divisiveness among cowives, power struggles between chiefs and cult leaders, and tensions between the generations. Though these social contexts are characteristically African, the crises and conflicts that arise in them are recognizably universal. They are the kinds of quandaries that characterize intersubjective life everywhere.

Relations between self and other—and by extension between those whom one regards as self and those whom one designates or dismisses as other—are always shot through with ambiguity and paradox. This is a function of what I have ventured to call the existential imperative, the need that every human being has to feel that he or she has some say over his or her own life, some space in which to exercise choice and judgment, some sense that, despite the finitude and contingency of human existence, his or her presence alters the way the world is constituted. Though this imperative may be voiced in terms of the primary, familial, or intimate *group* with which an individual identifies, or in terms of an abstract idea that articulates such an identity—such as "nation" or "country"—the dynamic is inescapably one of intersubjectivity. Listen to any politician pronouncing on any international issue and one quickly sees that the sensibilities and language games of *interpersonal* life provide the ways in which we think, experience, and negotiate international relations.

Though terms such as *freedom, dignity* and *human rights* are the ways we gloss the existential imperative, it goes by other names in other societies and finds oblique expression in myths and proverbial wisdom. But everywhere the unflagging dialectic of amity and rivalry, love and hate, closure and openness, identity and difference, acceptance and denial is driven by the same human desire for some kind of balance between autonomy and anonymity. And this interplay between the need to stand out and the need to belong governs not only relations between self and other but relations between self and symbol, subject and object, person and thing.

Lévi-Strauss was right: the universal can never be located in the *content* of relationships, for content is always culturally variable and historically contingent. But to locate the universal in the structure of the mind involves too great a departure from the world of lived experience in which contradictions are seldom a matter of logic, and where conceptual antinomies are very often matters of life and death. Structure has to be understood transitively *and* intransitively, as an ongoing process in which concepts, objects, and persons are all implicated. It has to be approached in a radically empirical way, as mediated by physical emotions, senses, gestures, and instincts, as well as by ideas and ideals. It betokens a world of quandaries and of struggle, where resolutions are always provisional, and justice, equity, and balance are always in doubt. Accordingly, structure reveals itself neither in the hidden recesses of the psyche nor in the transpersonal field of history and culture, but in the forms of encounter, interaction, exchange, and dialogue in everyday life. Consider the field of kinship relations. Whereas Lévi-Strauss argued that the kinship nexus may be analyzed *logically and semantically* as a language (1963, 31–54), the structure of elementary kinship relations must also be understood *existentially* as a dynamic interplay between self and others in ever-altering contexts of identification. Only in this way can the subject of kinship and marriage—once the defining field of social anthropology—be rescued from the formalism that has deprived it of any reference to human experience (cf. Trawick 1990, 118–54). Rather than logical relations born of the unconscious and universal structures of Mind, I have endeavored to speak of existential quandaries born of the universal structures of lived sociality. Thus, the mediated dyad that gives triadic form to kinship (mo/fa/child), to the three-generational developmental cycle (grandparent/parent/grandchild), and to interpersonal relations (I/Thou/third party) also governs the tripling of events and character in narrative (protagonist/antagonist/deuteroagonist), the triune in religious iconography, the tripartite structure of rites of passage and separation trauma, and the recurring triadic form of scientific models. Social, emotional, logical, and syntactic worlds are always inextricably conjoined.

But the test of anthropological understanding is wordly, not epistemological. Its truth lies in its capacity to help us see that plurality is not inimical but necessary to our integrity, so inspiring us to accept and celebrate the manifold and contradictory character of existence in the knowledge that any one person embodies the potential to be any other. As Terence's famous stoic dictum has it, *humani nil a me alienum puto*—being human, nothing human is alien to me.

The argument is for a view of Being as complex, ambiguous, and indeterminate. It is analogous to the argument ecologists make *against* genetically engineered and global monocultures and *for* indigenous biodiversity as the only effective way of sustaining life on earth. And it echoes the argument Michael Oakeshott makes in his famous essay on conversation. The task of science, he writes, is not to deliver us from the polyphony of Babel but to accommodate disparate voices, disagreeing with being disagreeable, as in conversation (Oakeshott 1991, 488–89).

Put otherwise, the task of ethnography is not to know the Other in any final sense nor even to know the self through the other. Nor is it to change the lives of others, or even to critique one's own culture. Its warrant and worth lie in its power to describe in depth and detail the dynamics of intersubjective life under a variety of cultural conditions in the hope that one may thereby be led to an understanding of how those rare moments of erasure and effacement occur when self and other are constituted in mutuality and acceptance rather than violence and contempt.

Stopped on a road in order to listen and take notes.

REFERENCES

Abu-Lughod, Lila. 1993. *Writing Women's Worlds: Bedouin Stories.* Berkeley: University of California Press.

———. 1996. "Honor and Shame." In *Things as They Are: New Directions in Phenomenological Anthropology.* Ed. Michael Jackson. Bloomington: Indiana University Press.

Adorno, Theodor. 1973. *Negative Dialectics.* Trans. E. B. Ashton. New York: Continuum.

———. 1974. *Minima Moralia: Reflections from Damaged Life.* Trans. E. F. N. Jephcott. London: Verso.

———. 1977–78. "The Actuality of Philosophy." *Telos* 31–34: 120–33.

———. 1978. "Subject and Object." In *The Essential Frankfurt School Reader.* Ed. Andrew Arato and Eike Gebhardt. Oxford: Basil Blackwell.

———. 1991. *Notes to Literature.* Vol. 1. Ed. Rolf Tiedemann, trans. Shierry Weber Nicholson. New York: Columbia University Press.

Anderson, Jon Christopher. 1984. "The Political and Economic Basis of Kuku-Yalanji Social History." Ph.D. diss. University of Queensland, Australia.

———. 1988. "All Bosses Are Not Created Equal." *Anthropological Forum* 5 (4): 507–23.

Appadurai, Arjun, ed. 1986. *The Social Life of Things: Commodities in Cultural Perspective.* Cambridge: Cambridge University Press.

Arendt, Hannah. 1958. *The Human Condition.* Chicago: University of Chicago Press.

———. 1973. *Men in Dark Times.* Harmondsworth: Penguin.

Bail, Kathy. 1997. "In the Driver's Seat." *Australian Magazine,* 8–9 Feb.

Bailey, F. G. 1983. *The Tactical Uses of Passion: An Essay on Power, Reason, and Reality.* Ithaca, N.Y.: Cornell University Press.

Bakhtin, M. M. 1981. *The Dialogic Imagination.* Ed. Caryl Emerson and Michael Holquist. Austin: University of Texas Press.

Baldwin, James. 1961. *Nobody Knows My Name: More Notes of a Native Son.* New York: Dell.

Barthes, Roland. 1977. *Image, Music, Text.* Trans. and Ed. Stephen Heath. New York: Hill and Wang.

Bateson, Gregory. 1958. *Naven.* Stanford, Calif.: Stanford University Press.

Becker, Ernest. 1975. *The Denial of Death.* New York: Free Press.

Beidelman, T. O. 1963. "A Kaguru Version of the Sons of Noah: A Study in the Inculcation of the Idea of Racial Superiority." *Cahiers d'études africaines* 3: 474–90.

Benjamin, Walter. 1968. *Illuminations.* Trans. H. Zohn. New York: Harcourt, Brace, and World.

Benveniste, Emile. 1971. *Problems in General Linguistics.* Trans. Mary Elizabeth Meek. Coral Gables, Fla.: University of Miami Press.

Berger, John. 1985. *The Sense of Sight: Writings of John Berger.* Ed. Lloyd Spencer. New York: Pantheon.

Berlin, Brent, and Paul Kay. 1969. *Basic Color Terms: Their Universality and Evolution.* Berkeley: University of California Press.

Berndt, Ronald M. 1969. *The Sacred Site: The Western Arnhem Land Example.* Australian Aboriginal Studies, no. 29. Social Anthropology Series, no. 4. Canberra.

———. 1979. "A Profile of Good and Bad in Australian Aboriginal Religion." Charles Strong Memorial Lecture. *Australian and New Zealand Theological Review* 12: 17–31.

Besnier, Niko. 1996. "Heteroglossic Discourses on Nukulaelae Spirits." In *Spirits in Culture, History, and Mind.* Ed. Jeannette Marie Mageo and Alan Howard. London: Routledge.

Biddle, Jennifer. 1991. "Dot, Circle, Difference: Translating Central Desert Painting." In *Cartographies: Poststructuralism and the Mapping of Bodies and Spaces.* Ed. Rosalyn Diprose and Robyn Ferrell. Sydney: Allen and Unwin.

Binswanger, Ludwig. 1963. *Being in the World: Selected Papers.* Trans. Jacob Needleman. London: Souvenir Press.

Bird, Charles S. 1976. "Poetry in the Mande: Its Form and Meaning." *Poetics* 5 (2): 89–100.

Bisilliat, J. 1976. "Village Diseases and Bush Diseases in Songhay: An Essay in Description with a View to a Typology." In *Social Anthropology and Medicine.* Trans. and ed. J. B. Loudon. London: Academic Press.

Blacking, John. 1973. *How Musical Is Man?* Seattle: University of Washington Press.

Bloch, Maurice. 1971. "The Moral and Tactical Meaning of Kinship Terms." *Man* 6 (1): 79–87.

Blumenberg, Hans. 1997. *Shipwreck with Spectator.* Trans. Steven Rendall. Cambridge, Mass.: MIT Press.

Bourdieu, Pierre. 1963. "The Attitude of the Algerian Peasant Toward Time." In *Mediterranean Countrymen: Essays in the Social Anthropology of the Mediterranean.* Ed. Julian Pitt-Rivers. Paris: Mouton.

———. 1977. *Outline of a Theory of Practice.* Trans. Richard Nice. Cambridge: Cambridge University Press.

———. 1992a. "Towards a Policy of Morality in Politics." In *From the Twilight of Probability: Ethics and Politics.* Ed. William R. Shea and Antonio Spadafora. Canton, Mass.: Science History Publications.

———. 1992b. "Pour un corporatisme de l'universel." Postscript to *Les Règles de l'art: Genèse et structure de champs littéraire.* Paris: Editions de Seuil.

———. 1996. "Understanding." Trans. Bridget Fowler. *Theory, Culture and Society* 13 (2): 17–37.

Bowlby, John. 1971. *Attachment and Loss, 1: Attachment.* Harmondsworth: Penguin.

———. 1975. *Attachment and Loss, 2: Separation and Anger.* Harmondsworth: Penguin.

Brandström, Per. 1990. "Seeds and Soil: The Quest for Life and the Domestication of Fertility in Sukuma-Nyamwezi Thought and Reality." In *The Creative Communion: African Folk Models of Fertility and the Regeneration of Life.* Ed. Anita Jacobson-Widding and Walter van Beek. Uppsala Studies in Cultural Anthropology 15. Stockholm.

Broom, Richard. 1982. *Aboriginal Australians: Black Response to White Dominance.* Sydney: Allen and Unwin.

Brown, Norman O. 1959. *Life Against Death: The Psychoanalytical Meaning of History.* Middletown, Conn.: Wesleyan University Press.

———. 1969. *Hermes the Thief: The Evolution of a Myth.* New York: Vintage.

Broyard, Anatole. 1992. *Intoxicated by My Illness, and Other Writings on Life and Death.* Ed. Alexandra Broyard. New York: Clarkson Potter.

Bruner, Jerome. 1976. "Nature and Uses of Immaturity." In *Play—Its Role in Development and Education.* Ed. Jerome Bruner, Alison Jolly, and Kathy Sylva. Harmondsworth: Penguin.

Buber, Martin. 1961. *Between Man and Man.* Trans. Robert Gregory Smith. London: Fontana.

Burridge, Kenelm. 1960. *Mambu: A Melanesian Millennium.* London: Methuen.

Byrne, Richard W. 1995. *The Thinking Ape: Evolutionary Origins of Intelligence.* Oxford: Oxford University Press.

Calame-Griaule, G. 1965. *Ethnologie et langage: La Parole chez les Dogon.* Paris: Gallimard.

Carter, Julie D. 1991. "Am I Too Black to Go with You?" In *Being Black: Aboriginal Cultures in "Settled" Australia*. Ed. Ian Keen. Canberra: Aboriginal Studies Press.

Chandogya Upanishad. 1965. *The Upanishads*. Trans. Juan Mascaró. Harmondsworth: Penguin Books.

Chattopadhyaya, D. P., Lester Embree, and Jitendranath Mohanty. 1992. *Phenomenology and Indian Philosophy*. New Delhi: Motilal Banarsidass.

Cissé, Youssef. 1973. "Signes graphiques, représentations, concepts et tests relatifs à la personne chez les Malinké et les Bambara du Mali." In *La Notion de Personne en Afrique Noire*. Ed. Germaine Dieterlen. Paris: Éditions du Centre National de la Recherche Scientifique.

Classen, Constance. 1993. *Worlds of Sense: Exploring the Senses in History and Across Cultures*. London: Routledge.

Classen, Constance, David Howes, and Anthony Synnott. 1994. *Aroma: The Cultural History of Smell*. London: Routledge.

Collmann, Jeff. 1988. *Fringe-Dwellers and Welfare: The Aboriginal Response to Bureaucracy*. St. Lucia: University of Queensland Press.

Connerton, Paul. 1989. *How Societies Remember*. Cambridge: Cambridge University Press.

Connolly, Bob, and Robin Anderson. 1987. *First Contact*. New York: Viking Penguin.

Cowlishaw, Gillian. 1988. *Black, White or Brindle: Race in Rural Australia*. Cambridge: Cambridge University Press.

Crapanzano, Vincent. 1988. "On Self-Characterization." *Working Papers and Proceedings of the Center for Psychosocial Studies*, no. 24. Chicago: Center for Psychosocial Studies.

Das, Veena. 1989. "Subaltern as Perspective." In *Subaltern Studies VI: Writings on South Asian History and Society*. Ed. Ranajit Guha. Delhi: Oxford University Press.

Davidson, Robyn. 1980. *Tracks*. London: Jonathan Cape.

Dawson, J. 1981. *Australian Aborigines: The Languages and Customs of Several Tribes in the Western Desert of Victoria, Australia*. Australian Institute of Aboriginal Studies, n. s., no. 26. Canberra.

De Certeau, Michel. 1988. *The Practice of Everyday Life*. Trans. S. Rendall. Berkeley: University of California Press.

Desjarlais, Robert R. 1992. *Body and Emotion: The Aesthetics of Illness and Healing in the Nepal Himalayas*. Philadelphia: University of Pennsylvania Press.

Devereux, George. 1967. *From Anxiety to Method in the Behavioral Sciences*. The Hague: Mouton.

———. 1976. *A Study of Abortion in Primitive Societies*. Rev. ed. New York: International Universities Press.

————. 1978. *Ethnopsychoanalysis: Psychoanalysis and Anthropology as Complementary Frames of Reference.* Berkeley: University of California Press.

————. 1980. *Basic Problems of Ethnopsychiatry.* Trans. Basia Miller Gulati and George Devereux. Chicago: University of Chicago Press.

Devisch, René. 1985. "Symbol and Psychosomatic Symptom in Bodily Space-Time: The Case of the Yaka of Zaire." International Journal of Psychology 20 (4–5): 589–616.

————. 1993. *Weaving the Threads of Life: The Khita Gyn-Eco-Logical Healing Cult among the Yaka.* Chicago: University of Chicago Press.

Dewey, John. 1958. *Experience and Nature.* New York: Dover.

Dilthey, W. 1976. *Selected Writings.* Trans. and ed. H. Rickman. Cambridge: Cambridge University Press.

Dixon, Robert. 1984. *Searching for Aboriginal Languages: Memoirs of a Field Worker.* St. Lucia: University of Queensland Press.

Dostoyevsky, Fyodor. 1961. *Notes from Underground.* New York: Signet.

Drewal, Margaret Thompson. 1992. *Yoruba Ritual: Performers, Play, Agency.* Bloomington: Indiana University Press.

Dussart, Françoise. 1988. "Warlpiri Women's Yawulyu Ceremonies: A Forum for Socialisation and Innovation." Ph.D. diss., Australian National University.

Edwards, Derek. 1978. "Social Relations and Early Language." In *Action, Gesture and Symbol.* Ed. Andrew Lock. London: Academic Press.

Elias, Norbert. 1994. *The Civilizing Process: The History of Manners and State Formation and Civilization.* Trans. Edmund Jephcott. Oxford: Blackwell.

Elkin, A. P. 1943. *The Australian Aborigines.* 2d ed. Sydney: Angus and Robertson.

Ellen, Roy. 1988. "Fetishism." Man 23 (2): 213–35.

Ellenberger, Henri F. 1958. "A Clinical Introduction to Psychiatric Phenomenology and Existential Analysis." In *Existence.* Ed. Rollo May, Ernst Angel, and Henri F. Ellenberger. New Jersey: Jason Aronson.

Erikson, Erik. 1968. *Identity: Youth and Crisis.* London: Faber

Esterson, Aaron. 1972. *The Leaves of Spring: A Study in the Dialectics of Madness.* Harmondsworth: Penguin.

Evans-Pritchard, E. Evans. 1937. *Witchcraft, Oracles and Magic Among the Azande.* Oxford: Clarendon Press.

————. 1956. *Nuer Religion.* Oxford: Clarendon Press.

Fabian, Johannes. 1983. *Time and the Other: How Anthropology Makes Its Object.* New York: Columbia University Press.

Fanon, Frantz. 1968. *The Wretched of the Earth.* Trans. Constance Farrington. New York: Grove Press.

Feil, Daryl K. 1983. "A World without Exchange: Millennia and the Tee Ceremonial System in Tombema-Enga Society (New Guinea)." *Anthropos* 78: 89–106.

Feld, Steven. 1982. *Sound and Sentiment: Birds, Weeping, Poetics, and Song in Kaluli Expression.* Philadelphia: University of Pennsylvania Press.

————. 1996. "Pygmy POP: A Genealogy of Schizophrenic Mimesis." *Yearbook for Traditional Music* 28: 1–35.

Fernandez, James. 1982. *Bwiti: An Ethnography of the Religious Imagination in Africa.* Princeton, N.J.: Princeton University Press.

Feyerabend, Paul. 1987. *Farewell to Reason.* London: Verso.

Finnegan, Ruth. 1967. *Limba Stories and Story-Telling.* Oxford: Clarendon Press.

Fiske, Alan Page. 1995. "Learning a Culture the Way Informants Do: Observing, Imitating, and Participating." Unpub.

Fonseca, Isabel. 1995. *Bury Me Standing: The Gypsies and their Journey.* New York: Knopf.

Fortes, Meyer. 1949. *The Web of Kinship among the Tallensi: The Second Part of an Analysis of the Social Structure of a Trans-Volta Tribe.* London: Oxford University Press.

————. 1969. *Kinship and the Social Order.* Chicago: Aldine.

————. 1975. "Strangers." In *Studies in African Social Anthropology.* Ed. Meyer Fortes and Sheila Patterson. London: Academic Press.

————. 1987. *Religion, Morality and the Person.* Ed. Cambridge: Cambridge University Press.

Foucault, Michel. 1970. *The Order of Things.* London: Tavistock.

————. 1977. *Language, Counter-Memory, Practice.* Trans. Donald F. Bouchard and Sherry Simon. Ithaca, N.Y.: Cornell University Press.

————. 1990. *The Use of Pleasure.* Vol. 2 of *The History of Sexuality.* Trans. Robert Hurley. New York: Vintage Books.

Fowler, H. W. 1984. *A Dictionary of Modern English Usage.* Ware, Hertfordshire, England: Omega Books.

Freeman, Derek. 1973. "Kinship, Attachment Behaviour and the Primary Bond." In *The Character of Kinship.* Ed. Jack Goody. Cambridge: Cambridge University Press.

————. 1983. *Margaret Mead and Samoa: The Making and Unmaking of an Anthropological Myth.* Canberra: Australian National University Press.

Freeman, Jane. 1997. "New Faces." In *Sydney Morning Herald,* 15 Jan.

Freud, Sigmund. 1957. *Standard Edition of the Complete Psychological Works of Sigmund Freud.* Trans. and ed. James Strachey. London: Hogarth Press.

Fromm, Erich. 1949. *Man for Himself: An Enquiry into the Psychology of Ethics.* London: Routledge and Kegan Paul.

————. 1973. The *Crisis in Psychoanalysis.* Harmondsworth: Penguin.

Geertz, Clifford. 1988. *Works and Lives: The Anthropologist as Author.* Stanford, Calif.: Stanford University Press.

Gergen, Kenneth J. 1991. *The Saturated Self: Dilemmas of Identity in Contemporary Life.* New York: Basic Books.

Giddens, Anthony. 1979. *Central Problems in Social Theory: Action, Structure and Contradiction in Social Analysis.* Berkeley: University of California Press.

Gilbert, Kevin. 1978. *Living Black: Blacks Talk to Kevin Gilbert.* Ringwood, Victoria, Australia: Penguin Books.

Godelier, Maurice. 1977. *Perspectives in Marxist Anthropology.* Trans. R. Brain. Cambridge: Cambridge University Press.

Goffman, Erving. 1963. *Behavior in Public Places.* Glencoe, Ill.: Free Press.

———. 1967. *Interaction Ritual.* New York: Doubleday.

———. 1971. *Relations in Public.* New York: Harper and Row.

Gottlieb, Alma. 1992. *Under the Kapok Tree: Identity and Difference in Beng Thought.* Bloomington: Indiana University Press.

Graumann, Carl F. 1995. "Commonality, Mutuality, Reciprocity: A Conceptual Introduction." In *Mutualities in Dialogue.* Ed. Ivana Marková, Carl F. Graumann, and Klaus Foppa. Cambridge: Cambridge University Press.

Guha, Ranajit. 1983. *Elementary Aspects of Peasant Insurgency in Colonial India.* Delhi: Oxford University Press.

———. 1989. "Dominance without Hegemony and Its Historiography." In *Subaltern Studies VI: Writings on South Asian History and Society.* Ed. Ranajit Guha. Delhi: Oxford University Press.

Halbwachs, Maurice. 1980. *The Collective Memory.* Trans. Francis J. Ditter Jr. and Vida Yazdi Ditter. New York: Harper and Row.

Hamilton, Annette. 1981. *Nature and Nurture: Aboriginal Child-Rearing in North-Central Arnhem Land.* Canberra: Australian Institute of Aboriginal Studies.

Hanks, William F. 1990. *Referential Practice: Language and Lived Space among the Maya.* Chicago: University of Chicago Press.

Harris, W. T., and Harry Sawyerr. 1968. *The Springs of Mende Belief and Conduct.* Freetown: Sierra Leone University Press.

Haviland, John. 1979a. "Guugu Yimidhirr Brother-in-Law Language." *Language and Society* 8: 365–93.

———. 1979b. "How to Talk to your Brother-in-Law in Guugu Yimidhirr." In *Languages and Their Speakers.* Ed. Timothy Shopen. Cambridge, Mass.: Winthrop.

Hegel, G. W. F. 1971. *Philosophy of Mind.* Trans. William Wallace. Oxford: Clarendon Press.

Heinz, Hans-Joachim, and Marshall Lee. 1979. *Namkwa: Life among the Bushmen.* Boston: Houghton Mifflin.

Heidegger, Martin. 1962. *Being and Time.* Trans. John Macquarrie and Edward Robinson. San Francisco: Harper Collins.

Herzfeld, Michael. 1987. *Anthropology through the Looking-Glass: Critical Ethnography in the Margins of Europe.* Cambridge: Cambridge University Press.

———. 1997. *Cultural Intimacy: Social Poetics in the Nation-State.* New York: Routledge.

Holquist, Michael. 1981. Introduction to *The Dialogic Imagination: Four Essys by*

M. M. Bakhtin, trans. Caryl Emerson and Michael Holquist, ed. Michael Holquist. Austin: University of Texas Press.

Horton, Robin. 1971. "African Conversion." *Africa* 41 (2): 85–108.

———. 1975. "On the Rationality of Conversion." *Africa* 45 (3): 219–35 and 45 (4): 373–99.

———. 1993. *Patterns of Thought in Africa and the West: Essays on Magic, Religion and Science.* Cambridge: Cambridge University Press.

Howes, David. 1991. "Olfaction and Transition." In *The Varieties of Sensory Experience: A Sourcebook in the Anthropology of the Senses.* Ed. David Howes. Toronto: University of Toronto Press.

Hultin, Jan. 1990. "The Conquest of Land and the Conquest of Fertility: A Theme in Oromo Culture." In *The Creative Communion: African Folk Models of Fertility and the Regeneration of Life.* Ed. Anita Jacobson-Widding and Walter van Beek. Uppsala Studies in Cultural Anthropology 15. Stockholm.

Hurston, Zora Neale. 1969. *Mules and Men.* New York: Negro Universities Press.

Husserl, Edmund. 1962. *Ideas: General Introduction to Pure Phenomenology.* New York: Collier.

———. 1970. *Cartesian Meditations.* Trans. Dorian Carins. The Hague: Martinus Nijhoff.

Hutchinson, Thomas J. 1861. "On the Social and Domestic Traits of the African Tribes; With a Glance at Their Superstitions, Cannibalism, etc. etc." In *Transactions of the Royal Ethnological Society of London* 1 (2): 327–40.

Illich, Ivan. 1973. *Tools for Conviviality.* London: Calder and Boyars.

———. 1975. *Celebration of Awareness.* Harmondsworth: Penguin.

Jackson, Michael. 1977. *The Kuranko: Dimensions of Social Reality in a West African Society.* London: C. Hurst.

———. 1982a. *Allegories of the Wilderness: Ethics and Ambiguity in Kuranko Narratives.* Bloomington: Indiana University Press.

———. 1982b. "Meaning and Moral Imagery in Kuranko Myth." *Research in African Literatures* 13 (2): 153–80.

———. 1983. "Knowledge of the Body." *Man* 18: 327–45.

———. 1986. *Barawa, and the Ways Birds Fly in the Sky.* Washington, D.C.: Smithsonian Institution Press.

———. 1989. *Paths toward a Clearing: Radical Empiricism and Ethnographic Inquiry.* Bloomington: Indiana University Press.

———. 1995. *At Home in the World.* Durham: Duke University Press.

———. 1996. Introduction to *Things as They Are: New Directions in Phenomenological Anthropology.* Ed. Michael Jackson. Bloomington: Indiana University Press.

Jacobson-Widding, Anita. 1979. *Red-White-Black as a Mode of Thought: A Study of Triadic Classification by Colours in the Ritual Symbolism and Cognitive Thought of the Peoples of the Lower Congo.* Uppsala: University of Uppsala Press.

James, William. 1950. *The Principles of Psychology*. 2 Vols. New York: Dover.

Jangala, Joe. 1994. "The Two Dogs." In *Yimikirli: Warlpiri Dreamings and Histories*. Trans. Peggy Rockman Napaljarri and Lee Cataldi. Sydney: Harper Collins.

Joas, Hans. 1993. *Pragmatism and Social Theory*. Chicago: University of Chicago Press.

Junod, Henri. 1927. *The Life of a South African Tribe*. Vol. 2. London: Macmillan.

Katzantzakis, Nikos. 1961. *Zorba the Greek*. London: Faber and Faber.

Keane, Webb. 1997. *Signs of Recognition: Powers and Hazards of Representation in an Indonesian Society*. Berkeley: University of California Press.

Keats, John. 1958. *The Letters of John Keats 1814–1821*. Vol. 1. Ed. H. E. Rollins. Cambridge: Cambridge University Press.

Keen, Ian. 1994. *Knowledge and Secrecy in an Aboriginal Religion*. Oxford: Clarendon Press.

Kermode, Frank. 1979. *The Genesis of Secrecy*. Cambridge, Mass.; Harvard University Press.

Kingsley, Mary H. 1897. *Travels in West Africa*. London: Macmillan.

Kone, Kassim. 1994. *Mande Zana ni Ntalen 1177: Bamanankan ni Angilekan na* (1177 Mande Proverbs in Bambara and English). Unpub.

Kleinman, Arthur. 1992. "Pain and Resistance: The Delegitimation and Relegitimation of Local Worlds." In *Pain as Human Experience: An Anthropological Perspective*. Ed. M.-J. DelVecchio Good, P. E. Brodwin, B. J. Good, and A. Kleinman. Berkeley: University of California Press.

———. 1995. *Writing at the Margin: Discourse between Anthropology and Medicine*. Berkeley: University of California Press.

Kuipers, Joel C. 1991. "Matters of Taste in Weyéwa." In *The Varieties of Sensory Experience: A Sourcebook in the Anthropology of the Senses*. Ed. David Howes. Toronto: University of Toronto Press.

Kundera, Milan. 1988. *The Art of the Novel*. Trans. Linda Asher. New York: Harper and Row.

La Barre, Weston. 1972. *The Ghost Dance: Origins of Religion*. New York: Dell.

Lacan, Jacques. 1966. *Écrits*. Paris: Editions de Seuil.

Laing, R. D. 1965. *The Divided Self: An Existential Study in Sanity and Madness*. Harmondsworth: Penguin.

Lakoff, George, and Mark Johnson. 1980. *Metaphors We Live By*. Chicago: University of Chicago Press.

Lange, Roderyk. 1975. *The Nature of Dance: An Anthropological Perspective*. London: Macdonald and Evans.

Langton, Marcia. 1993. *"Well, I Heard it on the Radio and I Saw It on the Television": An Essay for the Australian Film Commission on the Politics and Aesthetics of Filmmaking by and about Aboriginal People and Things*. Sydney: Australian Film Commission.

Lawrence, Peter. 1964. *Road Belong Cargo: A Study of the Cargo Movement in the Southern Madang District of New Guinea*. Manchester: Manchester University Press.

Leder, Drew. 1990. *The Absent Body*. Chicago: University of Chicago Press.

Lederman, Rena. 1986. *What Gifts Engender: Social Relations and Politics in Mendi, Highland Papua New Guinea*. Cambridge: Cambridge University Press.

Lee, Dorothy. 1976. *Valuing the Self: What We Can Learn from Other Cultures*. Englewood Cliffs, N.J.: Prentice-Hall.

Lefebvre, Henri. 1991. *Critique of Everyday Life*. Vol. 1. Trans. John Moore. London: Verso.

Le Goff, Jacques. 1993. *Intellectuals in the Middle Ages*. Trans. Teresa Lavender Fagan. Oxford: Basil Blackwell.

Lévi-Strauss, Claude. 1963. *Totemism*. Trans. Rodney Needham. Boston: Beacon Press.

———. 1963. *Structural Anthropology*. Vol. 1. Trans. Claire Jacobson and Brooke Grundfest Schoepf. New York: Basic Books.

———. 1966. *The Savage Mind*. London: Weidenfeld and Nicolson.

———. 1973. *Tristes Tropiques*. Trans. John and Doreen Weightman. London: Jonathan Cape.

———. 1990. *The Naked Man*. Vol. 4 of *Mythologiques*. Trans. John and Doreen Weightman. Chicago: University of Chicago Press.

Lévy, Bernard-Henri. 1995. "An Interview with Michel Foucault." In *Adventures on the Freedom Road: The French Intellectuals in the twentieth Century*. Trans. and ed. Richard Veasey. London: Harvill Press.

Levy, Robert L. *Tahitians: Mind and Experience in the Society Islands*. Chicago: University of Chicago Press.

Lienhardt, Godfrey. 1961. *Divinity and Experience: The Religion of the Dinka*. London: Oxford University Press.

Livingstone, David. 1961. *Missionary Correspondence 1841–1856*. Ed. I. Shapera. Berkeley: University of California Press.

Loos, Noel. 1982. *Invasion and Resistance: Aboriginal-European Relations on the North Queensland Frontier 1861–1897*. Canberra: Australian National University Press.

Lowry, Malcolm. 1979. *Hear Us O Lord from Heaven Thy Dwelling Place*. Harmondsworth: Penguin.

Luckmann, Thomas. 1970. "On the Boundaries of the Social World." In *Phenomenology and Social Reality*. Ed. Maurice Natanson. The Hague: Martinus Nijhoff.

———. 1972. "The Constitution of Language in the World of Everyday Life." In *Life-World and Consciousness: Essays for Aron Gurwitsch*. Ed. Lester E. Embree. Evanston, Ill.: Northwestern University Press.

Luria, A. R. 1968. *The Mind of a Mnemonist: A Little Book about a Vast Memory*. Trans. Lynn Solotaroff. New York: Basic Books.

Luria, A. R., and F. Ia. Yudovich. 1971. *Speech and the Development of Mental*

Processes in the Child: An Experimental Investigation. Ed. Joan Simon. Harmondsworth: Penguin.

Lutz, Catherine A. 1988. *Unnatural Emotions: Everyday Sentiments on a Micronesian Atoll and Their Challenge to Western Theory.* Chicago: University of Chicago Press.

Lyotard, Jean-François. 1984. *The Postmodern Condition: A Report on Knowledge.* Trans. G. Berrington and B. Massumi. Minneapolis: University of Minnesota Press.

MacGaffey, Wyatt. 1977. "Fetishism Revisited: Kongo Nkisi in Sociological Perspective." *Africa* 47 (2): 172–84.

———. 1990. "The Personhood of Ritual Objects: Kongo Minkisi." Etnofoor 3 (1): 45–61.

———. 1994. "African Objects and the Idea of Fetish." In *Peabody Museum of Archaeology and Ethnology* 25: 123–32.

MacIntyre, Alasdair. 1984. *After Virtue: A Study in Moral Theory.* 2d ed. Notre Dame, Ind.: University of Notre Dame Press.

Maddock, Kenneth. 1988. "Myth, History and a Sense of Oneself." In *Past and Present: The Construction of Aboriginality.* Ed. Jeremy R. Beckett. Canberra: Aboriginal Studies Press.

Mahuika, Api. 1975. "Leadership: Inherited and Achieved." In *Te Ao Hurihuri, The World Moves On: Aspects of Maoritanga.* Ed. Michael King. Wellington: Hicks Smith.

Malkki, Liisa H. 1995. *Purity and Exile: Violence, Memory, and National Cosmology among Hutu Refugees in Tanzania.* Chicago: University of Chicago Press.

Malinowski, Bronislaw. 1974. *Magic, Science and Religion and Other Essays.* London: Souvenir Press.

Mannheim, Bruce, and Dennis Tedlock. 1995. Introduction to *The Dialogic Emergence of Culture.* Ed. Dennis Tedlock and Bruce Mannheim. Urbana: University of Illinois Press.

Mannoni, Otare J. D. 1956. *Prospero and Caliban: The Psychology of Colonialization.* Trans. P. Powesland. New York: Praeger.

Marsden, Maori. 1975. "God, Man and Universe: A Maori View." In *Te Ao Hurihuri, The World Moves On: Aspects of Maoritanga.* Ed. Michael King. Wellington: Hicks Smith.

Marx, Karl. 1964. *Pre-Capitalist Economic Formations.* Trans. J. Cohen. London: Lawrence and Wishart.

———. 1970. *Capital.* London: Lawrence and Wishart.

———. 1953. *Die Frühschriften.* Ed. S. Landshut. Stuttgart: Dietz.

Marx, Karl, and Friedrich Engels. 1947. *The German Ideology.* Ed. R. Pascal. New York: International Publishers.

Mauss, Marcel. 1954. *The Gift: Forms and Functions of Exchange in Archaic Societies.* Trans. Ian Cunnison. London: Cohen and West.

————. 1973. "Techniques of the Body." *Economy and Society* 2: 70–88.

McConnel, Ursula. 1931. "A Moon Legend from the Bloomfield River, North Queensland." *Oceania* 11 (1): 9–25.

McNaughton, Patrick R. 1988. *The Mande Blacksmith: Knowledge, Power, and Art in West Africa.* Bloomington: Indiana University Press.

Mead, G. H. 1934. *Mind, Self and Society.* Chicago: University of Chicago Press.

Meggitt, M. J. 1964. "Male-Female Relationships in the Highlands of Australian New Guinea." American Anthropologist 66 (4, pt. 2): 204–24.

————. 1966. "Gadjari among the Walbiri Aborigines of Central Australia." *Oceania* 36 (4): 22–147.

————. 1968. "Literacy in New Guinea and Melanesia." In *Literacy in Traditional Societies.* Ed. Jack Goody. Cambridge: Cambridge University Press.

Merleau-Ponty, Maurice. 1962. *Phenomenology of Perception.* Trans. Colin Smith. London: Routledge and Kegan Paul.

————. 1964. *The Primacy of Perception.* Ed. James Edie. Evanston, Ill.: Northwestern University Press.

————. 1965. *The Structure of Behaviour.* Trans. A. L. Fisher. London: Methuen.

————. 1968. *The Visible and the Invisible.* Ed. Claude Lefort. Trans. Alphonso Lingis. Evanston, Ill.: Northwestern University Press.

Miller, James. 1993. *The Passion of Michel Foucault.* New York: Simon and Schuster.

Momoday, N. Scott. 1996. "The American West and the Burden of Belief." In *The West: An Illustrated History.* London: Weidenfeld and Nicolson.

Montaigne, Michel de. 1948. *The Essayes of Montaigne.* Trans. John Florio. New York: Modern Library.

Morphy, Howard. 1991. *Ancestral Connections: Art and an Aboriginal System of Knowledge.* Chicago: University of Chicago Press.

Munn, Nancy D. 1970. "The Transformation of Subjects into Objects in Walbiri and Pitjantjatjara Myth." In *Australian Aboriginal Anthropology.* Ed. R. Berndt. Nedlands: University of Western Australia Press.

————. 1973. *Walbiri Iconography: Graphic Representation and Cultural Symbolism in a Central Australian Society.* Ithaca, N.Y.: Cornell University Press.

Myers, Fred R. 1986. *Pintupi Country, Pintupi Self: Sentiment, Place, and Politics among Western Desert Aborigines.* Washington, D.C.: Smithsonian Institution Press.

————. 1988. "Burning the Truck and Holding the Country: Property, Time and the Negotiation of Identity among Pintupi Aborigines." In *Hunters and Gatherers 2: Property, Power and Ideology.* Ed. Tim Ingold, David Riches, and James Woodburn. Oxford: Berg.

Nagel, Thomas. 1986. *The View from Nowhere.* New York: Oxford University Press.

Nandy, Ashis. 1988. *The Intimate Enemy: Loss and Recovery of Self Under Colonialism.* Delhi: Oxford University Press.

Nihill, Michael. 1986. "Roads of Presence: Social Relatedness and Exchange in Anganen Social Structure." Ph.D. diss., University of Adelaide.

Oakeshott, Michael. 1933. *Experience and Its Modes.* Cambridge: Cambridge University Press.

——. 1991. *Rationalism in Politics and Other Essays.* New ed. Ed. Timothy Fuller. Indianapolis: Liberty Fund.

Oates, Lynette F. 1993. *Kuku-Yalanji Dictionary.* Australian Institute of Aboriginal and Torres Strait Islander Studies. Albury, N.S.W.: Graeme van Brummelen.

O'Brien, Tim. 1990. *The Things They Carried.* Boston: Houghton Mifflin.

Odin, Steve. 1996. *The Social Self in Zen and American Pragmatism.* Albany: State University of New York Press.

Onians, Richard Broxton. 1951. *The Origins of European Thought.* Cambridge: Cambridge University Press.

Papoušek, Mechthild. 1995. "Origins of Reciprocity and Mutuality in Prelinguisitc Parent-Infant 'Dialogues.' In *Mutualities in Dialogue.* Ed. Ivana Marková, Carl F. Graumann, and Klaus Foppa. Cambridge: Cambridge University Press.

Pierson, William D. 1976. "Puttin' Down Ol Massa: African Satire in the New World." In *Research in African Literatures* 7 (2): 166–80.

Pomonti, Jean-Claude. 1980. "The Ivory Coast: Clouds over a Model State." In *Guardian Weekly,* 2 Mar. p. 14.

Povinelli, Elizabeth A. 1993. *Labor's Lot: The Power, History, and Culture of Aboriginal Action.* Chicago: University of Chicago Press.

Povinelli, Daniel J., and Timothy J. Eddy. 1996. *What Young Chimpanzees Know about Seeing.* Monographs of the Society for Research in Child Development, no. 247. Chicago: University of Chicago Press.

Powell, Anthony. 1951. *A Dance to the Music of Time.* Boston: Little, Brown.

Rabinow, Paul. 1996. *Essays on the Anthropology of Reason.* Princeton, N.J.: Princeton University Press.

Rank, Otto. 1936. *Truth and Reality.* Trans. Jessie Taft. New York: Knopf.

Rawls, John. 1971. *A Theory of Justice.* Cambridge, Mass.: Harvard University Press.

Reade, Winwood. 1873. *The African Sketch-Book.* Vol. 2. London: Smith, Elder.

Reik, T. 1966. *The Compulsion to Confess: On the Psychoanalysis of Crime and Punishment.* New York: Wiley.

Reser, Joseph P. 1979. "A Matter of Control: Aboriginal Housing Circumstances in Remote Communities and Settlements." In *A Black Reality: Aboriginal Camps and Housing in Remote Australia.* Ed. Michael Heppell. Canberra: Australian Institute of Aboriginal Studies.

Reynolds, Vernon. 1976. *The Biology of Human Action.* San Francisco: W. H. Reading.

Riesman, Paul. 1977. *Freedom in Fulani Social Life: An Introspective Ethnography.* Chicago: University of Chicago Press.

Rimbaud, Arthur. 1957. *Illuminations.* Trans. L. Varese. New York: New Directions.

Rittenberg, Sidney, and Amanda Bennett. 1993. *The Man Who Stayed Behind.* New York: Simon and Schuster.

Róheim, Géza. 1971. *The Origin and Function of Culture.* New York: Doubleday.

Rorty, Richard. 1989. *Contingency, Irony, and Solidarity.* Cambridge: Cambridge University Press.

Rose, Deborah Bird. 1992. *Dingo Makes Us Human: Life and Land in an Aboriginal Australian Culture.* Cambridge: Cambridge University Press.

Rose, Gillian. 1978. *The Melancholy Science: An Introduction to the Thought of Theodor W. Adorno.* London: Macmillan.

———. 1995. *Love's Work: A Reckoning with Life.* New York: Schocken.

Rosser, Bill. 1985. *Dreamtime Nightmares: Biographies of Aborigines under the Queensland Aborigines Act.* Canberra: Australian Institute of Aboriginal Studies.

Roth, Walter E. 1897. *Ethnological Studies among the North-West-Central Queensland Aborigines.* Brisbane: Edmund Gregory.

———. 1903. North Queensland Ethnography: Superstition, Magic, and Medicine. Home Secretary's Department, Brisbane, Bulletin No. 5. Brisbane: G.A. Vaughan, Govt. Printer.

———. 1907. "North Queensland Ethnography: Burial Ceremonies and Disposal of the Dead." *Records of the Australian Museum Sydney.* Bulletin no. 9: 365–403.

———. 1910. "North Queensland Ethnography: Social and Individual Nomenclature." *Records of the Australian Museum Sydney.* Bulletin no. 18: 79–106.

Rowley, C. D. 1972. Outcasts in White Australia. Harmondsworth: Penguin.

Rumsey, Alan. 1994. "The Dreaming, Human Agency and Inscriptive Practice." *Oceania* 65: 116–30.

Sacks, Oliver. 1986. *The Man Who Mistook His Wife for a Hat.* London: Picador.

Sahlins, Marshall. 1965. "On the Sociology of Primitive Exchange." In *The Relevance of Models for Social Anthropology.* Ed. Michael Banton. London: Tavistock.

———. 1976. "Colors and Cultures." *Semiotica* 16 (1): 1–22.

———. 1985. *Islands of History.* Chicago: University of Chicago Press.

Said, Edward. 1994. *Representations of the Intellectual.* New York: Pantheon.

Sansom, Basil. 1982. "The Aboriginal Commonality." In *Aboriginal Sites, Rights and Resource Development.* Ed. Ronald M. Berndt. Perth: University of Western Australia Press.

Sartre, Jean-Paul. 1948. *The Emotions: Outline of a Theory.* Trans. Bernard Frechtman. New York: Philosophical Library.

————. 1956. *Being and Nothingness: An Essay on Phenomenological Ontology*. Trans. Hazel Barnes. New York: Philosophical Library.

————. 1964. *Words*. London: Hamish Hamilton.

————. 1968. *Search for a Method*. Trans. Hazel Barnes. New York: Vintage.

————. 1981. *The Family Idiot: Gustave Flaubert 1821–1857*. Vol. 1. Trans. Carol Cosman. Chicago: University of Chicago Press.

————. 1982. *Critique of Dialectic Reason 1: Theory of Practical Ensembles*. London: Verso.

————. 1983. *Between Existentialism and Marxism*. Trans. John Matthews. London: Verso.

Sayers, E. F. 1927. "Notes on the Clan or Family Names Common in the Area Inhabited by Temne-Speaking People." *Sierra Leone Studies* 12, o.s.: 14–108.

Schieffelin, Edward L. 1991. "The Great Papuan Plateau." In *Like People You See in a Dream: First Contact in Six Papuan Societies*. Ed. Edward L. Schiefflin and Robert Crittenden. Stanford, Calif. Stanford University Press.

Schutz, Alfred. 1967. *The Phenomenology of the Social World*. Trans. George Walsh and Frederick Lehnert. London: Heinemann.

————. 1970. *On Phenomenology and Social Relations: Selected Writings*. Ed. Helmut R. Wagner. Chicago: University of Chicago Press.

————. 1973. *Collected Papers*. Vol. 1. Ed. Maurice Natanson. The Hague: Martinus Nijhoff.

Serres, Michel. 1983. *Hermes: Literature, Science, Philosophy*. Ed. Josué V. Harari and David Bell. Baltimore: Johns Hopkins University Press.

Sharp, Richard Lauriston. 1968. "Hunter Social Organisation: Some Problems of Method." In *Man the Hunter*. Ed. Richard Lee and Irven DeVore. Chicago: Aldine.

Shipton, Parker. 1989. *Bitter Money: Cultural Economy and Some African Meanings of Forbidden Commodities*. Washington, D.C.: American Anthropological Association.

Simmel, Georg. 1950. "The Stranger." In *The Sociology of Georg Simmel*. Trans. and ed. K. H. Wolff. New York: Free Press.

————. 1950. *The Sociology of Georg Simmel*. Trans. and ed. Kurt H. Wolff. Glencoe, Ill.: Free Press.

Simmons, William S. 1976. "Islamic Conversion and Social Change in a Senegalese Village." *Ethnology* 18 (4): 303–323.

Skinner, Elliott P. 1963. "Strangers in West African Societies." *Africa* 33 (4): 307–20.

Soyinka, Wole. 1975. *The Man Died: Prison Notes of Wole Soyinka*. Harmondsworth: Penguin.

Stern, Daniel. 1985. *The Interpersonal World of the Infant: A View from Psychoanalysis and Developmental Psychology*. New York: Basic Books.

Stoller, Paul. 1989. *The Taste of Ethnographic Things: The Senses in Anthropology.* Philadelphia: University of Pennsylvania Press.

———. 1992. *The Cinematic Griot: The Ethnography of Jean Rouch.* Chicago: University of Chicago Press.

———. 1995. *Embodying Colonial Memories: Spirit Possession, Power, and the Hauka in West Africa.* New York: Routledge.

Strathern, Marilyn. 1972. *Women in Between: Female Roles in a Male World, Mount Hagen, New Guinea.* London: Seminar Press.

Straus, Erwin, W. 1966. *Phenomenological Psychology.* New York: Basic Books.

Sutton, Peter, and Bruce Rigsby. 1979. "Linguistic Communities and Social Networks on Cape York Peninsular." In *Australian Linguistic Studies.* Pacific Linguistics Series C, no. 54, ed. S. A. Wurm. Canberra.

Sutton, Peter. 1988. "Myth as History, History as Myth." In *Being Black.* Ed. Ian Keen Canberra: Aboriginal Studies Press.

Tamisari, Franca. 1997. "Body, Vision and Movement: In the Footprints of the Ancestors." Unpub.

Taussig, Michael. 1980. *The Devil and Commodity Fetishism in South America.* Chapel Hill: University of North Carolina Press.

Tindale, Norman B. 1959. "Totemic Beliefs in the Western Desert of Australia, Part 1: Women Who Became the Pleiades." In *Records of the South Australian Museum* 13 (3): 305–32.

Thomas, L. V. 1973. "Le Pluralisme cohérent de la notion de personne en Afrique noire traditionnelle." In *La Notion de personne en Afrique noire.* Ed. Germaine Dieterlen. Paris: Éditions de Centre National de la Recherche Scientifique.

Thomson, Donald F. 1935. "The Joking Relationship and Organized Obscenity in North Queensland." *American Anthropologist* 37 (3): 460–90.

Todorov, Tzvetan. 1993. *On Human Diversity: Nationalism, Racism, and Exoticism in French Thought.* Trans. Catherine Porter. Cambridge, Mass.: Harvard University Press.

Tournier, Michel. 1988. *The Wind Spirit: An Autobiography.* Trans. Arthur Goldhammer. Boston: Beacon Press.

Trawick, Margaret. 1990. *Notes on Love in a Tamil Family.* Berkeley: University of California Press.

Trevarthen, Colwyn, and Penelope Hubley. 1978. "Secondary Intersubjectivity: Confidence, Confiders and Acts of Meaning in the First Year." In *Action, Gesture and Symbol.* Ed. Andrew Lock. London: Academic Press.

Trotter, J. K. 1898. *The Niger Sources.* London: Methuen.

Tuan, Yi-Fu. 1977. *Space and Place.* Minneapolis: University of Minnesota Press.

Turnbull, Colin. 1965. *Wayward Servants: The Two Worlds of the African Pygmies.* New York: Natural History Press.

Turner, Victor. 1970. *The Forest of Symbols.* Ithaca, N. Y.: Cornell University Press.

United Nations Development Programme (UNDP). 1996. *Human Development Report 1996.* New York: Oxford University Press.

Von Sturmer, John. 1981. "Talking with Aborigines." *Australian Institute of Aboriginal Studies Newsletter* 15: 13–30.

Wagner, Roy. 1967. *The Curse of Souw: Principles of Daribi Clan Definition and Alliance in New Guinea.* Chicago: University of Chicago Press.

———. 1980. *The Invention of Culture.* Chicago: University of Chicago Press.

———. 1986. *Symbols That Stand for Themselves.* Chicago: University of Chicago Press.

Wallace, Phyl, and Noel Wallace. 1977. *Killing Me Softly: The Destruction of a Heritage.* Melbourne: Thomas Nelson.

Weiss, Brad. 1996. *The Making and Unmaking of the Haya Lived World: Consumption, Commoditization, and Everyday Practice.* Durham N.C.: Duke University Press.

Werbner, Richard P. 1989. *Ritual Passage, Sacred Journey: The Process and Organization of Religious Movement.* Washington, D.C.: Smithsonian Institution Press.

White, Edmund. 1993. "1983." In *twenty-one Picador Authors Celebrate twenty-one Years of International Writing.* London: Picador.

Wiener, Norbert. 1948. *Cybernetics; or Control and Communication in the Animal and the Machine.* Cambridge, Mass.: MIT Press.

Winnicott, D. W. 1974. *Playing and Reality.* Harmondsworth: Penguin.

Wiredu, Kwasi. 1996. *Cultural Universals and Particulars: An African Perspective.* Bloomington: Indiana University Press.

Witherspoon, Gary. 1977. *Language and Art in the Navajo Universe.* Ann Arbor: University of Michigan Press.

Witkowski, Stanley R., and Cecil H. Brown. 1977. "An Explanation of Color Nomenclature Universals." *American Anthropologist* 79 (1): 50–57.

———. 1982. "Whorf and Universals of Color Nomenclature." *Journal of Anthropological Research* 38 (4): 411–20.

Wolf, Eric R. 1982. *Europe and the People without History.* Berkeley: University of California Press.

Young, Michael W. 1971. *Fighting with Food: Leadership, Values and Social Control in a Massim Society.* Cambridge: Cambridge University Press.

———. 1983. *Magicians of Manumanua: Living Myth in Kalauna.* Berkeley: University of California Press.

Younge, Gary. 1997. "Black, White and Every Shade Between." *Guardian Weekly* 156 (22): 23.

Zahan, Dominique. 1974. *The Bambara.* Leiden: E. J. Brill.

———. 1979. *The Religion, Spirituality, and Thought of Traditional Africa.* Chicago: University of Chicago Press.

INDEX

aboriginal Australians: assimilationist policies, 138, 141; avoidance behavior, 151–53, 159–60, 161, 180; as belonging to the land, 199; Belyuen community, 176; children taken from their parents, 141, 150; circumspective style of talking, 147; on ghosts, 160–67; grievances as settled by, 148–49; hard and soft lives contrasted by, 155–56; initiative avoided by, 159–60; insiders and outsiders distinguished by, 144–45; *jawun,* 145, 154–55, 184; memory in contemporary foraging, 150; mythology and life stories fused by, 132, 133, 140, 176; the past as conceived by, 139–40; Pitjantjatjara, 126, 127, 143; Proserpine River aboriginals, 177n; scapegoating, 160; sense of loss among, 162; the stolen generation, 141; stories of, 175–83; on storms, 167–71, 179; on tracks as embodying the ancestors, 192; Tully River aboriginals, 177n; vernacular use during foraging, 150; weather as root metaphor for, 168; and whites, 130–31, 138, 141–44, 147, 150, 153, 173, 178–80, 182–83, 201; on whites as ghosts, 167; women's reaction to rape, 142–43; Yankuntjatjara, 125, 126, 127. *See also* Dreaming, the; Kuku-Yalanji; Pintupi; Warlpiri

abortion, 20

abstraction, 35, 195, 200–202

Abu-Lughod, Lila, 35, 205

active life. See *vita activa*

Adama, 118

Adam and Eve, 113, 118, 178

Adorno, Theodor: on abstractions, 195, 200; on the essay, 34; *Minima Moralia,* 36; on parataxis, 36n; on power of thought as limited, 190; on the subject, 8; on the task of thought, 204–5

affinity. *See* in-laws

African-Americans, 124, 140

African peoples: Azande, 47, 48, 49; BaKongo, 76; Bamana thought, 14, 26, 68n; Bambara, 63–64, 81; BaMbuti, 14; Beng, 14; Dinka, 70; Dogon, 26; Fang, 120; Haya, 53–54; Jelgobe Fulani, 4; Kung, 121; Limba, 120; Luo, 49; Macha Oromo, 46; Mande, 7, 23n; Sukuma-Nyamwezi, 45, 46–47; Tallensi, 9n.5; Thonga, 121; Yaka, 86; Yoruba, 192. *See also* Kuranko; Ndembu

ghosts (*continued*)
  separation anxiety, 163, 164; white people likened to, 167
Giddens, Anthony, 8n
gift exchange: fetishes contrasted with
  gifts, 78, 79; *gift* as also word for poison, 49; gifts incorporating something of
  oneself, 72; Kuranko view of, 68; Mauss
  on spirit of the gift, 8, 81; reciprocity in,
  8–9
Gilbert, Kevin, 143
globalization, 109
global world: intersection with local world,
  3; Kuranko adopting Islam for dealing
  with, 73–75; reducing to scale of the local world, 174–75; roads connecting people to, 89; sacrifice redressing loss of balance between local world and, 72
God: as distant, 46–47; Kuranko adopting
  Islamic, 73–75; sacrificing to, 71, 72
Godelier, Maurice, 82
Goffman, Erving, 6, 159
going native, 97
Gopie Ataiamelaho, 110–11
Gottlieb, Alma, 14
Granites, the, 134, 135
grass tree burning, 169–70
Graumann, Carl F., 6
Greene, Graham, 37
guardian angels (*kanda malika*), 79
gueth makech (bitter money), 49
Guha, Ranajit, 144n, 202
Guugu-Yimidhirr, 151
gypsies, 192

Halbwachs, Maurice, 140
half-siblings, 42
hallucinogenic mushrooms, 171
Ham, 114, 120, 121
Hamilton, Annette, 181
Hanks, William F., 11, 192
Harrist sect, 120
Haviland, John, 151
Hawa, 118
Haya, 53–54
Hegel, Georg Wilhelm Friedrich, 9, 192

Heidegger, Martin, 3, 16n
hermeneutic circle, 4
Hermes, 167
Herodotus, 133
Herzfeld, Michael, 32n.18, 93, 191, 199
Hides, Jack, 111n
history. *See* past, the
Holocaust, the, 140
home, 20, 137, 175
homeorrhesis, 19
Horton, Robin, 74
Howes, David, 85, 182
Hubley, Penelope, 11n
Hughes, Robert, 108
Hultin, Jan, 46
humanism, 5, 179, 190, 191, 193, 205–6
Hume, David, 18
Hurston, Zora Neale, 124
Husserl, Edmund, 94, 191
Hutchinson, T. J., 119

I and Thou relationship, 10, 32n.19, 45,
  131
identity: aboriginal loss of, 162; amity as
  not a simple function of, 191; essentializing discourse about, 199; Kuranko clan
  myths merging, 40–42; the Kuranko on
  going beyond the particular without losing, 38; land as a focus of, 127; narrative mediating reinvention of, 24; non-
  Western peoples on, 7; politics of, 205;
  relationships as involved in, 17–
  18; smell as metaphor for group, 182;
  of the Warlpiri, 131–32. *See also*
  self
identity thinking, 194, 199, 205
Illich, Ivan, 34, 193
impotence, male, 50
incantations, 79–80
incest, 40n, 159, 171n
Indian philosophy, 7
individual, the: as dialectically irreducible
  for Sartre, 27; the individual subject as
  dead, 55, 58–60; as microcosm, 25;
  Sartre on, 8. *See also* self
individualism, 164